J. Ramsay MacDonald

LIVES of the LEFT is a new series of original biographies of leading figures in the European and North American socialist and labour movements. Short, lively and accessible they will be welcomed by students of history and politics and by anyone interested in the development of the Left. *general editor*   David Howell

published: **J. Ramsay MacDonald**   Austen Morgan
James Maxton William Knox
Karl Kautsky Dick Geary

forthcoming, to include: **Big Bill Haywood** Melvin Dubofsky
A. J. Cook Paul Davies
Aneurin Bevan Dai Smith
Thomas Johnston Graham Walker
Eugene Debs Gail Malmgreen
R. H. Tawney Anthony Wright
Ernest Bevin Peter Weiler

To the memory of my father
Daniel Morgan 1918–1977

J. Ramsay MacDonald

Austen Morgan

Manchester University Press

Copyright © Austen Morgan 1987

Published by Manchester University Press,
Oxford Road, Manchester, M13 9PL, UK
27 South Main Street, Wolfeboro, N.H. 03894-2069, USA

British Library cataloguing in publication data
Morgan, Austen
  J. Ramsay MacDonald. —(Lives of the left)
  1. MacDonald, James Ramsay
  2. Prime ministers — Great Britain — Biography
  I. Title   II. Series
  941.083'092'4   DA566.9.M25

Library of Congress cataloguing in publication data applied for

ISBN 0 7190 2168 5 *hardback*
ISBN 0 7190 2169 3 *paperback*

Printed and bound in Great Britain by
Robert Hartnoll (1985) Ltd., Bodmin, Cornwall

Contents

Acknowledgements

I would like to thank David Howell, the series editor, for asking me, in, appropriately, Leicester, to write this political biography of Ramsay MacDonald. David has been everything an author could want, and I can only hope I helped make his editorial life rewarding and enjoyable. Alec McAulay of Manchester University Press was quick to guide me on to, hopefully, the right lines, and all his colleagues have been efficient and pleasant. Sue Dent took an early interest in MacDonald, and Emma Laybourne helped with picture research; the National Portrait Gallery allowed me into its recesses, and accepted elaboration on socialist art history. Andy Fairclough has been prepared to think the unthinkable with me over the years, and he even read a draft of the book. Ramsay MacDonald, to be honest, lacks street credibility in the culturally conscious north London of today and, more so than with other projects, the researching and writing of this book was a lonely form of existence. John Hampson kept me informed about the rest of the world, and sometimes in work. The British Library in Bloomsbury and Public Record Office at Kew allowed me in from the cold, and intellectual outdoor relief continues to be provided, on demand, by the British Library of Political and Economic Science at the London School of Economics. I have shamelessly plundered primary and secondary sources and, since only direct quotations are referenced in the notes, I am greatly indebted to many historical actors and scholars. My other debts are continuing. Paul Morgan and Sheila Harvey provided me with a home from home, alongside Daniel and Edwin, and my mother, Veronica Morgan, was supportive at a time when there was little to show. Shelley, Dan, and Nell, who was perplexed at my sudden interest in hamburgers, did their best to mitigate the ravages of a less salubrious part of the new Islington. Sammy kept watch. None of the afore-mentioned bears any responsibility for the argument of this book, which remains uniquely my own.

Abbreviations

ASE	Amalgamated Society of Engineers
BSP	British Socialist Party
ILP	Independent Labour Party
JRM	James Ramsay MacDonald
LRC	Labour Representation Committee
MEM	Margaret Ethel MacDonald
OMS	Organisation for the Maintenance of Supplies
PRO	Public Record Office
RMP	Ramsay MacDonald Papers
SDF	Social Democratic Federation
SDP	Social Democratic Party
TUC	Trades Union Congress
UDC	Union of Democratic Control

Introduction

In the early morning of Monday, 24 August 1931, a tall, conservatively dressed, elderly man with hair turning white was observed walking in London's St James's Park, Westminster with a young woman. The couple were Sheila MacDonald, an Oxford undergraduate, and her 64-year-old father, James Ramsay MacDonald, the British Prime Minister.

He had headed his first government in 1924 as leader of the Labour Party in parliament, and, in 1929, the political organisation of the British working class secured his return to 10 Downing Street with a second minority administration. Ramsay MacDonald, as he was universally known, had come a long way from the cottage on the edge of the Scottish Highlands in which he had been born, at a time when Lord Derby was considering the Second Reform Bill.

Civil servants on their way to work in Whitehall that summer morning would have recognised the nation's elected leader as a man stooped under strain. The inquisitive might have caught his Scottish brogue as he talked with his youngest daughter. Most likely, they were discussing the national crisis, which would mark a turning point between the First and Second World Wars in British political history; during the parliamentary recess, London bankers had seemingly become alarmed at the continuing run on the pound.

MacDonald might have intimated, during what was his regular walk before breakfast, that he had made a critical personal decision – one that would determine his historical reputation and rock the Labour Party to its foundations. He was due at Buckingham Palace at 10.00 a.m., a short drive up the Mall, for a meeting with George V and the leaders of the Conservative and Liberal Parties.

The Wall Street Crash of 1929 had occurred several months after MacDonald returned to office. In the ensuing international recession, unemployment in Britain soared from its characteristic post-war level of over ten per cent. The second Labour government was rendered impotent by its acceptance of free-trade orthodoxy. It rejected the radical solution of a revenue tariff as the problem loomed of a budget unbalanced by, as it was seen, the cost of unemployment benefit.

In the late spring of 1931, an international financial crisis saw a run on sterling. The publication of the supposedly independent May Report on Britain's public finances on 31 July, with its recommendation of a twenty-per-cent cut in unemployment benefit, reduced the confidence of international bankers further.

MacDonald was forced to return to London on 11 August. The Bank of England demanded action to balance the budget within fourteen days. The idea of devaluation was hardly envisaged, since keeping Britain on the gold standard was considered to be virtually a national obligation of all governments. For two weeks, ministers struggled to produce a budget satisfactory to international bankers.

On Sunday, 23 August, the cabinet split. A majority, including MacDonald, supported a set of tax increases and expenditure savings, including a ten-per-cent cut in unemployment benefit. A minority, led by Arthur Henderson, the Foreign Secretary, opposed this cut, taking a stand with the TUC. Thereupon, the second Labour government decided to resign, but the cabinet allowed MacDonald to advise the King to call a meeting of the three party leaders. It was assumed that there would be an immediate transfer of power to a Conservative government with Liberal support.

However, the Prime Minister was committed to the decision that he had forced through cabinet. He felt it would be difficult to revert to leadership of the opposition, given the TUC's hostility to any cuts. During his walk with Sheila the following morning, he may have ruled out the idea of supporting an emergency government as an independent member below the gangway. This left only a third possibility. At Buckingham Palace that Monday, the King, Stanley Baldwin, and Herbert Samuel quickly persuaded MacDonald to head a temporary 'national government' to save the pound; its members were to be drawn from the three parties. The Labour cabinet was taken by surprise at its last meeting at noon on 24 August. The Prime Minister accepted that he would get little support from his party.

Three former colleagues joined him in the new cabinet. However, it was opposed from the start by the Labour movement. Philip Snowden's emergency budget was passed by parliament in September. It led to the Invergordon 'mutiny' and, given a continuing lack of confidence, the British government was soon forced off the gold standard. The cataclysm MacDonald, and the whole governing class, had feared never came. International bankers quickly adjusted to a new era of currency management.

Working-class hostility increased, when the Prime Minister decided to seek a mandate for the national government. In the election that October, MacDonald was responsible for the parliamentary routing of the Labour Party. A general import tariff was agreed by parliament in March 1932, and the free traders resigned from the government in September. MacDonald would remain in Downing Street until 1935, as the head of a virtual Conservative administration.

Labour was supposed to be more than a bourgeois political party. Yet, in the 1931 parliament, the years of the means test, the man who had been leader of the party from 1911 to 1914 and again from 1922 was indistinguishable from the Tories. Socialists dismissed the ageing Ramsay MacDonald as a traitor to the party, the working class and their political ideology. It was all the more poignant in that he was seen by some as having betrayed his own political antecedents, having become a Socialist in 1885 and the founding Secretary of the Labour Representation Committee – later the Labour Party.

No doubt his lengthy career contains the seeds of 1931. However, before that fateful Monday morning, few, if any, seriously predicted that MacDonald would act the way he did. On the contrary, if he had become a victim of the proverbial Whitehall bus just before the August crisis, he would be remembered as one of the great leaders of the party.

He had become an anti-Marxist Socialist in London in the mid-1880s, with an uncritical attitude towards the British state. He came to work for Independent Labour representation when the trade unions were still implicated in Liberalism. When the organised working class began to break away from the Liberal Party, MacDonald retained his connections with middle-class radicalism. He was elected to parliament in the Liberal landslide of 1906 and became the fourth, and most impressive, leader of the Parliamentary Labour Party.

In 1914, when he resigned the leadership rather than vote for war credits, he took a more or less principled stand. MacDonald associated with bourgeois radicals and anti-war Socialists, while a trade-union-dominated Labour Party responded to the call of patriotism and other Socialists succumbed to social chauvinism. This was to be the high point of his political career as a Socialist. Henderson, who had become the key organisational figure in the Labour movement, acted in accordance with the wishes of the Labour Party. He served in the wartime coalitions but also prepared the party to fight the 1918 election independently. The faction of Labour led by George Barnes, which stayed in the Lloyd George government, did not survive the early 1920s. There was a lesson here, if MacDonald had cared to note it.

After the war, Labour profited from Liberal divisions, attracting some middle-class Liberals as well as sections of the working class. It was Labour's misfortune in the 1920s to be lured into office when it lacked a parliamentary majority. Few members queried MacDonald's goal of proving that Labour could govern responsibly. He was not unimpressive as Prime Minister in the area of foreign affairs, being an arriviste in the governing class. However, domestic political mistakes led to the precipitate defeat of his first administration. In 1931 he experienced the second major climacteric in his political career. This time, MacDonald clung to his position as Prime Minister, while he allowed the financial crisis to overwhelm him. The Labour Party had to be rescued by the TUC, the trade-union leadership refusing to allow the working class to pay further for an apparently collapsing Capitalism.

MacDonald's unexpected decision in 1931 resembled Lloyd George's throwing over of the Liberal Party in 1916. Each advanced his personal position by claiming to put country before party at a time of national crisis. However, it was not so obvious that Lloyd George had fatally wounded the Liberal Party in 1916, while in 1931 it seemed that Ramsay MacDonald had destroyed Labour's chances of ever becoming a majority ruling party. As things were to turn out, the Lloyd George coalition of 1916-22 largely destroyed the Liberal Party, while the national governments of 1931-40, followed by the wartime coalition, did not prevent the Attlee governments of 1945-51 nor those of Wilson and Callaghan in the 1960s and 1970s.

His erstwhile political associates, many of whom lost their seats in 1931, found it cathartic to create a myth of MacDonaldism – an overblown image of human failing which did injury to the historical figure who had commanded a huge following in the 1920s. The myth still survives. When, in October 1976, Tony Benn circulated the minutes of August 1931 to his cabinet colleagues in order to warn another Labour government against cutting benefits, his action 'caused a great deal of anger'.[1] No

Labour leader dare risk being accused of MacDonaldism. While politically understandable, this intellectual prejudice has obscured the complex of radicalism, trade unionism and Socialism, which was the making of the Labour Party as the anti-Tory force in British politics. This is evident in the way the historical literature on MacDonald has been shaped largely by his decision to form the national government.

He first came to cultural attention in the 1920s, as a potential Prime Minister. Mary Agnes – Molly – Hamilton, who became a Labour MP in 1929, produced impressions in 1923 and 1925 as 'Iconoclast', the two volumes being updated in a single book in 1929 under her own name.[2] Though in the genre of character examinations, these works were politically prescient; she had been a 'devotee' until 1924 and it was MacDonald's conduct during the election that year which led her to become '[a] loyal but critical follower'.[3] In contrast, the Labour journalist, Herbert Tracey, produced a biography in 1924 which portrayed Mac-Donald as the ideal leader of the working-class movement.[4] He was still 'Labour's Man of Destiny' five years later, when another journalist, Hessell Tiltman, produced a second biography.[5] Also in 1929, Egon Wertheimer, the London correspondent of *Vorwärts*, described him as 'the outstanding figure of International Socialism' in a book which praised the Labour Party for being non-Marxist. 'Like Lenin. . . he is the focus of the mute hopes of a whole class,' wrote Wertheimer. However, he also saw MacDonald as 'mov[ing] to-day in a personal vacuum that is almost painful to behold'.[6] Despite such limitations, MacDonald, then, was treated as a hero on the edge of greatness.

From 1931 he would be a simple anti-hero. In the *Political Quarterly,* Sidney Webb/Lord Passfield, who had supported Mac-Donald on the unemployment benefit cuts, portrayed the gestation of the national government as 'a single drama, in all its development foreseen in advance, it is safe to say, only by the statesman who was at once its author, its producer, and its principal actor'.[7] A conspiracy theory – involving MacDonald alone! – was an understandable reaction to electoral defeat but it distorted the Prime Minister's fundamental indecisiveness in 1931. It also, of course, excused the Labour party of any responsibility for its leader's behaviour. There was a second argument, namely that MacDonald had been socially corrupted by the ruling class. This was repeated by Harold Laski later in 1932, in an article in *Harper's*: 'Timid, indecisive, vain of applause, he shrank from the price of unpopularity among a society he had growingly come to esteem.'[8] The idea was reinforced by Philip Viscount Snowden in his autobiography in 1934, when he quoted MacDonald as having said on 24 August 1931: 'To-morrow every Duchess in London will be wanting to kiss me!'[9] The husband of Ethel was hardly immune from such criticism and, indeed, it was the former Labour Chancellor who had done so much to split the party.

Four years later, MacNeill Weir, who had been MacDonald's Parliamentary Private Secretary from 1924, eventually succeeded in publishing his near-six-hundred-page *Tragedy of Ramsay MacDonald*,[10] after having made 'some very drastic alterations'.[11] Though Weir had not been unsympathetic in 1931, he attributed MacDonald's political treachery to careerism pure and simple. The book, which became the classic exposition of the MacDonald myth, attributed the crisis to the political motivation of British bankers.

When MacDonald died suddenly in late 1937, the BBC could find no one to give an historical assessment. Harold Nicolson, who had been a political ally, declined a publisher's request to write an official biography. Molly Hamilton attempted an appreciation in the *Atlantic Monthly,* and she later admitted, in her autobiography, that 'it took years for the Labour Party to get him out of its system'.[12] In his war memoirs, Lloyd George had recalled MacDonald as a pacifist,[13] but Winston Churchill saw him as the companionable adversary of Stanley Baldwin.[14] In 1939 the Oxford historian, Godfrey (Lord) Elton, who had supported MacDonald to the end, published his *Life*.[15] Malcolm MacDonald retained his father's papers and this would-be official biography was a poor attempt at objectivity. It included, however, a subtle apologia for MacDonald's wartime abstentionism. Elton only took the story up to 1919 and he never produced the second volume. In the classic polemic against appeasement, *Guilty Men* (1940) by 'Cato', MacDonald and Baldwin were jointly credited with 'conduct[ing] . . . a great empire. . . to the edge of national annihilation'[16] in the inter-war years. In the same year, Howard Spring fictionalised MacDonald as Hamer Shawcross in *Fame is the Spur*. Michael Redgrave played him in the film version in 1947.

By then Ramsay MacDonald, only ten years dead, belonged to the historical past. In 1952 an American scholar, Benjamin F. Sacks, sympathetically constructed MacDonald's Socialist project with extracts and commentaries.[17] (It would be 1972 before Bernard Barker published the only selection of his writings.)[18] The appearance of Beatrice Webb's *Diaries,* in which she described MacDonald as, among other things, an 'accomplished substitute for a leader',[19] provided ammunition for Socialist intellectuals. (So also would Harold Nicolson's very different diaries in 1966.)[20] The 1950s also saw two monographs – a useful account by Lyman of the first Labour government,[21] and a highly argumentative defence of MacDonald in 1931 by Bassett.[22]

Francis Williams published a long essay in 1965,[22] and in the 1970s there were two scholarly articles on MacDonald by Mowat[24] and Lloyd.[25] The centenary of MacDonald's birth in 1966 awakened some interest in the almost forgotten Labour Prime Minister. Newspaper articles were commissioned from Malcolm MacDonald and his sister, Ishbel. Malcolm, who was representing his country in former colonies, organised a commemorative lunch in the House of Commons on 12 October. This was sponsored by 'Manny' Shinwell, and addressed by the Prime Minister, Harold Wilson. A scholarly account of the second Labour government was published by Skidelsky the following year.[26] With Malcolm more interested in writing about his travels, his father's papers were handed over to an academic-turned-pro-European Labour MP, David Marquand.

In 1977 the official biography, *Ramsay MacDonald,* finally appeared.[27] It distilled MacDonald's extensive papers, material from the Public Record Office and other primary and secondary sources into 903 pages. Marquand admired his subject's 'realism' but MacDonald's role in 1931 was discussed critically.

It is interesting that MacDonald has not been rehabilitated by the modern Keynesians of the Social Democratic Party. By the time of its formation, of course, the left of the Labour Party was preoccupied with ensuring that there would be no repetition of the Wilson and Callaghan governments. In terms of Labour's historical consciousness, it would seem that the high point of the Attlee years has come to obscure the earlier period of Mac-Donaldite treachery.

This book makes no claims to academic originality. It is a short political biography, commissioned for inclusion in a series aimed at readers and students, often with a cursory knowledge of British history and occasionally a strong interest in left-wing politics.

It is written from an independent Socialist position and out of an intellectual commitment to Marxism. I have been concerned less with reinforcing the negative reputation Ramsay MacDonald enjoys throughout the Labour movement and more with understanding a British political figure who was, arguably, his country's most important Socialist.

MacDonald maintained to the end that he was a Socialist. This is clearly preposterous, even by the standards of his own politics from the 1880s. From 1894 he was to be loyal, first to the idea of a Labour party and then, from 1900, to the actual organisational expression of Labourism. At no point after 1931 did he seriously attempt to return to the Labour Party, though it must be admitted that he predicted in 1935 that 'a Socialist Party'[28] would appear in British politics.

Such a claim raises important questions about the meaning of Socialism, the nature of British bourgeois-democratic politics and the character of a declining Imperialist state before and after the First World War. I have only been able to allude to such issues but, suffice to say, MacDonald's Socialism was as politically meaningless after 1931 as it had been practically rhetorical when he led Labour to become a party of government.

My aim has been to provide a readable, fair account of an extensive political career which saw MacDonald rise to the top of British, and international, politics. His private world is explored only insofar as this may inform the political narrative.

I have been extremely dependent on Marquand's weighty tome; it is the one and only serious book on MacDonald. *Ramsay MacDonald* provided a template which allowed me to construct my own account. Primary material spills out of Marquand's extremely generous flow of text. However, I have reworked the MacDonald Papers, now deposited in the Public Record Office in London, and examined most of Marquand's other primary and secondary sources as well. In the last ten years there has been a phenomenal growth in 'Labour history', though it must be admitted that little serious attention has been paid to the first Labour Prime Minister.

Given my different political and intellectual starting-points, I obviously see significant events differently. This brief volume may be taken as a critique of the official biography but, since it has been written outside the context of academic life, I have not felt moved to take Marquand's book apart. Rather, I have tried to reconstruct the life of Ramsay MacDonald against the enormous condescension of posterity on the British left.

In 1914 MacDonald threw over the party leadership rather than support the war. In 1931 the party expelled him when he clung to office during the financial crisis. An understanding of this contrast should also tell us something of the Labour Party, and help identify the trajectory of MacDonaldism in the years since 1931. This is a topic not only of intellectual interest but also of continuing political relevance.

1   *A British socialist, 1866–1906*

James Ramsay MacDonald was born, illegitimately, at 11.30 p.m. on 12 October 1866 in Lossiemouth, a small fishing port on the Morayshire coast in north-east Scotland, to Anne Ramsay and John Macdonald.

His father hailed from Highland stock, and he had been a ploughman on a farm some miles away. He then moved on to become a foreman. His mother had been a domestic servant on the same farm and she gave birth in her mother's cottage close to the sea. Isabella Ramsay came from a local family of small farmers, and she had raised her four children on her earnings as a seamstress, having left her husband's baker's shop in the county town of Elgin. Mother and daughter were strong in character; while John and Anne may have planned to marry, it is possible that Isabella was against the match. This was in spite of her firm Calvinist beliefs. The young couple, however, were exonerated by their local free kirk as they were not living in sin, in a rural area which had a high incidence of births out of wedlock.

Three weeks later, Anne registered her son as 'James McDonald Ramsay'. However, he was to become known at school as 'J. Macdonald', his mother remaining 'Miss Ramsay' to Lossiemouth folk. He was to be called 'Jamie' by his peers but known at home as 'Ramsay'. It was not until much later that the name 'James Ramsay MacDonald' evolved.

He was brought up at his grandmother's, his mother working as a fisherwoman and in the fields. Anne Ramsay, however, relied mainly upon her earnings as a dressmaker. 'Ramsay' grew up a lively child, but recalled having 'one of the most violent tempers ever known'. 'As far back as I can remember, I had a grudge against the world wrankling in me.' MacDonald attributed this to the hostility of respectable relatives and neighbours towards his mother and himself: 'All my early memories are frightfully wretched to me.' His father, who became a farmer, was not in evidence and his son saw him only once 'leading some horses out of a cattle show in Elgin'.[1] In 1875 'Jamie' went on to the Drainie parish school, where he was profoundly influenced by the dominie, James Macdonald. The young 'MacDonald' read his bible and noted Gladstone's Midlothian victory in 1880. He left school before his fifteenth birthday but returned in late 1881 as a pupil teacher. He did some farm work in the summer but MacDonald was hardly the 'ploughboy' of later mythology.[2] He founded a local field club to pursue his interest in science, and continued to read English literature. He also became secretary of the debating society in Lossiemouth. By his nineteenth year he was intellectually precocious, a critic of aristocratic social and political power. His agrarian radicalism exhibited, in the mid-1880s, traces of Socialism.

MacDonald was a product of Lossiemouth, a remote town which expanded with the capitalisation of fishing and farming in the third quarter of the nineteenth century. It was a place to which he returned regularly (even after his mother's death in 1910). He was unable to confront his illegitimacy (and it was 1915 before it was revealed, by a political opponent). Most likely an absent father – John Macdonald had died by 1896 – handicapped his future relations with men. His sensitivity stemmed from his mother and grandmother, Ramsay being the only child in their household. They, however, as self-employed women, averted his social destiny in the growing working class. His petty-bourgeois potential was underpinned by a solid education, one of the benefits of birth in rural Scotland in the mid-1860s. Mac-Donald's penchant for learning remained an enduring characteristic. His religiosity – he was a Scottish Presbyterian – was less otherworldly; it was more a personal philosophy. At the age of eighteen he was an insecure individual with driving ambition, a combination which made for a contradictory personality. He was to admit over a decade later: 'Something is constantly saying to me that I will do nothing myself but that I will enable someone else to do something.'[3]

He stood a little under six feet, and his nervous energy was to keep him trim for many a year. He was never to lose his love of the outdoors but, though he possessed physical courage, he felt '[he was] not going to live to be very old'.[4] (MacDonald became a hypochondriac, though he was not to suffer unduly from ill health, and, although he developed a taste for tobacco, he was to be abstemious with alcohol.) He had an oval face and sallow complexion with a 'broad and square' forehead, straight nose and 'ordinary' chin. MacDonald's hair was dark and wavy, his deep brown eyes had a piercing quality, and he was to wear a broad moustache throughout his life. He was extremely handsome as an adult and was to develop a bohemian edge to his conventional appearance in the 1890s. His soft Scottish accent expressed a romantic persona and the regional diction was not an obstacle to national communication.

It was not long before 'James Macdonald' was looking further afield than Lossiemouth.

In mid-1885 he left home to become assistant to a Bristol clergyman who planned to establish a boys' and young men's guild. Social work was to be his profession in this provincial centre but Socialism became his vocation within a short time. He joined the Marxist Social Democratic Federation (SDF) of H. M. Hyndman, having sought out the local branch. This was several months after William Morris in London had broken away to form the Socialist League. In October, MacDonald lectured to the branch after organising a small library for members. He had also attempted open-air propaganda and, in the time left over from work and politics, he studied the geology of the area.

It was during his time in Bristol – the city where Ernest Bevin was to discover trade unionism – that MacDonald became an active Socialist. His appointment at St Stephen's Church, however, proved short-lived and he was back in Lossiemouth towards the end of the year. In small-town Scotland he began to break away from the Marxism of an autocratic Hyndman.

MacDonald planned to establish a branch of the SDF in this far-flung spot. However, he had been critical of slanders about other Socialists in *Justice,* the Federation's paper, and when the 'Tory gold' scandal broke in early December, following Hyndman's (and H. H. Champion's) acceptance of funds to run two candidates to the detriment of Liberals in the general election of 1885, he took the view that they 'lacked a spirit of fairness' and were 'unscrupulous'.[5] The SDF's sectarianism and poor internal democracy led MacDonald to propose an alternative 'Socialist Union of Young Men' in the *Christian Socialist,*[6] a paper established by the Land Reform Union, and, after he was to move to London, he assisted C. L. Fitzgerald in organising this further breakaway. The demise in late 1886 of the *Socialist,* the new Union's paper, which MacDonald helped edit, signalled the failure of this more electorally orientated group. Thus ended MacDonald's short-lived connection with proletarian socialism, albeit admittedly rightward-moving.

He had moved to London in early 1886. Unemployment was reaching a peak and it was May before MacDonald obtained a permanent job as an invoice clerk in a city warehouse (an occupation he was to declare in 1906). He appears to have joined the Fabian Society at about this time, George Bernard Shaw recalling that he took him for an army officer! Certainly, MacDonald was to be impressed by unsentimental and practical middle-class socialists, though he noted that 'the spirit of Socialism. . . [was

also] stirring the lower ranks of labour to discontent'.[7] He fought
on the street for the right of free speech on 'Bloody Sunday' (13
November 1887) when police and troops prevented
demonstrators reaching Trafalgar Square in defiance of a public
ban: 'I. . . broke my hat and got my coat torn'.[8] MacDonald had
begun attending science evening classes, with the aim of obtaining
a scholarship from the South Kensington Museum. However, a
breakdown from overwork saw him back in Lossiemouth by
January 1888.

Land agitation in Ireland and Scotland had helped revive
Socialist ideas in the 1880s, and MacDonald was familiar with
Henry George's *Progress and Poverty* (1879), which advocated a
single tax on land values. The new Socialist organisations, however, failed to transcend sectarianism, because independent working-class politics were weak. Two miners had been returned to
parliament in 1874 as Liberals, and the number of Lib-Lab MPs
– as they were to be called – rose to eleven in 1885 following
the third reform act's enfranchisement of householders outside
the boroughs; miners were well placed to impose their candidates
on Liberal constituency organisations. Gladstone's democratic
internationalism of 1880 had been tarnished by repression in
Ireland and abroad, while Chamberlain's new strategy of social
reform at home could not sustain the class alliance of Liberalism.
However, it was the crisis over home rule for Ireland in 1885-6
which saw the exeunt of the Whigs and Chamberlainite Radicals
from the Party, leaving the Gladstonian majority with a new
constitutional cause to champion as the parliamentary opposition.
Liberalism was to continue as the focus of progressive politics,
even for Socialist critics such as MacDonald.

In 1885, he had helped an 'advanced radical' oppose the sitting
Liberal in Elgin and Nairn; the recently enfranchised rural workers of Morayshire ensured the latter's defeat in the following
year. By the spring of 1888, MacDonald was back in London

working as private secretary to Thomas Lough, the Irish-born 'Liberal and Radical' candidate for West Islington, who had founded the Home Rule Union some months earlier. Lough, an Ulster Nonconformist and tea merchant in London, was a loyal follower of Gladstone, and it is possible MacDonald had known him before his enforced return to Lossiemouth. The 21-year-old Scot entered the world of metropolitan middle-class Liberalism but also moved among the radical and Labour figures who dominated the local party. He was already using the name 'James R. Macdonald', probably to distinguish himself from the Scottish SDFer, James Macdonald, who had been active in London for some time.

By the end of 1887, MacDonald had become involved in the Scottish Home Rule Association and, as London Secretary, he received the names of four local contacts from Edinburgh. It is a historical coincidence that one of these, J. G. Weir, lived at Upper Frognal Lodge in Hampstead, the very house that he was to buy forty years later after he had been Prime Minister! Weir resigned as London Chairman in May 1888 and the branch effectively collapsed the following year 'owing to lack of financial interest on the part of the Scots'.[9] By about 1890, MacDonald's practical interest in Scottish devolution had ceased, though in 1892 he was to be mooted as a home rule candidate for Peterhead. The following February, he heard Gladstone's speech in the Commons on the second – Irish – home rule bill, from a seat in the public gallery behind the Prince of Wales (the future Edward VII).

It was, however, as secretary of the association that he had written to support James Keir Hardie in the Mid-Lanark by-election of April 1888. When the local Liberal caucus rejected the Lanarkshire miners' leader, Hardie decided to run as an independent Gladstonian 'Labour and Home Rule' candidate. The Irish in the constituency refused to support him and Hardie went on to found the Scottish Labour Party in August. MacDonald, however, continued to adhere to the perspective of 'recon-struct[ing] . . . Liberalism',[10] and he helped an 'Advanced Liberal' win the by-election in Morayshire in late 1889.

MacDonald, of course, was still a Socialist and in early 1890 he stood in for Shaw as a Fabian speaker. Sidney Webb also found Lough's secretary useful in his attempts to permeate the London Liberals with municipal Socialism.

Politics, however, did not dominate MacDonald's life and he was, at this time, much preoccupied with the individual.

He was attracted to the Fellowship of the New Life, a group of ethical Socialists who had spawned the Fabian Society. In 1891 MacDonald became secretary of its co-operative house in Bloomsbury, living there for a time. He was later Secretary of the Fellowship and his association was to last until its end in 1898.

MacDonald wrote a semi-autobiographical novel in Blooms-bury, possibly called *For Love's Sake*. It was not to be published, though he seems to have had some success with shorter pieces. This fiction appeared pseudonymously before his political writing. He also continued to do social work, though he cannot have had much time after the early 1890s. He seems to have left Lough's employ at the beginning of 1891 but there does not appear to have been any political falling-out because MacDonald was being sounded, unsuccessfully, in May 1892 for the post of Liberal agent in Mid-Hertfordshire. He had shown little interest in the upsurge of 'new unionism', crowned by the London dock strike of 1889, yet this aided Keir Hardie's return for West Ham South as an independent candidate in the general election of 1892. MacDonald's four year involvement with middle-class radicals and Socialists in the capital does not seem to have made him any less unhappy.

He became a free-lance journalist in his twenty-fifth year, writing mainly for any Liberal papers which would take his work. He also toured as a Fabian lecturer. In July 1892 he went to

Dover to help the Lib-Lab candidate in the general election. Following the expected return of the Conservative, MacDonald became the progressives' prospective candidate. On entry into electoral politics, he described himself as in the 'Labour' interest. While he envisaged Labour as a partner with the Liberals in a future 'progressive' party, he theorised an age of social reform in his first published pamphlet, *The New Charter* (1892). His 'Programme of working class politics' included a number of political reforms, land nationalisation as envisaged by Henry George, proposals to deal with poverty and the enactment of the eight-hour day. This was a series of Lib-Lab parliamentary demands but it was informed by Fabianism: 'The Labour Party is no class champion. In politics it is frankly democratic, in economics it is co-operative, in social theory it has thrown aside the metaphysical individualism of the old Radicals, which is so unreal that it has never been experimentally tried.'[11] There is no doubt that Mac-Donald saw himself as a Socialist, but he was still on the left-wing of the Liberal Party.

He nursed the constituency for nearly twenty months. In April 1894, he was put forward as a possible Lib-Lab contestant for the second – Conservative - seat in Southampton. The local Liberal caucus, however, fought off this working-class challenge in an unscrupulous manner. As a result, MacDonald resolved to run at the next general election as an independent 'Labour' candidate in the city. In June he helped another London journalist, Frank Smith, in the Attercliffe by-election in Sheffield, after the Liberals there refused to support a well-known local trade unionist. This was one of the first electoral struggles of the Independent Labour Party (ILP) which had been founded at Bradford in January 1893. Southampton, followed by Attercliffe, was decisive in changing MacDonald's view of the Liberal Party. On 15 July 1894, he applied for membership of the ILP, telling Hardie, whom he had met only shortly before, that 'Liberalism, and more particularly local Liberal Associations, have definitely declared against Labour'.[12] It was a letter of great personal, and historical, significance. MacDonald made no reference to Southampton, though, the following day, he agreed to run on behalf of the local Lib-Labers, who were moving over to the ILP: 'Our movement is neither a party nor a class movement, but a national one, and as such it must be presented to Southampton.'[13]

This movement was called 'Labourism' by a speaker at the first conference of the ILP. MacDonald had been a Socialist since 1885 but it took him nine years to break organisationally with Liberalism. In 1894, he emulated the stand of Keir Hardie at Mid-Lanark six years before.

The importance of this, irreversible, rupture in loyalty should not be underestimated. However, it obscured considerable political continuity on the part of former left-wing Liberals. They still saw politics in terms of capturing parliamentary seats. Whatever the Socialist ideological critique of Liberalism, the champions of Independent Labour representation sought to become the progressive party of the British state. This was to involve the political emergence of the working class but the character of this important historical shift was barely imagined by the Socialists. Marxism was not in the mainstream of the British left, where trade unionism was to be a major force; rather, social reform was to be accommodated with – at best – radicalism in a new third constitutional party.

MacDonald was to have a leading role in shaping this political project, in the shadow of the party which had once been Gladstone's, but these events lay in the future – where the historical outcome was still to be determined.

The Southampton ILP failed to win trade-union support for MacDonald's candidature over the following twelve months and, on the eve of the general election in July 1895, the Liberals selected the Trades Council's President to run in tandem with

their sitting member. In his first parliamentary contest, Mac-
Donald only secured 867 votes, the other twenty-seven ILP candidates also being unsuccessful. His intervention, however, led
to the return of both Conservatives. In December one was unsea-
ted for corrupt practices. It was thought that MacDonald might
run in the ensuing by-election, as the National Executive[14] of the
ILP was to advise. Later that month, he met the defeated MP
with the Liberal Chief Whip in London and agreed not to stand,
in return for a clear field at the next available opportunity. This
secret deal nearly backfired on MacDonald, as the Southampton
ILP became resigned to a position of neutrality in the forthcoming
contest. He ran the risk of widespread disapproval from fellow
Socialists, though such political horse-trading had probably been
common in the London Liberal Party. The Liberal was returned
by a narrow margin in early 1896, an SDF candidate, in the
absence of MacDonald, polling 274 votes. Nothing more was
heard of the informal agreement. While he was to be associated
with Southampton until 1900, MacDonald had moved on as a
parliamentary candidate by the time of the general election later
that year.

As a relatively new member of the ILP, he had criticised the
party from a right-wing perspective and contrived to ignore its
leadership. He was to be an irritant for the Fabian junta when
he launched a challenge from the left in the 1890s after several
years in the society.

In early 1894, MacDonald had been elected to the Executive
of the Fabian Society. He was soon urging his colleagues to reach
an 'understanding' with the ILP leadership in time for the local
government elections in London. However, a meeting of 'the
principals' over dinner in January 1895 proved unproductive.[15]
The Webbs remained aloof in the general election, the first fought
by the ILP. However, a leaflet by MacDonald was published as
a Fabian tract and Beatrice described him later as one of their

'lower middle class' followers.[16] The following spring, he clashed with the Webbs over the administration of the Hutchinson Trust, which managed funds bequeathed to the society mainly for propaganda purposes. MacDonald was then working as a trust lecturer in the provinces but Sidney had used some of the money to launch the London School of Economics in 1895. The trustees then decided to endow a library for the school. MacDonald, in contrast, wanted an organiser appointed, effectively to Fabianise the ILP. Beatrice Webb saw this as the use of Fabian funds to build the ILP and believed that the 'brilliant young Scot' was motivated by his rejection as a lecturer at the London school.[17] MacDonald fought the issue on the Executive but he secured only a Pyrrhic victory. The society maintained its course of trying 'to make the *thinking* persons socialistic'.[18]

The Fabians were committed, also in 1896, to opposing 'frivolous' – mainly ILP – candidates, in a society report drafted by Shaw for the London congress of the second International in July. MacDonald was to be a delegate from the Executive. Already, an ally of his had secured the removal of passages in the report which would have been offensive to most continental Socialists. However, a meeting of members failed to prevent the draft being published as a Fabian tract. Later, MacDonald was unsuccessful when he tried to have the pamphlet withdrawn. He was to be less prominent in the society in 1897. In the county council elections in March 1898, when he failed to win South Hackney as an ILP candidate, Beatrice Webb expressed contentment at the restoration of Fabian influence among the London 'progressives', as the anti-Tory alliance in municipal politics was called.

MacDonald's real ideological home from the early 1890s had been the Rainbow Circle. This was a small, regular discussion group, comprising radical and Socialist intellectuals. He was one of the first secretaries. Members read papers on the great issues of progressive politics and it is likely that he acquired many of his ideas in this milieu. In 1895 he summarised the previous year's discussions, noting that the common thread was opposition to the 'Manchester School'.[17] Early the following year, he apparently originated the idea of a monthly publication, the *Progressive Review,* to be edited by J. A. Hobson, the radical economist, and William Clarke, one of the contributors to *Fabian Essays* (1889). MacDonald was Company Secretary. The editors were strongly anti-jingoist and the first editorial in October 1896 hinted that the Liberal Party would have to move to the left to survive. In December, however, the *Review* carried an attack on the party by Keir Hardie. The circulation was never large and Clarke blamed this on MacDonald. In July 1897 relations between them broke down. MacDonald's defiance of his curt dismissal contributed to the company's demise and the last issue appeared in September.

Meanwhile, both his private and public life had been transformed by Margaret Ethel Gladstone.

She had been born on 20 July 1870 in Pembridge Square, Bayswater. Her father was a professor of chemistry and he had been active as a Liberal in London politics. His Scottish nonconformity inspired an interest in social work. Her mother, who had died shortly after the birth, was the daughter of a Presbyterian minister born in Ulster and the niece of Lord Kelvin. Margaret Gladstone became involved in evangelicalism and progressed to social work in the East End. By 1895 she was a Socialist and almost certainly in love with the ILP candidate for Southampton.

Margaret met MacDonald in June that year and was to join the ILP the following April. He proved a diffident suitor, posing his 'unitarianism' as an obstacle. Nevertheless, the relationship grew. In July 1896 he proposed on the steps of the British Museum. MacDonald alluded to their different social backgrounds, though not, apparently, to her private income or lack of domestic experience. Margaret's father took steps to find out about his prospective son-in-law. MacDonald asked his mother to get some proper flower-pot saucers in expectation of a visit by Margaret to Lossiemouth but insisted that 'none of the ordinary ways of the house [was to] be disturbed'.[20] His mother still called him Ramsay, and this forename was passed on to his betrothed; its use outside the family probably dates from 1896. The young couple – MacDonald was thirty and Margaret twenty-six – were married in November, and they had a week's honeymoon in the west country.

They made their home a flat at 3 Lincoln's Inn Fields in Holborn. This was a compromise between MacDonald's desire for a house in the suburbs and Margaret's for 'a simple life among the working people'.[21] They were to have a comfortable existence. Margaret contributed something under five hundred pounds a year and MacDonald had his free-lance earnings. It was, however, the household of a modest rentier, the Gladstone family having investments in domestic and empire municipal and railway stock. Margaret Ethel MacDonald offered above all emotional security and was to provide her husband with his first real experience of family life. She, of course, had grown up motherless and Anne Ramsay was to be an important figure. The marriage was a political partnership, albeit an uneven one. Margaret continued with her own public work, but she also coped with her husband's social awkwardness. About once every three weeks, they were 'at home' to progressive trade unionists and Labour activists, Socialist leaders and radical intellectuals and later to foreign Socialists, dominion Labour leaders and colonial nationalists. These gatherings were important for MacDonald's political career. The many visitors over the coming years were to find a flat which was far from tidy and a hostess unconcerned about personal appearance. This was in spite of the presence of servants.

There was, of course, a succession of children – Alister (1898), Malcolm (1901), Ishbel (1903), David (1904), Joan (1908) and

Sheila (1910) – though Margaret was not to allow the rearing of three sons and three daughters to swamp her many activities.

Anne Ramsay was a great help and she had the children for the summer in Lossiemouth. When all the family were there on holiday, they would attend the free kirk. In London, MacDonald's ethical Socialism militated against doctrinal affiliation; the sabbath, however, was marked by a certain seriousness.

New-found economic security allowed MacDonald to share his wife's taste for foreign travel. In August 1897 they sailed to North America for several months. The MacDonalds returned home impressed by democratic political stirrings in the United States.

This was more the observation of a British radical – a Mac-Donald scathing of 'the shallow, optimistic man who could not see much difficulty in reconstructing English society',[22] even though he had been a member of the ILP for three years. He attended his first annual conference in 1896 and was runner-up in the Executive elections. On the sudden death of a member, he was brought onto the National Administrative Council.

MacDonald was unsympathetic to what he recalled as 'a Left Wing purist section'[23] in the ILP, committed to the idea of a Socialist Party. However, he was a representative of the ILP in negotiations in 1897 with the SDF about amalgamation. The idea of Socialist unity was popular in both parties but the Hardie leadership scuppered rapprochement at the following year's conference. In 1898, when there was a further discussion of Socialist unity, MacDonald took the view that '[ILP] tolerance should not show itself by surrender [to the SDF].[24]

In 1896 at the International Socialist Congress, however, he had been aligned, as a Fabian delegate and secretary of the British section, with the Hyndmanites. The issue was whether anarchists should be admitted and the Socialists of Europe voted for their exclusion. Hardie and Tom Mann were in the minority who favoured admission, and MacDonald was to describe them as taking 'a sentimental view'.[25]

On the question of anarchism, he was in the mainstream of international Socialism but, when it came to Socialist unity, Mac-Donald and Hardie were very much on the right.

As an ILP delegate from Southampton, he was not prominent at party conferences (unlike 'Mrs. J. R. MacDonald' who was to represent various branches from 1900). However, his repeated election to the Executive allowed him to consolidate his position on its sub-committees. He joined Hardie, J. Bruce Glasier and Philip Snowden – the three former being illegitimate Scots – in the 'big four' leadership of the party. They constituted a group of journalist-politicians (Hardie had lost his parliamentary seat in 1895) who tended to eclipse the trade-union figures in the ILP. In 1899 MacDonald had to refuse nomination for the post of Chairman.

He had been critical of Hardie's hostility to all Liberals after the 1895 election rout for the ILP, but, by January 1899, the two were agreed on a policy of contesting twenty-five seats at the next general election, it being hoped that the Liberals would allow Labour a free run in return for parliamentary support under a Campbell-Bannerman government. In three years he had helped reverse the independent tendency of the ILP.

The outbreak of the South African war in October 1899 increased the Socialists' dependence on the radicals. They were to campaign for an immediate peace, while the Conservative government secured the support of the Liberal Imperialists – and the neutrality of the party proper. Pro-war jingoism was resisted by the ILP (and SDF) but support for the Boers raised the thorny question of a British defeat. By 1901, ILP members were to be sensitive to criticisms of rank-and-file British soldiers. MacDonald was at one with the 'little-England' Liberals, accepting Hobson's intellectual condemnation of financial Imperialism. Many

Socialists simply considered this symptomatic of Capitalism and the protection of Lloyd George from a Glasgow mob in March 1900 was organised by Keir Hardie.

By then, MacDonald had been defeated within the Fabian Society. A majority of members refused to pronounce on the war, though Shaw favoured 'annexations provided we introduce our higher social organization there'.[26] In April 1900, the Executive noted the resignation of thirteen supporters of the peace campaign, including MacDonald; the Webbs' apolitical conception of Socialism had finally become unacceptable to a Gladstonian Socialist. MacDonald quit the intellectual nest of Fabianism after fourteen years, at what was to be a decisive moment for the ILP.

As a Socialist party, it emphasised the goal of Labour representation. Hardie had worked from 1887 to break the unions from Liberalism but it took the employers' counter-attack of the late 1890s, under a Conservative government, to produce a breakthrough. This came when, in 1899, the Trades Union Congress (TUC) agreed to call a congress 'to devise ways and means for securing the return of an increased number of labour members to the next Parliament'.[27] Members of the ILP in the railway servants' union had created this opportunity and it was seized by Hardie and MacDonald. The big coal and cotton unions, however, remained wedded to their sectional politics as the TUC invited 'all the co-operative, socialistic, trade unions, and other working organisations'[28] to a conference in the Memorial Hall, London on 27/28 February 1900.

There were 117 trade-union delegates, who were joined by representatives of the Fabians, ILP and SDF. The Hyndmanites took a principled stand for class-war Socialism, which was to lead to their departure a year later. Hardie, in contrast, proposed 'a distinct Labour group in Parliament, who shall have their own whips, and agree upon their policy'.[27] This largely organisational idea was not unacceptable to the Parliamentary Committee of the TUC. The conference then established a Labour Representation Committee (the LRC). There had been similar initiatives in the past and it was not entirely obvious that this committee would be any more successful. The 33-year-old MacDonald was appointed Secretary, there being no other likely office-holder. He was to work with an Executive, on which Socialist organisations were allocated five of the twelve seats. This was to be 'the political committee of the combined forces',[30] since the unions and Socialists would run and, in particular, finance their candidates separately. It was MacDonald's political responsibility to co-ordinate this federal United Labour Party. In 1900, its head office was to be a room in his Holborn flat.

The new LRC endorsed ten ILP candidates (one jointly with the SDF) and four union general secretaries. In the September/October ('khaki') general election, the (Socialist) Hardie was returned for Merthyr Boroughs in the company of (the railway servants' Liberal) Richard Bell for Derby. This new, and divided, parliamentary party was overshadowed by the nine Lib-Lab MPs also returned in 1900. MacDonald had become the ILP candidate for Leicester in October 1899. In the general election he secured 4,164 votes against two sitting Liberals, (one of whom was Henry Broadhurst – the first working man to have achieved government office) but his intervention saw the Conservative capture the other seat. At the time, there were 278,000 trade unionists affiliated to the LRC. The decision of the law lords in July 1901 on the Taff Vale case against the railway servants, however, was greatly to alarm trade-union leaders. Increasingly, they were to accept the necessity of independent parliamentary representation.

To some extent the ILP had become redundant in February 1900 but the leadership, including MacDonald, considered that its mission was to push the LRC towards complete independence. As for the members of the party, they insisted that the political goal of Socialism should be kept to the fore.

The LRC was unique as a working-class party in Europe. It was a strange political animal, conceived by the ILP out of the trade-union movement. This was at a time when the unions were being incorporated into Capitalism through collective bargaining. The British version of a proletarian movement stood at two structural removes from the continental Socialist parties. Firstly, the ILP had emphasised the means of Labour representation but it failed to make the unions its motive force in the 1890s. Secondly, when the unions began to move, albeit within the world-view of Liberalism, Hardie envisaged a parliamentary party 'to promot[e] legislation in the direct interests of labour'.[31] It was understood that Labour would co-operate with the liberals. There was no mention of Socialism as a guiding ideology and a parliamentary Labour group was hardly a complete expression of Labourism. There was no mass, organised party, as such, and the ILP was to fill this absence for many a year. In the early 1900s, Liberalism was to be revived as the anti-Conservative force in British politics. This was when MacDonald sought to construct the Labour Alliance – of Socialists and trade unionists – in selected constituencies, in order to make socialism the progressive force in the state. British Socialism, however, was not clearly defined and his project was difficult to realise through trade unionism in the Edwardian era.

In its first year, the LRC attracted the new unions of the unskilled. The Amalgamated Society of Engineers (ASE) affiliated in 1902, to be joined by the textile workers the following year. By 1903, MacDonald spoke formally for 861,000 trade unionists. This was already a majority of the organised movement, though it was to be 1909 before the miners finally broke away from the Liberal Party. He had received a small payment in 1901 but it was 1904 before the secretary was granted an annual salary of £150 (with £100 for an assistant). In the same year, the LRC moved to a two-room office at 28 Victoria Street. The affiliated bodies had contributed ten shillings (50p) for every thousand members but this annual subscription was increased at the 1903 conference. A compulsory political levy was also established (modelled on that of the miners in 1901) to pay MPs £200 a year and help with election expenses.

In August 1902, a (Liberal) cotton-weavers' secretary, David Shackleton, was returned for Clitheroe. Philip Snowden had with-drawn as the ILP candidate and the local Liberals allowed the LRC an uncontested by-election victory. The following March, Will Crooks of the coopers' union defeated the Conservative in Woolwich in a campaign mounted by the local trades council. The ILP branch muted its Socialist politics. Four months later, the iron-founders' Arthur Henderson was returned as LRC can-didate for Barnard Castle; he had been Liberal agent there since 1896 and pushed the candidate of his former party into third place behind the conservative.

MacDonald still had his eye on the London County Council. In February 1900 he had run unsuccessfully as a Labour and Progressive candidate in Woolwich. He was in tandem with a radical, the anti-Tory forces tending to remain united in the capital. The ILP conference criticised him but Hardie did not find it unacceptable. MacDonald was elected for Central Finsbury in a by-election the following year, having been selected at a meeting of 'the Progressive and Labour interests' in the area. He defended the progressive alliance in his election literature: 'The issues are not those of party politics but of the efficient govern-ment of London'.[32] With the help of other Labour councillors, he challenged Sidney Webb in his municipal fief of technical education for being too pro-government. This, and his identifica-tion with the ILP, prevented MacDonald from becoming a governor of University College, London. The Webbs also had the last laugh, when absence abroad disqualified him from the register and re-election in 1904. He suspected political foul play and was angry when he was not consulted about his successor by the Progressive Association.

From mid-1903, the parliamentary Labour group was five strong. Bell, however, was to drift back to his old party and the LRC moved to reprimand Shackleton and Henderson in June 1904 for allegedly supporting the Liberal in a by-election. Mac-Donald struggled to exercise political control over the Labour MPs, while serving on the ILP Executive. As early as October 1901, Glasier had counselled him not to resign: 'We have no man [in the ILP], and there is none in the Trades Unions to take your place'.[33] He criticised Shackleton in 1903 for not adopting a full status quo ante-Taff Vale position in parliament, when he (MacDonald) was insisting that only the LRC could bring about the restoration of trade-union legal immunity. This may have encouraged hostile talk at the TUC about middle-class Socialists and even rumours of MacDonald's resignation for not being a working man (or trade-union official). Towards the end of the year, Glasier was urging him to stay until after the general election – at which point he might become Secretary of the ILP. In February 1905, however, the LRC and TUC agreed to support each other's parliamentary candidates. This concordat raised the possibility of ILPers (through the LRC) having to work for Lib-Labers (endorsed by the TUC), but MacDonald, and Keir Hardie, knew that this was unlikely.

The Secretary of the LRC had already reached a secret under-standing in 1903 with the Liberal Chief Whip, Herbert Gladstone. Labour was to be allowed a free run in a given number of con-stituencies, in return for Liberal and Tory working men, who were affiliated to the LRC, voting for the return of a Liberal government.

Gladstone was interested merely in damage limitation. Mac-Donald, however, was engaged again in realpolitik, though this time as chief engineer of Labour independence. However, he practised political diplomacy nationally in order to achieve an entente with the Liberals, when local caucuses would only back down if there was pressure from Labour activists. Nevertheless, there is no doubt that MacDonald wanted a new, third party in British politics. It is equally certain that he saw the LRC as a Socialist-inspired trade-union nucleus which was, in time, to attract radicals into a new democratic alliance. This force would be committed to social reconstruction from within a Gladstonian political tradition. In 1898 MacDonald had helped found the Society of Ethical Propagandists. In this context he argued that the task of democracy was 'to modify the fabric of society, to make the art of government the greatest of the arts'. Ethics were to give the individual 'a central place in the collectivist scheme'.[34]

In the short (five-year) term of the 1900 parliament, Mac-Donald was the one ILP leader with a well-worked-out vision of the LRC's future. He also had the political ability not unduly to offend trade-union leaders or liberals with 'wild-cat [political] candidatures'.[35]

The Labour Party had been formed to bring about social reform; it was an unfortunate accident of history that the Memorial Hall conference took place several months after the Conservatives' Imperialism provoked the South African war.

MacDonald's opposition to the violence of the British state abroad was largely moral. It derived from the Gladstonian politics of external non-intervention and his support for the Boer republics fell short of what was later called a pacifist position. In September 1900 he tried to avoid the issue during the general election. This may have been justifiable as an electoral tactic, given the Leicester Conservatives' jingoism, but it was based, ultimately, on MacDonald's national patriotism; he believed it was right to oppose a government's foreign policy, but, once the state was engaged in military action, he felt that it was wrong to criticise his nation when it might be under threat.

It therefore followed that politics could only be resumed after the war. In August 1902 he and Margaret left for South Africa in order to study the consequences of the British victory. They spent much of their four months as political travellers interviewing leading figures on the British and Boer sides. MacDonald wrote for the (London) *Echo* and the *Leicester Pioneer* (an ILP paper) and, on his return, he was to expand these pieces in the book, *What I Saw in South Africa* (1902). (This volume, incidentally, was the first to carry the name J. Ramsay MacDonald, by which he was subsequently known.) He reported that the Transvaal and Orange Free State had been laid waste in the war but Afrikaner nationalism still flourished. 'The first step to the consolidation of the British Empire in South Africa',[36] he concluded, was reconciliation with the Boers. This required, as an absolute precondition, the replacement of Milner as High Commissioner. Looking further forward, he saw future British administrations leading native blacks to rudimentary self-government. At least, he mentioned the African majority but it was occluded in his dream of an integrated white colony. Many years later, his book was to be praised for having 'a. . . statesmanlike. . . moderation of tone'.[37]

MacDonald had been a free-lance journalist for a decade and his own political writing appeared from 1895. In the early 1900s he used an anonymous column in the *Echo* to further his work for the LRC, but he was also ambitious to be the author of Socialist books. A proposal in 1899 to edit a series funded by the Hutchinson Trust had been dismissed by Sidney Webb, though MacDonald was to produce a Fabianesque volume on women in the printing trades in 1904. The following year, he started a more-theoretical 'Socialist Library' series for the ILP. The second volume was his *Socialism and Society* (1905), written after he had taken a stand on the right at the Amsterdam Congress of the International. He had been a Socialist for twenty years and his ideas were well formed. They fell into three politico-intel-lectual categories.

Firstly, he championed what he was keen to call a 'British School of Socialism'.[38] This was to be post-Marxist and the most advanced Socialism in Europe. MacDonald, of course, had sloughed off all talk of 'the coming revolution'[39] as early as 1886/87 and he looked forward to the Europeans doing the same.

In *Socialism and Society,* he dismissed the Marx (and Engels) of contemporary English reputation. MacDonald argued that Marx had challenged Utopian Socialism with his notions of 'the economic basis of history, surplus value and the class war'; he had failed, however, to achieve a 'scientific' critique, given 'the metaphysical and logical faults of the Hegelian dialectic'.[40] Iron-ically, Engels's Socialist historiography of 1892 in *Socialism: Utopian and Scientific* was used to demolish Marx's supposed historicism. There is no doubting MacDonald's iconoclasm but it was a theoretically unsophisticated attempt to lay the ghost of Marxism.

Secondly, he rejected the classical English Liberal tradition. MacDonald argued that it had completed its historical mission but, at the same time, he was opposed to a decisive rupture in British progressive politics.

He had rejected metaphysical individualism in 1892 (in *The New Charter*) but later he distinguished the old radicals' 'atomic individualism' from what he called 'organic individualism'.[41] The nineteenth century saw the demise of Liberalism, he argued con-veniently in 1899, and the twentieth century would see a new political era. This was to be the age of 'social reform'.[42] The laissez-faire economics of the Manchester school had failed to avert chaos in the market and there was a need to develop a notion of 'social liberty'. This, however, sounded similar to Lloyd George's 'new Liberalism'. MacDonald's key concept, of course, was 'society'. Unfortunately, the father of English sociology was Herbert Spencer, who had been a cerebral anti-Socialist in his later years. MacDonald was ultimately a proponent of Social Democracy (as the term was understood in the second International). He acknowledged that 'Constitutional Reform was still necessary',[43] but did not accept that his socialism implied a structural break with a non-interventionist Gladstonian Liberalism.

The third category was the doctrine of evolution. This was used, in *Socialism and Society,* to intellectually despatch Marxism and also to resolve MacDonald's political contradiction with Liberalism.

Evolution was a notion of eighteenth-century materialist philosophy. It assumed a natural-scientific form through geology and then the biology of, in particular, Lamarck. The philosophical individualist, Herbert Spencer, announced in the 1850s that evolution was a principle of universal applicability and, in 1859, Charles Darwin's *Origins of Species* gave it a firm foundation in the natural world.

Darwinian evolutionism became a lingua franca of late-nineteenth-century social thinkers. Indeed, Marx was pressed into the mould by an executorial Engels. However, the political fatalism implied by Social Darwinism made the doctrine just as attractive to the right.

The young MacDonald had been interested in geology and biology and he would have been immersed in Social Darwinism from the 1880s. In his first major work, he wrote that 'Socialism could [only] be placed on a definitely scientific foundation' after Darwin. Marx, he dismissed again, on the grounds that 'the Hegelian dialectic is too shallow for biological evolution'.[44] MacDonald's own scientific Socialism, however, was nothing more than a melange of social organicism and anti-revolutionary sentiment.

He was a collectivist, as the term was understood by the Fabians. However, he saw the evolution of society substructuring an historical continuum. This was unlike some Fabians, who were simply antithetical to individualism. Capitalism might have run its historical course, according to MacDonald's politics, but, in terms of his theory, there could be no abrupt changes in history. Therefore, he waited intellectually for the emergence of Socialism. However, the crude inevitability of much contemporary Marxism saw MacDonald generate antithetical statements of voluntarism; the world was knowable only insofar as it was changeable within the terms of British politics.

MacDonald was as much of a historicist as the Marxists he rejected, all Socialists believing, not without some empirical justification, that history was on their side. Indeed, classical Liberalism had viewed history in the same way, with its central notion of 'progress' – a concept which was transliterated as 'evolution' in the Socialist theory of J. Ramsay MacDonald.

All this was some way from the toddling LRC which shared in the Liberal revival of the early Edwardian years.

An important section of the opposition party had opposed the Boer war and Liberalism as a whole benefited from the peace. The reality of Imperialism revealed in South Africa began a reaction against the government. When the Rand mine-owners – with government connivance – introduced indentured Chinese labour in 1904, there was an outburst of Liberal indignation and a trade-union concern for the price of emigrant labour. At home, the Education Acts of 1902 and 1903 had aroused nonconformist opinion against the Conservatives' concessions to religious interests. Democrats were further offended because locally elected school boards were replaced by county (borough) education authorities. In 1903 the Colonial Secretary, Joseph Chamberlain, created another rift in British politics. Following a visit to South Africa, he came out in favour of tariff reform. This forced many Liberal Unionists into the 'free trade' camp, alongside the Liberals, compelling Balfour to declare the issue an open question for his ministry.

It was the Chamberlainite threat to free trade which had speeded MacDonald's understanding with Herbert Gladstone, though the promise of a general election in 1903 proved premature. The delay, however, allowed things to mature. For thirty years, the existence of Lib-Lab MPs had been due to the power of sectional trade unionism within regional Liberalism. In 1903, however, the central leadership of the party contracted a relationship with the LRC, treating it as the political wing of the trade-union movement. This response was to see a radical shift in the form of political subordination for Labour. Active local Socialists were encouraged by MacDonald to push forward trade-union candidates. In London, the LRC Secretary was in regular contact with the Liberal Chief Whip. Gladstone, however, was less able to pressure local Liberals to stand aside. His writ did not run in Scotland, while the Liberals in Wales and Yorkshire made few concessions to the advocates of Labour independence. In fact, the LRC did best in Lancashire, where the Conservatives had been traditionally strong. Thus, Labour was admitted onto the political stage of parliamentary politics by the Liberal opposition but only where it was believed that it might challenge the Tories more effectively.

MacDonald secured the adoption of fifty LRC candidates, twenty-two of whom were given a clear run by the Liberals. Ten were in tandem with Liberals in two-member constituencies and only eighteen against Liberals – some of whom were unofficial – in three-cornered contests. Forty were sponsored by trade unions and all except Stanton Coit, the American ethical preacher, were working-class by origin. The ILP ran only a minority of the Labour candidates. In Leicester, MacDonald was this time twinned with Broadhurst. The local Liberals had been pressured not to run a second candidate and the Trades Council endorsed the Lib-Laber and ILPer.

The Progressives' opportunity finally came in December 1905

when Balfour resigned. The new Prime Minister, Campbell-Bannerman, called an election for the following January/February. The issues of tariff reform, education, Chinese labour and, to a lesser extent, home rule for Ireland were debated on the hustings. The LRC had little scope to put forward a distinct social programme. The Liberals secured a landslide victory, with 401 seats to the Conservatives' 157. The pro-government vote included twenty-four Lib-Labers, who were mainly miners.

Twenty-nine LRC candidates were also returned. This included nine in English two-member constituencies and only five who fought Liberals (some of whom were unofficial). Within the Labour group, the ILP secured seven seats, though many of the trade-unionists elected also belonged to the party. There were only two Labour MPs from Scotland. In England, the election of candidates was determined by the local strength of trade-unionism; the LRC secured a bloc of twelve seats in Lancashire, in part a response to the cotton towns' opposition to tariffs.

Broadhurst and MacDonald were returned for Leicester. They received 13,999 joint votes, the sitting member securing 14,745 to the latter's 14,685 votes. There could be no clearer demonstration of the indistinguishability, in popular consciousness, of working-class Liberals and Independent Labourists. Both were Labour men and they were going to support the Liberals, albeit with different degrees of enthusiasm.

It took MacDonald fourteen years to get elected to the House of Commons. If political ambition was his only motivation, it is likely that he would have secured a Liberal seat much earlier. In the 1906 electoral landslide, he found himself in parliament with Hardie and Snowden (Glasier was never to become an MP). The principal trade-union representatives were Henderson, Shackleton and J. R. Clynes. The twenty-nine Labour men were, of course, considerably overshadowed by the huge Liberal majority but it is, nevertheless, the case that this general election saw the parliamentary breakthrough of the LRC. It was a force capable of attracting working-class Liberals into a new Labour party but, by the same historical reckoning, this new challenger could be returned to the political ghetto if the Liberal elite chose, and was able, to reassert its dominance of progressive British politics.

2   *Labour in parliament, 1906–18*

Immediately after the 1906 election, the 39-year-old Ramsay MacDonald wrote: 'Everybody is asking: "What does it all mean? What does the Labour Party want? What will it do?"' He predicted that the new party '[would] have a hand in the making of history'.[1] No doubt he was delighted but, in the Executive report which he almost certainly wrote, the LRC's Secretary must have known he was being rhetorical.

The new party was to cut a poor figure in parliament. From 1910, when Britain would be enveloped in political crisis, Labour was to become even more dependent upon the Liberals. The European war of 1914-18, however, was to wrought a sea-change in British society. Labour was to join the wartime coalition governments of Asquith and Lloyd George, MacDonald having resigned the leadership of the party in 1914. Paradoxically, Labour was to emerge stronger in 1918, but only because of a split in the Liberal Party.

The Parliamentary Labour Party in the new House of Commons was thirty strong, the additional member being a Durham miner whose candidacy had come too late to gain official Labour approval. However, the Campbell-Bannerman government, with a huge bloc of 400 seats, had an overall majority of 130. If all the remaining twenty-three Lib-Labers were to defect, the Liberals would still have a substantial majority.

Keir Hardie was elected Chairman, in a contest with David Shackleton which ran to a third vote. It was MacDonald who tipped the balance; he had sought to abstain as Secretary of the LRC but the real reason was his lack of confidence in Hardie as a parliamentarian. MacDonald was then elected Secretary by the Labour MPs and he assisted Arthur Henderson as whip. In 1908 the chair was to rotate to Henderson and, two years later, he was succeeded by the former ASE Secretary, George Barnes. MacDonald was to consider Labour's third leader a 'disastrous failure'[2].

In 1906 the LRC, on the recommendation of its Executive Committee, became the Labour Party at its annual conference after the election.

The next year, Hardie established the principle of an MP's individual conscience, thereby legitimising his own political individualism. Labour delegates had agreed that 'the time and method of giving effect to [conference] instructions [should] be left to the Party in the House, in conjunction with the National Executive'. (The new party was to be decidedly 'parliamentarist', a term used later by an as-yet-unknown Lenin).[3] In the discussion, Hardie stated that they 'desired to be nothing but the servant of the movement as a whole'.[4]

Its trade-union MPs had little interest in Socialist politics, and their bureaucratic duties were to intrude upon political work. The parliamentary party established a number of committees, MacDonald convening that on education (Thomas Lough was a junior minister in the department). Labour was committed, in principle, to secular education but the Liberal government adopted the nonconformist solution of 'simple Bible reading' in state schools. In parliamentary debates, MacDonald argued that this would not foster a real spirit of religion. Labour was offered representation on one of two parliamentary committees but Hardie unsuccessfully demanded a seat on all of them. The party was considered the left-wing of Liberalism and, on one occasion, the government Chief Whip even offered to bring members to an important division.

They had to vote for many government proposals, in accordance with Labour's commitment to 'a progressive policy at home and abroad'. 'On great questions of public policy a reasonable amount of freedom of action [was] allowed Members.'[5] On what were considered legitimate Labour matters, the party and the trade-union group could exercise influence with suggested amendments. Taff Vale was reversed with the Trades Disputes Act of 1906 but the provision of school meals did not go far enough to satisfy Labour MPs. As for other social and political questions, Labour was dependent upon the ballot for private members' bills – and the support of radical MPs. An honourable defeat was the likely parliamentary outcome.

From time to time, Labour opposed the government. However, by the 1907 conference, Hardie eschewed 'running amok at the Treasury Bench'.[6] MacDonald had wanted a quiet first session, so that members could learn the ways of the house. He maintained that 'Governments [were] not afraid of Socialist speeches. . . [but] of successful criticism in details'.[7]

The party, not unnaturally, found it difficult to project its pressure-group image, as the reality of Liberal parliamentary dominance became evident. However, a serious trade depression brought about an increase in unemployment. Pete Curran won the Jarrow by-election in July 1907 and, significantly, Victor Grayson was returned for Colne Valley as an Independent Socialist. With the Conservatives' 1905 measures due to expire, MacDonald, who sat on the Central Unemployment Body for London, introduced a TUC-supported 'Right to Work' bill in July 1907. This envisaged maintenance for the unemployed and the creation of employment by the state. The bill got no further than a first reading but it was reproduced in a MacDonald pamphlet used in the 'Right to Work' campaign during the winter of 1907/8. It was reintroduced by a Liberal the following March, only to be denied a second reading by 267 votes to 118.

Labour's second parliamentary session had seen no major legislative reforms. However, the enactment of old-age pensions was promised for 1908. This was the year Lloyd George became Chancellor of the Exchequer and Winston Churchill moved to the Board of Trade, under the premiership of Asquith. Expectations of social reform were raised. In 1909 the miners finally affiliated to Labour. The parliamentary party, by a stroke of the pen (as it were), increased to forty-six members. However, Lib-Labism was far from extinct in the coalfields.

In 1906 MacDonald had finally become Chairman of the ILP. He was thus able to preside over the Socialist scrutiny of Labour's parliamentary apprenticeship. At the following year's conference, he defined Socialism as 'a guiding idea for legislation, for administration, for all constructive work of a social character'.[8] The goal of a Socialist society was thereby theoretically liquidated in parliamentary evolutionism. He soon tired of Socialist criticism as such, and longed for 'a sane laborious policy of reconstruction having for a background an active platform of idealism.'[9]

Labour still feared a revival of Lib-Labism. When the Colne Valley ILP selected Victor Grayson as its parliamentary candidate without seeking the endorsement of the trade unions locally, Labour's Executive Committee refused to endorse him. The ILP leaders had also been opposed to this Socialist firebrand but, when he narrowly won the three-cornered contest, the party decided to pay his salary as an MP. Henderson, as Chief Whip, remained hostile to Grayson but MacDonald attempted to integrate him into the Labour Party, to prevent further damage to the Labour Alliance.

Grayson, however, became a crusading preacher in parliament and outside but the reference back, at the ILP's 1908 conference, of the Executive's report was defeated by 336 votes to 104. MacDonald was cheered by delegates at the close. Some ILP branches had co-operated in unemployment agitation with the Social Democratic Party (the renamed SDF), after Labour's leaders declined to further challenge the Liberals. They gradually came to favour Socialist unity through supporting SDP by-election candidatures, though these resulted in Conservative gains. In November 1908, Grayson publicly snubbed Hardie by refusing to appear on the same platform. The leadership of the ILP, however, regained the initiative at the 1909 conference, only to be faced with a partial reference back. Thereupon, the 'big four' resigned from the new Executive, to the chagrin of most of the delegates.

Subsequently, MacDonald was to write that 'the qualities that made [Grayson] popular were those of instability'.[10] This, of course, was to dismiss Socialist criticisms of the Labour Party. Certainly, Grayson would show himself to be unreliable in later years. He lost his parliamentary seat in the first 1910 election but the following year, he led a section of the ILP into the British Socialist Party (BSP), an amalgam of Social Democrats, dissatisfied members of the ILP and independent Socialists.

Hardie responded to the scenes at the 1909 ILP Conference by publishing his *Confession of Faith in the Labour Alliance*, when Labour was even more dependent on the Liberal government. This was in spite of the fact that he was critical of the party's performance. Four new members of the ILP Executive retorted the following year with their so-called 'Green Manifesto', *Let Us Reform the Labour Party*, but the left wing of the ILP was unable to commit the party to a more radical strategy.

By the end of the 1906 parliament, then, the Labour Party had failed to dissociate itself from the Liberals. From the point of view of ILP members, this lack of independence meant that Socialism counted for little. As for MacDonald, he had been privately critical of the trade-union MPs, who made poor parliamentarians, yet he was part of an ILP leadership committed to the Labour Alliance, and determined to see off its Socialist critics. The resolution of this contradictory position in which he found himself lay in advancing a conception of Socialism which was practically indistinguishable from parliamentary radicalism.

The 1906 Labour Party Conference had been told that several MPs would visit 'our Colonial brethren' that autumn, in order to further 'co-operat[ion] with them in establishing the Empire upon a basis of international peace and goodwill'.[11] In August, MacDonald and his wife left, on their own, for a tour of Canada, Australia and New Zealand. They did not return from this political mission-cum-holiday until January 1907. The MacDonalds visited local legislatures, studied socio-economic conditions in these self-governing colonies and established relations with trade-union and Labour leaders. They also stopped off at a number of other places, such as Ceylon.

After their return, MacDonald published *Labour and the Empire* (1907), a book he hoped would form the basis of Labour's Imperial policy. This short work acknowledged that classical Liberalism had been internationalist until the 'cosmopolitan trading class' built an empire in the name of Imperialism. It proclaimed 'Socialism... [as] the next world movement'.[12] MacDonald opposed Liberal and Conservative Imperialists, and he hoped that Labour would influence the government 'to democratise the personnel of the Imperial machine'.[13]

This was a position which fell far short of the anti-Imperialism which was to become a major force in the twentieth century.

MacDonald believed, basically, in the reform of the British Empire. He wanted the implementation of 'an Imperial standard' based on 'moral... qualities of justice, honour, and administration', 'expressing the idea that the Empire is organic and develops its forms'.[14] His intellectual evolutionism also induced political fatalism in external affairs. However, MacDonald theorised the community of nations known much later as the white British Commonwealth. He envisaged 'our daughter states' freely accepting the responsibilities and privileges of 'the British hegemony'[15], and argued for an 'imperial conference' in London to transact the business of empire.

This was less Social Imperialism (to use another Leninist term), since MacDonald saw 'friendly co-operation between the Labour Parties of the Empire. . . [as] an essential first step to a genuine Imperial unity',[16] and more Liberal British Nationalism.

As for the non-white 'dependencies' of the Empire, he accused all leading nations of having 'sent their exploiters. . . to aid the development of. . . backward peoples'. He saw a future British Imperial conference 'assum[ing], on behalf of the whole self-governing empire, responsibilities for the subject races' government, education, and development'.[17]

In late September 1909, he and Margaret sailed for India, where they travelled widely. However, the parliamentary crisis necessitated their return in late December. The following year, MacDonald published *The Awakening of India*, a book that was soon reissued in a popular paperback edition. It was a sympathetic travelogue; he had been enchanted by India's Hindu culture, which appealed to his romantic spirit. MacDonald opposed the British cultural domination of dependent peoples and welcomed the burgeoning national consciousness of India.

However, there was little trace of later notions of self-determination.

Nevertheless, he was a critic of the British Raj. He saw Anglo-Indians as a degenerate ruling class and called for a strengthened India Office in London. He looked forward in 1910 to a Viceroy 'steeped in Liberal traditions';[18] this representative of the monarch, MacDonald hoped, would not simply tinker with the administration of government, but would infuse it with a new spirit of Indian reform. He described 'the Indian multitudes [as] passive' but noted that 'our education of the Hindu has set going a political evolution in which anarchism is the sequel of oppression'.[19] MacDonald believed that this could be contained by constitutional nationalism. He was unsympathetic to the separatist-inclined Muslim minority, and hinted that the government had practised divide and rule tactics. However, he expressed optimism about Indian unity. MacDonald looked forward to 'responsible government'[20] in the provinces, leading in time to a federal Indian government. He tended – like Hardie, who had visited the sub-continent the year before – to see the native states as nuclei of self-government. He expected Lord Morley's current reforms to culminate eventually in parliamentary government. However, 'for many a long year British sovereignty [would] be necessary for India, for the warring elements in Indian life need a unifying and controlling power'.[21]

Recent nationalist agitation, basically, had been uncongenial for a benign MacDonald, who saw even Indian politics in terms of the Palace of Westminster.

He had theorised Socialist politics for Britain in his two-volume *Socialism and Government* (1909), the eighth title in the ILP's 'Socialist Library' series. Contemporary preoccupations were evident in MacDonald's disavowal of 'those who would degrade the House of Commons by an exhibition of conduct... like what marked the life of the London vestries'[22] – a clear reference to Grayson's suspension in 1908.

MacDonald continued his critique of Marx and Engels. He dismissed 'as inadequate and inaccurate' their view of 'the State as the political instrument of capitalist oppression'. The theory of class war, he argued, '[made] every epoch and its institutions mere excrescences of class mischief'.[23] Indeed, he described 'the class struggle [as] far more akin to Radicalism'.[24]

He further negotiated his relationship with Liberalism, having claimed that [its] political philosophy and work... [had] now become the patrimony of the Socialist'.[25] MacDonald retained a Liberal view of democracy when he defined the state as 'the organised political personality of a sovereign people – the organisation of a community for making its common will effectual by political methods'.[26] However, like many British Socialists, he underplayed the need for political reform when he claimed elsewhere 'that the whole people of the country (not all the individuals yet, but taken as a mass) now rule'.[27]

MacDonald turned again to the notion of evolution. (It is a little known fact that he suggested the title of *Evolutionary Socialism*, when he edited the 1909 English translation of Eduard Bernstein's 'revisionist' text for the 'Socialist Library' series.) He had asserted, in another place, that 'the history of the British Parliament [was] the history of evolution of popular liberty in this country',[28] a view with which all parliamentarians would have concurred. Evolutionism was deployed, in *Socialism and Government*, to explain 'the domination of the classes which is the history of civilisation hitherto, [as] a natural and rational progression. . . of broadening political and economic freedom' but political history was intellectually liquidated when the state was portrayed as 'not the instrument of a class but an organ of Society'.[29]

It is certainly true that 'Socialism [would] be led again and again into quagmires unless it harmonise[d] its politics with its sociology, and unifie[d] its theories of political and industrial organisation'.[30] However, when *Socialism and Society* (1905) was used by MacDonald as the foundation of his second major work, it simply became a two-volume tour of a derivative political philosophy, lacking any notion of a specifically Socialist strategy under British constitutionalism.

Labour had been given an inauspicious start in 1906, when the political tide was flowing in the Liberals' direction. Nevertheless, its parliamentary emergence and the secessionary tendencies of the Lib-Labers brought what is considered a Liberal counter-strategy into play three years later. With little prompting from the Parliamentary Labour Party, Churchill tackled unemployment by establishing 'Labour Exchanges'. He also set up 'Trade

Boards' to determine wages in sweated industries. These reforms, whether by design or not, threatened the role of trade unionism. In April 1909 Lloyd George had announced his so-called people's budget, which included limited measures for taxing the rich. It won the enthusiastic support of the Labour Party. However, when the House of Lords vetoed it in November, the government was presented with a constitutional issue. It was one to which all progressive forces would certainly rally.

Asquith immediately called a General Election for January/February 1910. However, the Liberals lost 125 seats, securing only two more than the Conservatives. This made the eighty-two Irish Party and forty Labour members a potential parliamentary force, as holders of the balance of power. Labour had run seventy-eight candidates, thirty of whom were returned in straight fights with Conservatives and seven in tandem with Liberals. It is certain that the spirit of the 1903 pact continued and no Labour candidate was returned when a Liberal was running in opposition. MacDonald came in a close second to the government candidate in Leicester, having fought a contest in support of the budget.

The 1909 Osborne judgment of the law lords greatly undermined Labour's financial future, given that it prohibited unions from funding political activity. Working-class independence counted for little in the 1910 parliament, dominated, as it was, by the problem of the Upper House. Hardie believed that it 'had almost ceased to count' and, as he told the ILP conference that year, 'he wanted to see a more vigorous and militant policy pursued'.[31] The national crisis was further complicated by the death of Edward VII in early May. However, Asquith's secret enlistment of the support of his successor, George V, required a second general election. In December, the two main parties secured 272 seats each; the Irish Party had eighty-four members returned, and Labour forty two. Fifty-six candidates had been run by the party and, in circumstances similar to the first 1910 election, only two candidates, both miners, were returned against Liberals.

In the new session, MacDonald was elected unopposed as Chairman of the parliamentary party. He had been unsure about standing, not least because he might have less influence than as Secretary. ILP friends, however, argued that he was the most capable Labour MP: 'You have powerfully helped to bring sanity and commonsense and construction into the British Socialist Movement. Your books, hastily written amid the pressure of other duties, have influenced thought. . . More than any other you have organised the Labour-Socialist Alliance.'[32] The illness of Barnes finally created a vacancy and it was agreed that Henderson would take over as national party Secretary in 1912. MacDonald was to remain on the Executive as Treasurer, this largely nominal post to be filled by election at the annual conference.

At the age of forty four, then, and with five years' parliamentary experience, he was in charge of a third party of forty-two members.

The Parliament Bill was reintroduced in the Commons in February 1911, providing for the enactment of legislation passed in three successive sessions. By August, the Lords had agreed to the limitation of its veto. The government was indebted to the Irish Party for its support and, in April 1912, a home rule bill was given its first reading. The United Kingdom was thereby plunged into a major constitutional crisis, from which the unionists were to secure the principle of partition in Ireland by September 1914.

In 1910 and 1911 the Webbs championed the minority report of the Poor Law Commission, to which they had been appointed by the Conservatives. MacDonald, in contrast, accepted the contributory principle in health and unemployment insurance. He thus welcomed Lloyd George's National Insurance Bill of 1911, which proposed to make friendly societies and trade unions 'approved' bodies for the scheme.

The parliamentary party supported the Insurance Bill in 1911. However, Snowden and Hardie continued to advocate the ILP policy of no contributions and nearly a quarter of Labour MPs voted against the government. MacDonald criticised the minority in his report to the party conference. He argued for increased parliamentary discipline, though he also defended Crooks's right to introduce an anti-strike bill.

Thus were laid the foundations for welfare Capitalism, in which the trade unions were given an institutional role. Labour under MacDonald in the early 1910s proved a poor critic of bureaucratic state control. At the time, however, the parliamentary party was the prisoner of a reforming government under threat from the Tories, but Social Liberalism seems to have satisfied all but active Socialists.

MacDonald had associated increasingly with Liberal MPs, and even ministers, from 1906 and the 'at homes' in Lincoln's Inn Fields were discontinued because of parliamentary sittings. These meant that he saw even less of his wife and growing family. Margaret also had her public commitments, in between confinements, 'women and children [being] her special care'.[33]

She had long been associated with the Women's Industrial Council, a body which investigated the conditions of women workers, especially in home industries. In 1910 she was a member of its Executive. However, she opposed the mooted idea of wages boards as a solution to the problem of low pay. This may have lain behind Margaret MacDonald's growing dissatisfaction with the council's paid secretary and, after a major internal row, she resigned from the organisation. Her husband was involved in the dispute as a member and he privately described his wife's adversary as a 'Catholic coward' who used 'Jesuit methods'.[34] She was also involved in the National Union of Women Workers, a body which lobbied on issues of concern to women. Margaret also worked for women's suffrage but she and her husband, like many Socialists, opposed the militant suffragists. This was on the grounds that they 'created no new movement',[35] the Pankhursts having moved away from Labour in the course of their campaigning. Margaret was still active in the ILP and in 1906 she had presided over the foundation of the Women's Labour League. This was an organisational attempt to bring women collectively into the Labour Party. She attended meetings of the International, latterly as a delegate from the Women's League, 'though most of the leading Socialist women of the Continent were against her'.[36]

According to her husband, Margaret MacDonald came to regret competitive parliamentary politics and valued the unique role of women at home and in work. The MacDonald's family life seems to have been content, '[their] home [being] a workshop of social plan and effort'.[37] A weekend cottage in Buckinghamshire had been acquired in 1905 and, in 1908, he had a house built for his mother in Lossiemouth. This was also the family's summer home.

Then, in 1910 and 1911, MacDonald's private world collapsed. His youngest son, David, died of diphtheria in early February 1910 at the age of five years. Eight days later, his mother died in Lossiemouth. Her son's illegitimacy was still a secret guarded from the outside world but she was not to see him become leader of the Labour Party. In April 1911 the national party Assistant Secretary, Jim Middleton, lost his wife. The death of Mary, who had been Secretary of the Women's League, greatly affected Margaret MacDonald. Three months later she succumbed to blood poisoning, an internal ulcer having burst. Margaret died of heart failure on 8 September. No clergy were present at the deathbed but religious addresses were given at her cremation in Golders Green and a church service held in Leicester. Her ashes were interred in Spynie churchyard, near Lossiemouth.

MacDonald wrote a short memoir for private circulation and he was persuaded to expand it into a book, which appeared in 1912. It is significant that he chose such a method to deal with his loss. Pain exudes from these two works but his public display of grief did not greatly help his private feelings. On the first anniversary of Margaret's death, as his second son, Malcolm, was to recall, 'he spoke to [them] about her, of course in a wonderful way, but with this terrible tear-stained agony of grief'.[38]

MacDonald was never to overcome the death of his wife, so soon after the loss of his mother and one of their children. It was with a numbed inner self that he led the Labour Party.

From 1909 there had been a deepening political crisis in Britain. In the immediate context of rising prices, freedom to picket and falling unemployment, there was an unprecedented wave of strike activity.

A railway strike had been narrowly averted by Lloyd George in 1907 but a brief national stoppage, during the Agadir crisis in 1911, led to union recognition. This aided amalgamation as the National Union of Railwaymen by 1913. The miners' eight-hour act of 1908 had further restricted earnings but, following the Cambrian Combine strike of 1910-11, a national stoppage in 1912 was successfully concluded when legislation was passed providing for district minimum wages. In 1910 a National Transport Federation had been formed. The following year, there was a series of transport struggles, most notably in Liverpool and London, but the gains in the capital were thrown away in 1912 through an abortive national transport strike. In 1913 railwaymen, miners and transport workers' leaders began to negotiate a 'triple alliance'. This was the year of the great lock-out in Dublin but it was to be June 1914 before there was tentative agreement about the threat of a general strike.

The National Insurance Act greatly aided the growth of trade unionism but the strike wave of the early 1910s was contemporaneously known as 'syndicalism', owing largely to the Socialist agitator, Tom Mann. It had a revolutionary connotation in France and the United States and, while the syndicalist goal of industrial unionism certainly stimulated new forms of working-class struggle, the trade-union gains often stifled spontaneity; the National Union of Railwaymen is a case in point. Syndicalist dogma tended to be anti-political but, in the circumstances of British Labourism's waning parliamentary profile, industrial action was seen by many as a way of revivifying Socialist politics.

Ramsay MacDonald did not concur. He saw parliamentary action as central, and as the means to the Socialist end – if such existed. Significantly, he did not come from the industrial working class. Nor is there any evidence that he belonged to a trade union. (When he was to agree to join the National Union of Journalists in 1927, MacDonald stated that he had been refused entry in the past on the grounds of being free-lance). However, the Labour Alliance, which was the basis of his Socialist strategy, was dependent upon trade-union leaders. In 1911, while working on the Insurance Bill with Lloyd George, he helped persuade the railwaymen to end their national stoppage in August; three months later, he intervened to prevent the settlement breaking down. The following year, MacDonald supported a minimum wage for miners, backing the government's legislation which was rushed through to bring the struggle to an end. He had criticised Churchill, as Home Secretary, over the behaviour of police and troops in the Liverpool transport strike. However, in 1912 he accused the London dockers' leaders of 'plunging the whole country into a state of unsettlement'.[39]

MacDonald supported workers' industrial struggles but he was against unofficial action promoted by rank-and-file militants. As a parliamentarian, however, he was concerned above all with the national interest.

'There is. . . a real unity called the nation, which endows the individual with traditions, with habits, with a system of social conduct',[40] he argued in *Syndicalism: A Critical Examination* (1912). This was a quick theoretical retort to revolutionary Socialism. MacDonald defined syndicalism as 'British trade unionism applied to revolutionary purposes'. He contrasted his own method of 'legislative moulding' with 'the passive force of social paralysis or the active force of riots'. 'British realism', he concluded, 'had been captured by French idealism'.[41] Once again, his argument came to rest on evolutionism: 'Society is in a process of change, and the workers who are toiling for greater justice are only retarding progress by following the wrong-doing of which they are victims rather than strengthening the social tendencies which make for their emancipation'.[42] *Syndicalism*, judging by the attention it received in the British press, was one of MacDonald's most popular books, his intervention being welcomed as an attempt by Labour's leader to condemn the forces unleashed in the strike wave.

The following year, he published *The Social Unrest: Its Cause and Solution*. This was a more sympathetic historical appreciation of Labour unrest; for example, he continued to defend a disciplined train driver mentioned in the text, even after the railway manager privately pointed out further facts. Indeed, MacDonald concluded that Britain had been close to a revolutionary breakdown between 1910 and 1912. The threat, of course, had passed and he was able to make general Socialist criticisms of contemporary workplace relations.

He had not rejected 'organised labour operating in the factory and workshop, keeping alive labour issues'[43] and, when the much less revolutionary notion of guild Socialism was developed later as a way of increasing workers' control in industry, he was to argue that it should be 'grafted on to a complete social economic organisation. . . merged in the true comprehensive Socialist idea of the civic community'.[44]

MacDonald was re-elected unopposed in each parliamentary session but, during his time in the Chair, the Labour Party was beset with difficulties.

There had been talk in 1910 of MacDonald joining the government but nothing came of this. He had a decided strategic view whereby Labour would attract the 'Socialistic radicals'[45] into a third party. In late 1911 he rejected any sort of coalition in the current parliament. Early the following year, MacDonald again turned down offers of a cabinet post. He argued that he could not support the Liberals 'through thick and thin' and that 'it would do great evil to the Labour Party'.[46] However, there was some talk of coalition government in the future.

Emmeline Pankhurst, of the Women's Social and Political Union, had emerged from a sympathetic ILP. However, the opposition of the Labour Party, from 1905, to votes for women householders saw the militant suffragists isolated from working-class politics. It was the non-militant suffragists, with whom Margaret MacDonald had been identified, who forced the Labour Party to shift in 1912, when votes for women became part of an electoral strategy to gain full adult suffrage. MacDonald helped negotiate joint electoral work with the Socialist wing of the suffrage movement. However, when George Lansbury, the ILP MP for Bow and Bromley, resigned in November in order to fight a by-election on the issue, the Labour leader expressed his opposition. Only Hardie actively supported his independent candidature, which resulted in the loss of a Labour seat to the Conservatives.

In December, MacDonald sailed for India as a member of the royal commission on its public services. He was away until May 1913. The members of the commission returned to the subcontinent in the autumn but it was to be 1917 before its report, recommending gradual Indianisation, was published. MacDonald was to develop this theme in his much-delayed *Government of India* (1919).

He had privately threatened, in June 1913, to withdraw from Leicester at the next general election. This was after the National Executive instructed the local Labour Party not to contest the second seat, following the resignation of the Liberal, and local ILPers went on actively to support a BSP candidate who was unsuccessful. In the by-election autopsy, MacDonald defended electoral realism, refusing to challenge the government when it might jeopardise his own seat in the future.

In March 1914, Labour's support was again sought by Lloyd George. This was on the eve of a planned government raid on the Conservatives over Ulster. Asquith reputedly offered a new electoral compact, further policy concessions and a seat for Mac-Donald in the cabinet if the government were returned. Mac-Donald and Henderson were keen to have an election on the opposition's resistance to home rule. However, the Curragh 'mutiny' weakened the resolve of the government and Hardie, on the National Executive, set out to kill any co-operation with the Liberals.

At the 1914 conference of the ILP, having missed the two previous gatherings, MacDonald took the Chair at an informal session. In a private debate, he denied the allegations of Fenner Brockway about an electoral agreement. Brockway had been prompted by Hardie. However, MacDonald would have returned to London by the time delegates agreed – by 233 votes to 78 – that Labour members should 'vote on all issues only in accord with the principles for which the Party stands'.[47] That year, the party celebrated its coming of age. The ILP had put down roots since 1906, though there had been a loss of members more recently. This may have been partly because of the Labour unrest, Lansbury's *Daily Herald* being an alternative focus of militant politics.

The trade-union and Labour leaders had countered with the *Daily Citizen*, its success being a measure of Labour's popularity. The party was growing as an organisation at a time when trade-union membership was rising. Labour benefited from the inauguration of state payments for MPs in 1911 but it was 1913 before the Trades Union Act allowed political funds once again. A substantial number of trade unionists voted against such funds in the required ballots and individuals could opt out of any payment. Between 1910 and 1914, its share of by-election votes increased, even though, by the end of this period, the parliamentary party was only thirty-seven strong. Some miners' seats, acquired by the Labour Party, when the Miners' Federation joined the Party in 1909, were lost. Some were regained by the Liberals on the deaths of sitting members. In other cases, nominally Labour members reverted to their former Liberalism. The government was also worried about working-class secession and the 1903 Gladstone/MacDonald entente was unlikely to be revived. Labour was undoubtedly a product of 'an acutely developed working-class consciousness',[48] but Labourist culture imposed limited political horizons and it was not yet clear that it could supplant the Liberal Party.

In 1911 Ramsay MacDonald had found a new fulcrum for his political balancing act. On the one hand, the trade-union majority of MPs was interested in supporting the government, while, on the other, an ILP minority was worried about the fate of Socialism. Lansbury, Snowden and Hardie made fundamentalist stands from time to time but they shared no coherent Socialist strategy. The idea of Socialist unity had waned, and a considerably weakened BSP sought to return to the Labour Party. The trade-union MPs would probably have welcomed, in 1914, an electoral arrangement with the Liberals, further reforms and participation in government. This, however, was tantamount to a return to the Liberal fold. Labour had the capacity to run a hundred or so candidates in the general election expected in 1915 but the Liberals were prepared to fight such a threat and the Conservatives likely to gain from division in the progressive camp. The Labour Alliance under MacDonald looked as though it could split, with some trade unions returning to the Liberal Party. A smaller Labour Party might indeed be more socialist, but MacDonald had written, in the ILP's *Labour Leader*, that 'Parliamentary policy [was] exactly that which the most revolutionary Socialist Party would adopt if it had forty members in the House of Commons'.[49]

There would be no such critical general election because, on 4 August 1914, Britain was to enter what became known as 'the Great War', a European conflict which dislocated the evolution of Capitalist society.

MacDonald was called back to London on 1 August by the government Chief Whip. Germany had declared war on Russia and he was told that Britain was now involved. The following day, Sunday, the British section of the International demonstrated its opposition in Trafalgar Square. MacDonald, meanwhile, was ensconced in 12 Downing Street. On Monday, 3 August, the Parliamentary Labour Party decided to oppose intervention. However, now that Germany had also declared war on France, the Foreign Secretary, Sir Edward Grey, won the assent of the Commons to his war policy. MacDonald argued, as Labour leader, that the United Kingdom was not in danger. However, with the experience of South Africa in 1899 uppermost in his mind, he accepted that war was now inevitable. The party's position, he insisted, almost for the historical record, was that 'the country ought to have remained neutral'.[50]

The next day, Britain declared war on Germany, much being made of the invasion of Belgium.

As Socialist internationalism crumbled into national patriotism, Labour's National Executive agreed on 5 August, by eight to four, that the party should aim 'to secure peace at the earliest possible moment'.[51] This sentiment was subsequently endorsed by Labour MPs. That evening, however, the parliamentary party decided, by a majority, that it would support the war credits, which were to be voted the following day. Thereupon, Ramsay MacDonald resigned in despair as its Chairman, though he remained on the National Executive as Treasurer.

It was a heroic political decision and he was to be cast in the role of national traitor for the duration. However, MacDonald was to find it difficult to express his political position.

MacDonald's resignation restored his reputation in the ILP. He was one of the party's five sponsored MPs (the exceptions being Clynes and James Parker) who refused to support the government. On 11 August the ILP issued 'a manifesto on international socialism', greeting German Socialists 'across the roar of guns'.[52] The party was to oppose the war mainly from a pacifist position. MacDonald, however, considered Tolstoyism an inadequate guide to politics. (He, of course, stood even further from what was to be called 'revolutionary defeatism' and noted that erstwhile Socialist opponents, such as Grayson, Robert Blatchford, editor of the *Clarion*, and Hyndman, rapidly became social chauvinists.) He had long been anti-Imperialist, hostile to the Russian autocracy, suspicious of the entente with France and supportive of German Social Democracy. He had opposed British militarism, voting in parliament against expenditure on arms, but it was Keir Hardie who had done much to promote the idea of an international general strike in the event of war. While Hardie failed to convince the International in 1910 and subsequently the Labour Party, MacDonald was prepared to endorse the notion of a general strike 'against an unpopular war'. This support for extra-parliamentary action, however, was highly qualified; MacDonald only favoured a national stoppage when opposition to war was 'regarded sympathetically by sections of all classes'.[53] In the jingoistic atmosphere of August 1914, his stand was to remain untested.

Arthur Henderson had temporarily assumed the Chair, while retaining the secretaryship of the national party. MacDonald's parliamentary colleagues, however, were reluctant to see him go. It was hoped that party unity could be maintained, even in the face of differences over the war. However, he rejected overtures from a deputation of fellow MPs and urged Labour 'to take up a distinctive position which will in due course be the rallying centre for those who will wish that this war should not have been fought in vain'.[54] He claimed that only a minority of the parliamentary party had opposed his view of the causes of war. This was to overlook the vote on 5 August for war credits but, given that MacDonald seemed to be admitting that it was polit-ically impossible to oppose war once it had started, there was a basis for continued unity if the pro-war majority mitigated its militarism. This was not to be the case. On 24 August the TUC agreed to an industrial truce; five days later, the Labour Party accepted a political truce. This involved participation in an all-party recruitment campaign. MacDonald was thrown into a quan-dary. With the ILP refusing to collaborate, even as the Germans advanced, MacDonald declined, in September, to appear on a recruiting platform in Leicester. However, his letter of apology to the mayor was couched as a paean on progressive warfare, and Henderson, for one, was led to hope that the party would unite.

For this he was to be criticised by the ILP executive and, privately, he came to regret the tone of ILP resistance to the war but he also continued to refuse entreaties to return to the Chair, the Labour Party having become increasingly anti-German. MacDonald effectively became one of a small number of anti-war members within the parliamentary party and he resolved to remain silent in the House of Commons.

He was not, however, totally inactive in the Labour movement.

On 4 August, at a representative meeting, the War Emergency Workers' National Committee had been established. Originally conceived as an anti-war body, it was created to safeguard working-class interests during the war. Henderson and two others represented the Labour Party and MacDonald was soon co-opted to the committee. Though he would attend regularly, 'he seems never to have asserted himself and he was at odds with the majority of the Committee on relief administration at the beginning of the war'.[55]

At the same time, he had also agreed to serve on the all-party relief committee set up by the government. In this capacity he helped allocate grants for war distress from the Prince of Wales Fund. MacDonald was not to resign from this until after the war when he lost his seat in parliament.

Isolated within the Labour movement, MacDonald's opposition found expression elsewhere.

There had been resignations from the government and a number of radical MPs opposed the war. Indeed, they outnumbered the five ILPers. Lloyd George, however, contrary to the expectations of those who remembered the Boer War, was to become a major promoter of militarism. Shortly after resigning the leadership of the party, MacDonald argued that Gladstone would have accepted Germany's guarantees of Belgian neutrality as it marched to war with France. On 10 August he dined with a number of dissident Liberals. Early the following month, MacDonald, Charles Trevelyan, an ex-junior minister, Norman Angell and E. D. Morel circularised likely supporters of 'parliamentary control over foreign policy'. It was MacDonald's view that the war had been brought about by 'the present system of European diplomacy by which international relations are settled by a few interested gentlemen, drawn from the aristocratic and capitalist classes, working in secret and making arrangements which are not accurately or fully reported to the public.'[56]

The resultant Union of Democratic Control (UDC) was inaugurated on 17 November. 'The UDC was not a "Stop-the-War" organisation, although it held that the outbreak of war might have been prevented if the people had been aware of what the Government was committing it to.'[57] This largely middle-class group sought to develop a democratic foreign policy. Such an enterprise could proceed during the war but it would not, of itself, bring the war to an end. The UDC looked forward to a negotiated peace settlement based on the principles of no annexations, parliamentary approval of all treaties, an international council in place of the European balance of power and agreement on disarmament (including the nationalisation of manufactories). MacDonald was to be prominently associated with the UDC, although he was only responsible for one of its pamphlets, *War and the Workers* (1915), and two leading contributions to the union's paper. However, the UDC represented the appropriate political response in his opinion; he believed in broad progressive alliances and was particularly aware of social democracy's weakness in foreign affairs.

Hardie had feared that the UDC might become a rival to the ILP. However, party branches began to affiliate to the major organisation against the war. Middle-class radicals were to derive a progressive foreign policy for the anti-war Socialists.

MacDonald's resignation was a personal release from frustration. On 2 August, walking home after dining with some members of the government, he '[felt] that a great break [had] come'.[58] The next day, however, he was predicting another '1906'. Like most British people, he was far from prepared for a continental war. He was soon being attacked in the press for his criticisms of Grey; it was alleged that his refusal to support the national effort encouraged the Germans and sowed doubts in neutral countries. This induced considerable strain and MacDonald drew further on his reserves of self-reliance. In the process, he became more and more isolated.

A Liberal MP privately suggested that he might lend his organising ability to the Red Cross ambulance volunteer corps. In early December, he left for Belgium, apparently to investigate the work of this body. MacDonald's intention, it seems, was to 'see the war'.[59] However, he was arrested and deported. He returned later with the correct permit and was taken on a tour of the front by his friend, Colonel Seely, a former Liberal Minister of War. It was his first and last direct experience of warfare.

MacDonald was once again a political propagandist but he was now 'the recipient of disgusting abuse',[60] though he was not to be imprisoned like E. D. Morel. In September 1915, Hardie died suddenly – of a 'broken heart',[61] it was said. MacDonald became the ILP's most public figure and the party was to organise larger appreciative meetings as the war dragged on. The depths of chauvinism were plumbed by Horatio Bottomley's *John Bull*; in September 1915, it revealed that MacDonald was 'the illegitimate son of a Scotch servant girl!'[62] The registered surname on the facsimile birth certificate came as a complete surprise to him. His only relief was that his mother was spared the exposure. Several dozen people wrote disapproving of Bottomley's actions, and MacDonald was well received as fraternal delegate at that year's TUC in Bristol. However, a number of good burghers in Lossiemouth were trying to rescind his membership of the local golf club. MacDonald put this down to long-standing hostility towards radicals and, in September 1916, he was to be expelled by a vote of three to one for his anti-war views.

In May 1915, Asquith had brought the Conservatives into the government. He invited Labour to join this coalition. The parliamentary party opposed the idea but the Executive was in favour. A joint meeting finally authorised Henderson, as Chairman, to take a seat in the cabinet, nominally as Education Minister; William Brace and George Roberts were given junior posts, in the Home Office and as a whip, respectively.

Thus the Labour Party became a prisoner of the war lords, unable to resist the conscription of workers into the munitions industry or military service.

It supported the establishment, in June, of the Ministry of Munitions under the control of Lloyd George. As the person in overall charge of armaments manufacture, he sought '[the] greater subordination [of] labour to the direction and control of the state'.[63] In order to increase production, the unions agreed to compulsory arbitration, the dilution of skilled labour and restrictions on the mobility of war workers.

The 1915 TUC, however, came out against military conscription, but only to the point when it might be enacted. Asquith introduced an alternative, whereby eligible men 'attested' their willingness to serve. Labour helped secure two and a half million signatures, in order to maintain voluntary conscription. In January 1916 the Liberal-dominated coalition government proposed to call up unmarried men of between eighteen and forty-one years of age. This idea had seen the resignation of the Home Secretary, Sir John Simon, and was to meet with the opposition of some thirty MPs. A special Labour Party Conference voted to resist Asquith's bill. However, its three members in government decided to delay consideration of resignation until after the party's annual conference at the end of the month. Then, delegates voted to give up the fight. In April, the parliamentary party came out against any extension of the Military Service Act. However, the Executive was forced to call off a special conference on the issue when the trade unions fell into line behind the government. Conscription for married men aged eighteen to forty one was forced through in the House of Commons.

Lloyd George, who was rapidly becoming the leading figure in the government, moved to the War Office in July and, the following month, Henderson was made Paymaster-General, outside the cabinet.

In December 1916, Asquith was brought down by his War Minister. Lloyd George thereupon formed a second coalition government. In so doing, he excluded many prominent Liberals. The Parliamentary Labour Party and, to a lesser extent, the Executive, backed Lloyd George. Henderson became a member of the small Conservative-dominated war cabinet, John Hodge and George Barnes took over the new Ministries of Labour and Pensions (the former with cabinet rank) and there were several junior posts for the Labour Party.

Lloyd George split the Liberals, irreparably as it turned out, on the question of the war's prosecution. As early as January 1916, however, MacDonald had '[begun] to doubt as to the future of the [Labour] Party'.[64] When Labour accepted universal military service, he wrote: 'In the history of reaction this chapter will be headed: "How we succeeded with Labour"'.[65] He argued, in December, that 'the policy of independence [was] no longer the policy of the party',[66] on the grounds that Lloyd George's coalition was less than an all-party national government. His belief that Labour could supplant the Liberals was being threatened by the war.

Despite differences over the war, Labour, as a party based on the trade unions, struggled to maintain internal unity throughout. At the 1916 ILP conference, MacDonald argued against the expulsion of its two dissident MPs. However, when Parker became a government whip in April 1917, the ILP was compelled to disown him. Earlier in the year, the Labour Party Conference had voted to abolish the federal principle in Executive elections, a move which was widely seen as an attempt to strengthen the power of the unions. Yet the same conference had already elected a new Executive under the old format. This included two anti-war Socialists from the ILP, a balance acceptable to Henderson. Mac-Donald was re-elected annually as Treasurer by the whole con-

ference and, despite his opposition to the government, he continued to carry out his duties on behalf of the party. However,
this was largely symbolic and, in early 1917, it seemed that a
split in Labour was only a matter of time.

In the course of the war the party's affiliated membership
roughly doubled. The TUC grew slightly less rapidly but, by the
end of hostilities, it was to have four and a half million members.
The rapid expansion of trade-unionism was due to the wartime
combination of low unemployment and high inflation, both of
which were created by the insatiable need for munitions. The
war effort required unprecedented state intervention in economic
and social life and even the recognition of trade unions. Many
Socialists thought politics were moving almost naturally in their
direction. Lloyd George's brand of state intervention required a
high degree of trade-union collaboration and, in the context of
a working class being reforged by a managed economy, it gave
rise to significant industrial unrest. On the Clyde, engineering
workers had, in 1915, struck for a wage increase and had subsequently fought against dilution. In May 1917 shop stewards
led an unofficial national strike of munitions workers. However,
this rank-and-file movement did not overcome a sectional
approach to Labour conscription. Early the following year its
leaders failed to mount a political strike for an immediate peace.
This industrial militancy inspired local ILPers, but nationally the
party declined; the BSP took an anti-war position in 1916 just
as it was admitted to the Labour Party. In contrast, other pre-war
left Socialists shared the jingoism of Hyndman.

Ramsay MacDonald still refused to countenance industrial
action, even though the handful of anti-war Socialist and radical
MPs was occluded by a formidable parliamentary alliance. In the
second month of the Asquith coalition, he wrote in the *Leicester
Pioneer*: 'those who can enlist, ought to enlist, those who are
working in munitions factories should do so whole-heartedly'.[67]

The following March, he told the House of Commons that, if his opposition to the war encouraged industrial militancy on the Clyde, 'I should wish. . . something [to] happen. . . which would destroy every particle of influence that I ever have had with the working men of this country'.[68] At heart, MacDonald did not believe that there was any basis for resistance when the country was engaged in war.

In January 1917 he published *National Defence: a Study in Militarism*. This was a short book which theorised his opposition to war. MacDonald rejected pacifism as sentimental. However, his own stand was probably moralistic and his belief in the innate peace-loving character of all peoples was certainly romantic. He dismissed the idea of a citizen army, which European Socialists had seen as a popular constraint on ruling-class militarism. Mac-Donald argued that even defensive forces conducted offensive wars. This was undoubtedly the case but it did not square with his own public position. He remained opposed to Britain's involvement in the European war, yet he had said on 7 August 1914: 'whatever our views may be of the origins of the war, we must go through with it'.[69] (Revolutionary defeatism would have been abhorrent to MacDonald. He was a parliamentarian, entrusted with the destiny of the British people, and (virtually) an English nationalist.)

He attributed the war to the triple alliance and triple entente, condemning the balance of power in international relations. He blew cold on the alternative idea of an armed League of Nations, insisting that much more could be achieved. MacDonald advocated what was being called the new diplomacy - the conduct of foreign policy in the open – but this democratic proposal, however worthy, remained rhetorical. (In December 1916 he had welcomed the pronouncements of the United States's President, Woodrow Wilson, on the post-war world: 'The note follows precisely the line of my suggestion and indeed some of his phrases are word for word what I said in the conversation [with an American official]'.[70]) MacDonald still stood some distance from practical, bourgeois politics and saw militarism as an inexorable historical force. Against its presumed logic of evolution, he posed the solution of disarmament. He saw each nation, at some point in the future, contributing to the process of pacification.

By way of political conclusion, however, MacDonald looked forward to a reassertion of Socialist internationalism: 'The working classes must build up a Labour international diplomacy. . . which will be enforced and guaranteed by peoples in every European Parliament working in union with each other, insisting upon knowing what their Foreign Offices are doing and pursuing a common policy decided upon by themselves at joint conferences held frequently.'[71]

On the outbreak of war, the International had been undermined. However, in 1915 its functionaries at The Hague made overtures to Labour but when they later visited London, in March 1916, they were told that the party officially stood for 'prosecution of the War to a victorious termination'.[72]

The allies were bent on defeating Germany but Lloyd George, soon after he became Prime Minister, articulated Britain's war aim as national self-determination. In April 1917 Wilson brought the United States into the war. Revolution had already broken out in Russia, the Tsar having abdicated on 2/15 March, when a provisional government, including Kerensky, was formed. On 14/27 March, the Petrograd soviet declared in favour of a peace without annexations or indemnities.

MacDonald was enthused by this bourgeois-democratic revolution. He looked forward to the soviet-inspired government pressing for a negotiated peace but he also feared that Russia might make a separate peace if it slipped from democracy. Socialists in the Labour Party summoned a convention in Leeds for 3 June. There, MacDonald proposed the resolution welcoming the Russian revolution; other motions suported the Petrograd declaration, the restoration of civil liberty and even the establishment of councils of workers' and soldiers' delegates.

British Labour wanted to keep Russia in the war, at all costs. To this end, Henderson had been sent on a government mission to Petrograd. On 10 June, seamen in Aberdeen refused to convey MacDonald to Russia. He wanted to persuade the Petrograd soviet that 'a democratic programme of peace'[73] should be presented to a forthcoming meeting of the International. Henderson returned to Britain in July, convinced of the need to support a negotiated peace. At a special conference on 10 August, Labour agreed to send delegates from the pro-war majority to Stockholm (minority representation was refused the ILP). It was accepted by the party's leaders that a meeting of allied, neutral and even enemy Socialists was necessary to maintain the position in Russia. This was too much for the government, in particular its Conservative members. Henderson was more or less forced to resign from the war cabinet, though Barnes took his place on behalf of Labour. The government insisted that passports would not be provided for British delegates to Stockholm and this helped sabotage the Socialist attempt at a peace conference. The Labour Party remained predominantly pro-war and, while an attempted Socialist intervention could not have arrested the continuing Russian revolution, it had resulted in Henderson being freed to concentrate on his job as Party Secretary.

On 25 October/7 November, the Bolsheviks seized power through the Petrograd soviet. The following day a decree on peace was issued. The revolutionary government in Russia, under Lenin, agreed to an armistice on 2/15 December and, on 3 March 1918, the soviet delegation was to sign the treaty of Brest-Litovsk without even reading it.

MacDonald had long warned about 'the danger of anarchy in

Russia',[74] but he was to support the Bolshevik régime until after the war. Henderson had drawn up a 'memorandum on war aims', with the assistance of Webb and MacDonald, and, with the publication by Trotsky of the allies' 'secret treaties', the British Labour movement formally came to accept a democratic peace at the end of 1917. It was Labour which forced Lloyd George into making an apparently sympathetic statement of war aims and, since the October Revolution had inspired Wilson's 'fourteen points' of 8 January 1918, the party began to reunite while still part of the coalition. Henderson still concentrated on the allied governments, while MacDonald, in contrast, was concerned with reviving democratic internationalism.

Henderson was still bitter about his departure from the government. Now with the expectation of a wider franchise and the evidence of Liberal disarray, he saw that Labour could become the second party of the state. The coalition had introduced a Representation of the People Bill, which would enfranchise men over twenty one years with six months' residence and women over thirty with an occupancy qualification, a major reform enacted in June 1918. MacDonald thought 'a new Democratic Party'[75] might emerge from the anti-war radicals. In *Socialism After the War*, published by the ILP in 1917, he had condemned the state Socialism of a trade-union-dominated Labour Party; as Treasurer, he was critical of the bureaucrats on the Executive, and, as an MP, he had seen his trade-union colleagues bought off by the government.

MacDonald tried to limit the power of the unions with their block votes, as a member of a Labour sub-committee drawing up a new party constitution. However, Henderson and Webb, who had joined the Executive in 1916, restricted the role of local Labour Parties – which were to recruit individual members for the first time. The whole party was to elect, at annual conference, an Executive of twenty four, the majority being trade unionists, with five from local parties and four from the new women's sections. When the constitution was agreed in January/February 1918 at the seventeenth annual conference, Socialists had only Webb's collective goal in Clause 4 as consolation.

Thus was born 'the People's Party'.[76]

In June, the eighteenth conference adopted *Labour and the New Social Order* as the party's programme. Drafted by Sidney Webb, it laid down principles of guaranteed employment, nationalisation, social welfare and popular education. Its actual proposals, however, were modest. The emphasis was on post-war reconstruction, the needs of society which would be met by the state. The party's trade-union leaders assumed that state intervention would continue after the war and MacDonald moved the conference resolution on 'increased production'. More importantly, the conference voted that Labour should break the political truce. With the allies about to launch an offensive on the western front, the party selected candidates for a general election expected before the end of 1918.

The Labour ministers, including Clynes who had become food controller in July, accused the Executive of breaking with the wartime coalition. Lloyd George and Bonar Law, the Conservative leader, were determined to continue with the government once the Germans had sued for peace in early October and while the combatants wrangled about the 'fourteen points'. On 7 November Labour's Executive met in the wake of the general election announcement. Clynes argued that Labour should remain in the government until a peace treaty was concluded. MacDonald, supported by James Maxton, an ILPer, successfully moved that the party's ministers should now resign. This view was to be endorsed by a special party conference. Germany signed the armistice on 11 November and, when parliament dissolved, Clynes and two other Labour ministers prepared to resign. However, Barnes led a group of four coalition Labourites, and their parliamentary supporters, into the election.

The 'coupon' contest was held on 14 December. It was virtually a plebiscite on Lloyd George's conduct of the war, with nearly eleven million men and women voting – a turnout of fifty-nine per cent. The government secured forty-eight per cent of this vote, just under half. However, it won 478 seats, the majority of its supporters being Conservative. Asquith, as leader of the opposition, was not returned and there were only twenty-eight Independent Liberals in the new parliament. Labour had run 361 candidates, but it only secured 59 seats – most of them being trade unionists. The party, however, achieved twenty-two per cent of the poll. Clynes was returned unopposed but Henderson and the prominent ILPers lost their seats. Leicester had been divided into three constituencies. MacDonald only gained 6,347 votes in the West Division, to his opponent's 20,510 votes. It was an irony, probably not lost on MacDonald, that the coalition candidate had once been a member of the SDF. He lost his parliamentary seat after twelve years because of his stand on the war. This was a cataclysm which had produced a profound change in Britain, including the fact that Labour, with not many more seats, was the main opposition force in parliament.

3   The challenge of Labour, 1918–24

Ramsay MacDonald suffered greatly during the war because of his politics; in July 1918 he had written in his diary: 'Four years indignity, lying, blackguardism, have eaten like acid into me. Were I assassinated before it is all over would give no one who has followed the attacks cause for wonder.'[1] Nevertheless, he recovered his political energy. Following the loss of his seat in Leicester, he wrote: 'I am truly sorry that my Parlia[mentary] and public work is broken, & that, though there are one or two good men in it, the Labour team is altogether inadequately equipped for the part it ought to play.'[2] He did not elaborate on what this role might be.

The 52-year-old defeated MP was clearly unimpressed with the new parliamentary contingent. However, 1918 was the year Labour became a major party, following the enfranchisement of seventy-eight per cent of adults. (It had won the support of more men and women, many first-time voters, than the Liberals in December 1910.) In the course of this parliament, Labour was to more or less see off the Liberals. MacDonald had almost lost his faith in the party and he was not to be centrally involved in this historic breakthrough. Little can he have realised that, within four years, the parliamentary party would more than double its membership of fifty nine, after which he was effectively to be elected leader of the opposition. He can hardly have envisaged that the party would then become a minority government in January 1924, and that he was to be Prime Minister.

At the end of 1918, however, he became a private individual once again. Though deprived of his £400 parliamentary salary and with the income from his wife's estate considerably reduced, MacDonald was able, in the immediate post-war years, to work as a writer and lecturer. It must have been with some satisfaction that he took to calling himself an 'author'.

A Dutch housekeeper had taken charge at Lincoln's Inn Fields after Margaret's death and in 1916 the family moved to 9 Howitt Road in Hampstead. This was a comfortable terraced house, close to Belsize Park underground station. MacDonald, perhaps because of his identification with the ILP, does not seem to have been well-received by all his middle-class neighbours. His oldest son, Alister, spent three years with the Friends' medical corp during the war. Following his marriage in 1922, when he was presumably still training to be an architect, he would present Ramsay with a granddaughter. Malcolm became head boy at Bedales, a public school in Hampshire, and in 1920 he was to become a student at Oxford University. The three daughters – Ishbel, Joan, and Sheila – were still at school. Family life was a source of considerable happiness but MacDonald still grieved for his wife and his son, David.

He was unable to accept Katherine Bruce Glasier's advice that he should remarry. After Margaret's death, he had associated with the daughter of the 8th Earl De La Warr, Lady Margaret Sackville (the young ninth earl was to be one of the first aristocratic members of a Labour government). In the early 1920s MacDonald was to appear close to Mrs Molly Hamilton. However, he found it impossible to respond to women in political love with him. To compound this, he had few male friends. He eschewed the company of individuals in the Labour movement, by and large preferring the society of self-made men, like himself. MacDonald was a solitary figure, whose passion for reading filled his house with books; later he would become a collector of furniture and paintings. His other interest, walking, was chronicled in his political journalism; articles which were to be collected as *Wanderings and Excursions* in 1925.

MacDonald, however, remained treasurer of the Labour party, and, in the context of the post-war settlement in Europe, this Executive position was to allow him to intervene in international Socialist affairs. Here, the October Revolution, which was introducing soviet Marxism to the world, would reshape the Socialist landscape.

He had a free vote as a member of the party's delegation to the International, which held its first post-war meeting at Berne in February 1919. At this time, Moscow was trying to establish a third, or Communist, International – the Comintern. Europe's Socialists, however, were concerned primarily with the post-war settlement. MacDonald successfully proposed that the delegations to a League of Nations, Wilson's key institutional proposal, should be subject to parliamentary control. He was elected, with others, to approach the peace conference on behalf of international Labour. However, his Socialist colleagues were to refuse to endorse the argument that the Treaty of Versailles, signed at the end of the peace conference, fell far short of the Wilsonian ideal of international democracy. In contrast, the Labour Party conference passed a resolution from MacDonald criticising the allied solution imposed on Germany, though, in July, only one radical, pro-Labour MP voted against Lloyd George when the treaty was approved by the British parliament.

The second International had succumbed to social chauvinism in August 1914 but in 1919 many anti-war Socialists, including MacDonald, looked forward to its reconstitution. This position was condemned as 'centrist' in March by the first congress of the Comintern in Moscow.

The Communist left espoused the dictatorship of the proletariat. At Berne, MacDonald had been concerned, above all, with international Socialist unity. Thus, he refused to support the majority Branting resolution, which declared in favour of parliamentary democracy. The pro-soviet position was enshrined in the minority Adler-Longuet resolution but this was equally divisive. MacDonald was to find it increasingly difficult to rally the forces of international Socialism. In October he concluded that 'the danger to the Second International [was] not the Third but sections in itself'.[3] He still distrusted the dominant section, which had supported the war, but, with the Comintern bent on 'split[ting] the most revolutionary elements from the "centre"... by mercilessly criticizing and exposing...[its] leaders',[4] he came to defend left-wing Social Democracy from the theory and practice of Bolshevism.

MacDonald was not unsympathetic to the soviet régime. As late as May 1919, he noted in his diary: 'Getting more and more struck with the work of Lenin as an administrator and his views of revolution.'[5] Some of this was evident in his *Parliament and Revolution* (1919), the twelfth volume in the 'Socialist Library' series. However, this work was mainly an attempt to reassert the agreed ideas of the pre-war International. Thus, he argued that 'a Parliamentary. . . majority [could] proceed to effect the transition from Capitalism to Socialism with the co-operation of the people'.[6] MacDonald's objection to Russian Marxism was that all revolutions eventually became tyrannical. (In September 1920 he was to visit, as part of a delegation from the International which also included Kautsky and Vandervelde, the Menshevik republic of Georgia, an independent state which would forcibly be incorporated by the soviet authorities the following February. He was subsequently to insist that the Georgians should be allowed to choose between the Mensheviks and Moscow.)

Just as he had opposed British Marxism from the 1890s, so he sought to save the ILP from Communism after the war. In April 1920 the party voted, against his advice, to withdraw from the now-moribund second International. This immediately raised the question of the third International, even though the ILP had not shown itself to be any more than a Social-Democratic formation. The Comintern, of course, considered the centrists the greatest obstacle to revolutionary advance and MacDonald was to be vindicated, at least in part, at the 1921 conference, when ILP delegates rejected the twenty-one conditions for affiliation to Moscow.

He had argued for an all-inclusive International, something in which the ILP still believed, but it looked unlikely that this could be the old pre-war organisation; at its Geneva conference in August 1920, the second International was shown to be little more than a right-wing rump. However, when its headquarters were transferred to the Labour Party in London, pending further negotiations, MacDonald and a trade unionist accepted the secretaryship of the skeletal organisation in November. He may have been tempted by the remuneration of £600, the British unions seeking to subsidise their version of international Socialism. However, he considered it a 'ridiculous sum',[7] and, though this was not known at the time, he only accepted the salary for a month or two. MacDonald believed the second International's prospects were poor and he convinced himself that he was only keeping it going to become an element in a new movement. This reconsolidation, it was quietly assumed, would not include Moscow. The ILP censured him but MacDonald convinced the party Executive to withdraw its reprimand. The logic of his centrism was, of course, that, once he had rejected Communism, he was thrown in the direction of right-wing Social Democracy. This was something the ILP attempted to avoid. In late 1920 it condemned Social Democracy as reformist and Communism as dogmatic. The institutional implication was the so-called two and a half International, the International Working Union of Socialist Parties which was established at a conference in Vienna the following February with the aim of attracting all Socialists.

MacDonald basically wanted an alternative to the Comintern which was not dominated by the right. The ILP agreed about the right but it wanted to attract back the Communists. This was at a time when the Comintern was still committed to the idea of world revolution.

In mid-1921, however, its third congress in Moscow embraced the united front in all but name. It looked like the log jam was breaking up. The Labour Party Conference had called for consultations with the Vienna Union. However, although MacDonald succeeded in luring these left Social Democrats to a conference in London with the party Executive, they refused to take part in any international conference without the Communists. A month later, he took the Chair at the 1917 Club, of which he was a member, on the occasion of a dinner in honour of Krasin and welcomed what was taken to be the leading Bolshevik's criticism of the Russian Revolution. It was to be April 1922, following the formal adoption in Moscow of the slogan of 'the united workers' front', before representatives of the three Internationals met in Berlin. (Radek observed of the British representatives that MacDonald, known as a member of the ILP, was prominent in the second International delegation, while the ILP, which was still affiliated to the Labour Party, was part of the Vienna contingent!) The right-wing Social Democrats extracted concessions from the Comintern's delegates but MacDonald, who had become increasingly anti-Communist, cannot have been too disappointed when the putative international united front, embracing all Socialists, was rejected by Lenin in Moscow. The way was now open for a rapprochement with the Vienna Union. In August, at a meeting of the second International's Executive in Prague, MacDonald resigned as joint secretary, his work largely completed. The following May the two wings of Social Democracy were to merge in Hamburg. The Labour and Socialist International, as this new organisation would be called, was to be a worthy successor of the body Lenin had sought to transcend from late 1914.

If MacDonald became an agent of the right in Labour's foreign dealings, in domestic politics the ex-parliamentarian acquired a left-wing reputation.

During the war he had intimated that 'the trade unions were now a terrible incubus on the Labour Party'.[8] He observed the growing number of anti-war radicals, though he was not in favour of them joining the ILP. In January 1919, however, MacDonald admitted that 'there [were] sections of the Labour Movement now more dead to everything towards which democracy calls "progress" than the snobbish middle class sections.'[9] This was hardly an argument for the Liberal Party, since it was evidently in historical decline. However, he was clearly disillusioned with the new, Webbian Socialist, Labour Party, though he still believed it would rally all progressive forces in time.

MacDonald was unenthusiastic when a Scottish miner, William Adamson, who had been elected to the Chair of the parliamentary party in 1917, was confirmed in the leadership for the 1919 session. The fifty-nine Labour members, augmented by one Co-operative and three Independent Labour MPs, were over-shadowed in the 1918 parliament, given that Lloyd George had the support of a huge phalanx of 478 supporters, the majority of whom were Conservatives. Though it greatly outnumbered the Asquithian Liberals, Labour failed to 'show that the Party [was] in effect the Chief Opposition'.[10] It was, however, to win half the by-elections, where seats changed hands, in the next four years. In late 1919, Henderson re-entered parliament. However, it was the Vice-Chairman, J. R. Clynes, who took charge of the growing parliamentary contingent in the 1921 session; the small group of three ILP MPs made little impression and the Socialists looked to the return of Snowden and MacDonald.

Earlier, in June 1920, MacDonald had agreed to advise Labour MPs on parliamentary tactics. However, when this highly irregular arrangement became public knowledge, the parliamentary party was forced to do without the experience of a former leader. He was angry at this rejection and confided that 'it might be better to make a new combination and "smash" the present Labour Party'.[11] This was a measure of his dissatisfaction with the trade unionists, who were at their most powerful in the Labour Party.

MacDonald had abandoned Leicester, after two decades' association, to become the prospective candidate for Aberavon, in Glamorgan. Largely at the insistence of Henderson, he was persuaded to stand for East Woolwich in February 1921, following the retirement of Will Crooks. It was understood that he would return to Wales for the general election. Despite the intervention of Horatio Bottomley, he was only narrowly defeated; he secured 13,041 votes to the 13,724 which went to the coalition candidate, a decorated military captain. East Woolwich, however, was the only seat Labour lost in the 1918 parliament, though no one, especially in the ILP, held it against MacDonald.

Beatrice Webb had observed him to be 'a restless and uneasy spirit' at the 1920 Labour Party Conference in Scarborough, 'generally in company with the ex-Liberal MPs who have joined the Labour Party and who are now posing as Left Wing.'[12] The conference still re-elected MacDonald to the treasurership each year, though he attended the Executive less frequently. However, Henderson summoned him, along with Webb, to a meeting with Clynes during the 1921 conference. The leader feared he might be asked to form a government if Lloyd George were to fall from power but this speculation about office only bemused Mac-Donald. Since becoming an official of the International, he had achieved a certain distance from the internal life of the party.

The contrary was the case in the ILP, a party whose role had been further diminished when Labour formally became Socialist. MacDonald continued to attend ILP annual conferences, as a delegate from Leicester. As an ex-MP, he supervised the post-war reorganisation of the party. This was at a time when local Labour Parties were attracting individual members. Though the ILP might be committed to international Socialist unity, it was less inclined to look to its left in domestic politics. As a member of Labour's Executive, MacDonald rejected the affiliation of the nascent Communist Party in September 1920 and on two subsequent occasions. He was to be denounced for this by Communist militants during the East Woolwich by-election. MacDonald had not been active in the ILP's leadership since 1909 but at the 1921 conference he was elected to the Executive with 471 votes, the next candidate receiving 270. This was a measure of his popularity with the members; he was known for his stand on the war and he spoke at many branch and other meetings from 1919.

MacDonald was ideologically pre-eminent in the ILP; Glasier had died in 1920 after a long illness. He continued to edit the party periodical, the *Socialist Review*, and the 'Socialist Library' series was resumed. He also produced regular pieces for the Glasgow *Forward* and other papers. MacDonald also kept up his output of books and pamphlets. He rejected 'the merely bureaucratic and materialist Socialis[m] of the Fabian and Economic Schools' in *Parliament and Democracy* (1920),[13] a third position which was analogous to the ILP's rejection of reformism and dogmatism in international Socialism. He restated his general theory, with the now fashionable and tame graft of guild Socialism, in *Socialism: Critical and Constructive* (1921),[14] and, in the pamphlet, *History of the ILP* (1922), MacDonald presented an exemplary statement of mainstream British Socialism. (It remains the best introduction to the totality of his mature thought.)

Labour had been robbed in the 1918 election. Though it had gained over a fifth of the vote, it secured only eight per cent of the seats. It is not surprising that proportional representation should have been most popular in the early 1920s; many Labour candidates were to declare themselves in favour of electoral reform and even MacDonald was forced to concede that the British system was not necessarily the most democratic. The low turn-out in 1918 had been attributed, in part, to inadequate registration. Electoral registers were brought up to date by the authorities after the war but, in a political system approaching mass democracy, the onus of securing high levels of working class voting was thrown on the Labour Party. At the local elections in November 1919, when the question of peace had been settled, it did surprisingly well. Labour even took control of a number of towns and began to show it could administer local government.

The wartime growth of the party had continued after the armistice. Labour's affiliated membership was nearly four and a half million in 1920, a figure that was to remain an all-time high for nearly three decades. The number of affiliated Socialists, however, continued to decline. Underlying this political strength was trade-union density. The TUC represented six and a half million trade unionists in 1920, the sustained growth of the movement seeing a doubling of the 1914 figure. The trade-union centre had also increased its functions. The TUC had taken an interest in foreign affairs from 1917 and, in 1919, it began to think about co-ordinating industrial action.

Underlying these developments was a post-war economic boom which created employment for the first demobilised soldiers. Apart from the low Socialist profile of the Parliamentary Labour Party, there was an objective basis to Ramsay Mac-Donald's political depression – in the immediate post-war years, the ideology of 'direct action' once again invoked the spirit of syndicalism, though this time the challenge came from left-wing trade-union officials. In 1918 the economy had been largely under state control. However, Lloyd George was successfully to negotiate the politics of post-war industrial conflict. In this he was greatly helped by a slump which began in mid-1920, from which date unemployment soared. By 1922, laissez-faire Capitalism was to be substantially restored.

There had been a police strike in London in August 1918 but an attempt the following year to defend trade-union organisation was smashed by the government. Troops had also been used in an unofficial strike of engineers on Clydeside (and in Belfast) in early 1919. The power of shop stewards in the industry was eroded by unemployment and finally destroyed by a lock-out in 1922. The threat of a miners' strike had produced the Sankey Commission in February 1919. However, in August, Lloyd George rejected any idea of nationalisation but the Government responded to the miners' demands on wages and hours. A joint TUC/Labour Party political campaign on nationalisation proved futile. In September, railwaymen had gone on strike against wage cuts. However, a 'negotiating committee' of other unions resolved the issue within seven days and the government agreed to maintain existing rates for a year. Transport workers were also active and in 1920 dockers secured a wage claim through legal arbitration. This was largely owing to the advocacy of Ernest Bevin, thereafter known as 'the dockers' KC'.

The miners, railwaymen and transport workers had been threatening sympathetic action through the machinery of the 'triple alliance'. In May 1920 London dockers refused to load the 'Jolly George' because it was carrying munitions to Poland. This forced the TUC and Labour Party to establish a 'council of action' in August, with a view to a general strike if the government intervened again in Russia. It seemed that the theory of 'direct action', whereby industrial power would be used to obtain political gains, was about to be put into practice. The Russian crisis passed, however.

Far from there being a political general strike, the 'triple alliance' was to be found wanting on an economic issue. Railwaymen and transport workers helped the miners secure a temporary wage increase in October. When the miners were locked out for refusing wage cuts after decontrol on 31 March 1921, the railwaymen and transport workers' leaders promised a sympathetic strike from Saturday, 16 April. However, the day before, J. H. Thomas of the National Union of Railwaymen and Robert Williams of the National Transport Workers' Federation abandoned their plans, forcing the miners to accept the cuts in late June. The term 'Black Friday' was used thereafter to signify the demise of working-class solidarity.

'Black Friday' was effectively the end of a period of unprecedented class struggle. This was evident in the fact that even MacDonald, after the 1919 Labour Party Conference, had toyed with the idea of 'direct action'. However, he quickly came to mock its advocates. He told *Forward* readers of his wait at a railway station, following a walk in the Cairngorms: 'We surveyed Messrs. Menzies' bookstall, stocked for the enlightenment of the world. We found it was being used for the dissemination of leaflets on "Direct Action". We took one and laughed and wept at its rubbish, invested in a Conrad, and so home to supper and bed.'[15] MacDonald, at least, was consistent, since he had dismissed mass action before the war as fundamentally irrational. However, his wartime unpopularity still showed in his antipathy towards the ruling class. Walking in London on Sunday, 10 April 1921, he listened to conversations in Hyde Park about the miners: 'These people would shoot us with even more pleasure than. . . the Germans. For after all, the quarrel with the Germans was with powers in whom they believed – of their own class. Kensington Gardens turned into a military camp and closed. Civil war spoke and stared us in the face.'[16] As yet parliamentarism was of little moment, especially coming from a jettisoned parliamentarian; in 1919-21 it was 'War Socialism' which the working class had failed to defend through industrial struggle.

This would have needed more than militant trade-unionism in the post-war years, since the British bourgeoisie was determined to return to the old order. One of the products of working-class industrial resistance was the establishment of a TUC General Council in 1921 but this also represented a tendency towards oligarchy. The left-wing union officials, whose mobilising ideology was 'direct action', had the clearest understanding of post-war history but they were disarmed by the significant loss of trade-union members in 1920-22. This had a commensurate effect on affiliations to the Labour Party, though industrial defeat may have increased its electoral appeal. Attention reverted to the strict world of politics, though few Socialists were attuned to the opportunity afforded by the coalition government's difficulties.

Suddenly, on 19 October 1922, Lloyd George resigned. That morning, in the wake of the Chanak crisis, Conservative MPs, meeting at the Carlton Club, had voted to bring down the coalition, the better to rule alone after a general election. Bonar Law took charge with a one-party, Conservative government and polling day was fixed for 15 November.

Asquith, who had been returned in a by-election in 1920, still led the Independent Liberals; even after the break-up of the coalition they remained opposed to Lloyd George's National Liberals. Liberal division was fundamentally a cause, and consequence, of the party's failure to make significant electoral inroads into the new working-class electorate. Given this, Labour was able, in the autumn of 1922, to mount 414 candidacies, in two-thirds of the seats in the reduced House of Commons. The ILP, which had been attracting at least some prominent middle-class radicals, accounted for an unprecedented 55 of these contests.

MacDonald had nursed his nonconformist, working-class constituency in South Wales. It seems that the ILP head office made an especial effort in Aberavon and rich friends ensured that it was to be the party's most expensive contest. He won the support of those he described as 'the middle mass of workers, well educated as a rule, religious, interested in the discussion of real issues',[17] the sort of people with whom he had identified throughout his life. MacDonald was returned with 14,318 votes to the Conservative's 11,111 and the National Liberal's 5,328 votes – forty-seven per cent of the electorate who voted.

Labour received twenty-nine per cent of the national poll, on a greatly increased turn-out. From 76 seats at the dissolution, it nearly doubled its representation to 142 in a 615-seat parliament. (One of its MPs was a Communist, and another had been elected without a contest.) It was, unquestionably, the second party of the state. The two Liberal Parties only secured 116 seats (54 for Asquith and 62 for Lloyd George), though their combined vote was nearly as large as Labour's. The Conservatives obtained the support of thirty-eight per cent of the electorate, but had an overall majority with 345 seats. Bonar Law remained in office with the same team of ministers.

Clynes had been re-elected Chairman of the Parliamentary Labour Party at the beginning of the 1922 session. The electoral breakthrough of that year, however, was attributed, by many Labour activists, to Henderson. (The national party Secretary, who was dogged by personal ill-fortune at general elections, had to wait until January 1923, when he was to be returned at a by-election.) Sidney Webb was one of the newly elected Labour MPs and he had done much in the preceding six years to shape the party's Socialist politics but the composition of the 1922 parliamentary party was of greater historical significance. The number of successful trade-union candidates was eighty five, an absolute increase but proportionate decline. Thirty-five ILPers were also victorious, and about half the party – on the basis of membership of the ILP – was nominally Socialist. More than one in five Labour MPs had a professional background and nine had been to public school. Socially, Labour showed signs of becoming an inter-class party, at least among its parliamentary representatives. Politically, it now comprised former Liberals committed to a UDC conception of foreign policy, a majority of trade unionists, most of whom saw parliament in terms of piecemeal social reform, and the Red Clydesiders, with the legacy of wartime militancy in Scotland. In the days after the election, Clynes failed, through negotiations with the Speaker of the House of Commons, to secure sole occupancy of the opposition front bench for Labour. This was something the re-elected MPs might have continued to tolerate but it was unacceptable to most of the new members. It was Ramsay MacDonald who articulated their view at a meeting of the parliamentary party on 21 November.

He had just returned from the political wilderness. Though he was to make a bid for the leadership, he did not expect to be immediately successful. At a meeting of ILP MPs, Emanuel Shinwell proposed that MacDonald should stand against Clynes. Only Snowden and Maxton voiced any objections. With the backing of the ILP, he secured sixty-one supporters in an open vote of the parliamentary party, to Clynes's fifty-six defenders. It was a close-run contest and MacDonald's victory was due apparently to the absence of over twenty trade-union MPs. He was then unanimously elected to the post of Chairman and Leader, and Clynes became Deputy Leader. The new titles signified Labour's intention of behaving as a major parliamentary party. However, MacDonald was to preside over far-from-united Labour ranks on the opposition benches.

'If [MacDonald] is not the best man for the post,' Beatrice Webb noted two days later, 'he is at any rate the worst and most dangerous man out of it!' Behind her critical observations – which have been plundered posthumously – there was, nevertheless, a recognition of his ability to fill the role of Labour leader: 'looked at impartially and without considering the way it was done, MacDonald's chairmanship has much to recommend it.'[18] He was very much the choice of ILP members in 1922. The trade-union MPs, however, quickly accepted their dependence upon his leadership. As for MacDonald, he felt closest to the former Liberals.

He had a social and political affinity with the middle- and upper-class recruits to the party, who were democratic inter-nationalists in the post-war world. He had long considered the radicals an important element for a progressive party. The trade-union leaders considered him a colleague. He had worked at a central level since 1900 and recently become a member of the new National Joint Council linking the Labour Party, TUC and Labour MPs. The ILP was attracted by his Socialism. This had been espoused in heavily qualified abstract writing and proclaimed in flowing platform rhetoric.

MacDonald was the best man to lead the Labour Party, at a time when it was trying to become the official opposition. This was because he attempted to mediate the three forces making for a mass parliamentarist party in 1922. He had not been impli-cated in parliamentary decisions for over eight years and it was a relatively new and untried Labour Party which eclipsed the divided Liberals on the opposition benches. However, there was considerable continuity in the politics of anti-Conservatism.

Labour's new leader had revived a British Socialist vision since the war, against a hegemonic Fabianism in the Labour Party and a disruptive Communism on the left. At the same time, he had carried out his undemanding duties as Treasurer of the party. The Versailles peace, meanwhile, was sowing the seeds of another war in Europe. Certainly, MacDonald's resurrected Gladstonianism cosmeticised Britain's declining Imperial status and he was compromised by standing for the reform of an empire that 'little Englanders' never wanted. His belief in the Labour Alliance had been waning since 1914, and he had difficulty forgiving the unions for their stand during the war. As for his post-war Socialism, it was to be strategically out of touch with the required restructuring of British Capitalism in the 1920s.

These factors determined the political nature of his leadership but it was the goal of official parliamentary opposition which circumscribed Labour's project. This was to be managed by a man with obvious personality limitations, to which Beatrice Webb frequently alluded in coming years.

MacDonald was greatly misunderstood by his contemporaries in the 1920s. None appreciated his psychological deterioration, the loneliness he had experienced for over a decade. Depression dug ditches round his being, leaving him isolated as a sensitive egocentric. He had earned his position in British politics and, at fifty-six, MacDonald was considered to be at the height of his powers. Hard work had been his personal strategy since leaving Lossiemouth but the private cost was high.

He was tremendously popular as an orator. This was at a time when mass politics stood on the eve of broadcasting, coinciding with the final approach to full enfranchisement. MacDonald had a quality which would be described, after Max Weber, as charisma. Indeed, Molly Hamilton saw him as 'more himself on the platform than in private'. The role was becoming the reality: 'MacDonald, on the platform, can stir the whole gamut of feelings: meet him and he is as secret as an oyster.'[19] Feelings did not cross-fertilise with ideas in his persona. The perceived romanticism of a MacDonald who tried so hard to be a rationalist, inspired discussion of 'the dualism of his make-up'.[20] (Later, his mixed Highland and Lowland origins would be cited as an explanation!) For all his political success as a speaker and writer,

MacDonald erected screens between himself and his associates: 'screens that suggest a sort of mystery that has awkward consequences for a leader of men. . . it limits his power to give to his followers the thrilling sense of shared adventure: prevents the creation of effective lieutenants; accounts for a great deal of disquiet and some suspicion.'[21]

MacDonald adopted a tough stance on the eve of the 1923 parliamentary session. Under Clynes, the Labour Party had been a harmonious interest group, overshadowed by a coalition government with internal differences. Following the 1922 election, Labour's new leader was determined to show it could become the opposition, despite the presence of the Clydeside contingent.

New members, such as Maxton and John Wheatley, brought their practice of the class struggle to the House of Commons. Initial skirmishings led MacDonald to insist that a would-be leader might 'have to save his Party and his cause by denouncing his followers.'[22] In May, nearly ninety Labour MPs voted against the suspension of Walton Newbold, the Communist member. The front bench abstained. However, only half of the parliamentary party later opposed the same fate befalling four ILPers. MacDonald had to be content with condemning the 'slap-dash' methods of the rebels.[23] The Clydesiders and their supporters were not revolutionary Socialists. Though some certainly harboured doubts about their parliamentary leader, there was no significant difference of strategy. 'The members of the ILP and their Trade Union colleagues', ran a report of ILP MPs to their 1923 conference, 'have re-created an interest in Parliament, and have focussed on Parliamentary affairs the attention of the country as a whole.'[24] They did, however, address the problem of how the material position of the working class could be improved when the Conservative government looked safe until 1926/27. Wheatley, who was emerging as a considerable political figure, proposed that MPs should not accept the hospitality of political opponents. This tactic was narrowly endorsed by ILP delegates but only after all reference to the King was removed. No doubt, MacDonald continued to attend political dinners in clubs and private houses where leaders of public opinion discussed the affairs of the nation. He had certainly shunned Beatrice Webb's Half-Circle Club for Labour wives, the most radical attempt to resist absorption by the governing class. (It was to be absorbed into the Parliamentary Labour Club in Tufton Street.)

In mid-July, MacDonald wound up the 'memorable [parliamentary] debate' on Socialism. Abstract statements of Labour's goal rallied most of its MPs, Snowden having originally proposed on 20 March that parliament should concentrate 'legislative effort. . . [on] the gradual supersession of the capitalist system'.[25] It was the first and only debate in the British House of Commons on Socialism.

In May 1923, Bonar Law had been forced to resign with a terminal illness. With Labour the de facto opposition in the Commons, it was accepted that Curzon, as a member of the Upper House, could not become Prime Minister. George V thereupon sent for the Midlands ironmaster, Stanley Baldwin, who was Chancellor of the Exchequer. The new Prime Minister made few changes in the government and held on to the Treasury. As Chancellor, he had agreed stiff debt repayments to the United States. When faced with a problem, he knew it was generally easier to bend. After a torturous period in Anglo-French relations, he was to acquiesce, as Prime Minister, in the occupation of the Ruhr.

Baldwin and MacDonald became party leaders within a few months of each other in 1922/23. Though no one could have known it at the time, they were to share the premiership through five general elections until 1937. Together, they helped recast British politics in a less antagonistic mould in the inter-war years.

In 1923 MacDonald was preoccupied with the issue of

reparations. He claimed that the benign face of government foreign policy was due to the influence of Labour. However, his attempt to conduct open diplomacy with allied Socialists failed to dent the Versailles settlement – as might have been expected.

Then, suddenly on 25 October, Baldwin came out in favour of protection, Bonar Law having declared that it was not an issue in the 1922 election. The King counselled against a general election, which would not otherwise have been necessary for three to four years, on the grounds that 'most countries. . . were in a chaotic and dangerous state'.[26] It was, therefore, left to Mac-Donald to move a censure motion on 15 November, in which he concentrated upon the government's handling of foreign affairs. The following day, the Prime Minister secured his dissolution. The election was set for 6 December 1923.

Stanley Baldwin jeopardised the Conservatives' parliamentary majority after a year. Tariff reform had divided both the party and the country in the past and the government had no mandate for undermining free-trade. It is possible that the Conservative leader, with experience as a manufacturer in the home market, was concerned simply to stop imports. He seems to have given little thought to the effects of foreign retaliation on unemployment. Baldwin, of course, had come to the premiership through Bonar Law's illness and he may have desired a mandate for his own national leadership. This implied that he could win such a general election. He must have known that there would be a rally in defence of free trade, as in the past, but he may have calculated that the opposition forces would be considerably divided. Lloyd George returned to the Liberal fold and Asquith was, once again, in charge of a united party. This, however, was the best way of seeing off the threat of Labour, which had emerged in the 1922 parliament.

MacDonald must have feared the revival of the old progressive party. While he had told the 1923 party conference that 'they had to get an absolute majority... before a Labour Government would stand a ghost of a chance',[27] a would-be opposition was required, by virtue of the nature of parliamentary government, to make a serious electoral bid for power.

Labour fought the contest mainly on the issue of unemployment. It also, of course, declared for free trade, since the 1923 election – virtually a referendum – was the only one with a mass electorate to be dominated by the question of protection. The electoral struggle was also unique in another way. This was the first occasion when MacDonald entered the lists as a potential Prime Minister. The symbolic effect of Labour standing at the gates of the British state cannot be underestimated. No doubt, this helped his return for Aberavon, with 17,439 votes; a sole opponent, a Conservative, obtained 13,927, so MacDonald, on the basis of his previous result, must have attracted some Liberal supporters.

The 1923 election, however, produced little change in the distribution of party support. The Conservatives lost 100,000 votes and Labour gained a similar number. The Liberals put on 200,000 votes, an underestimate of their improvement since some of their 1922 total was provided by Lloyd George supporters who had no Conservative opponent, but popular support was not proportionately reflected in the allocation of seats. The government lost over 80, having 258 members returned, Labour secured 191 seats, a gain of nearly 50, and the Liberals had 159 – a gain of over 40 seats. However, since about half of Lloyd George's former supporters lost to Labour, Asquith secured something of a Liberal come-back. The party did marginally better than Labour but MacDonald widened the parliamentary gap. This was an unprecedented result for the two-party system which had been built up in Britain, because three single-party governments were theoretically possible, given parliamentary alliances, to say nothing of at least two possible coalitions.

The general election was an undoubted political defeat for the Conservatives. Asquith, if anybody, was the moral victor but Labour was now definitely the second party. The King, who was perennially concerned about stability, prevailed upon Baldwin to remain in office and meet the new House of Commons on 8 January 1924 (on the grounds that the sovereign was not bound directly to accept the verdict of the polls).

Winston Churchill, who had lost his seat as a Liberal, was to presumably speak for many when he claimed that 'the enthrone-ment in office of a Socialist Government would be a serious national misfortune such as has usually befallen great States only on the morrow of defeat in war'.[28] Various Tory peers suggested a change in party leadership so that the Conservatives might remain in power with a measure of support from the Liberals. Baldwin, however, who had spoken so vociferously at the Carlton Club against Lloyd George, had his mind set against any return to coalition politics. As for Asquith, he saw no advantage in allying with protectionists, especially when free trade had been endorsed by the electorate. On 18 December 1923, in a speech which was reported by *The Times,* he told Liberal MPs that it was they who 'really control[led] the situation' and 'if a Labour Government [were] ever to be tried. . . it could hardly be. . . under safer conditions'.[29]

The leaders of the two bourgeois parties, then, were remark-ably sanguine. Neither saw any advantage in allying with the other and both believed that they could make party gains by not seeking office. That Christmas, the representatives of the organised working class waited at the gates. The British political elite, despite having fought over protectionism, appreciated that a minority Labour government, which was the most likely out-come when the new parliament met, was bound to fail sooner rather than later.

This possibility had been put to MacDonald, who must have

been surprised at his electoral good fortune (a mere year after his return to parliament). However, a consensus quickly emerged that Labour should take office – indeed, no serious consideration was to be given to any other alternative. MacDonald was told that there would be no panic in the City of London, and Haldane, who had been Lord Chancellor under Asquith, reassured him about the House of Lords; the armed forces, however, would be 'more difficult'. On 10 December, MacDonald met Clynes, Thomas, Henderson, Snowden and Webb at the latter's house in Grosvenor Road, Millbank. Labour's leaders were 'unanimous that moderation and honesty [would be] our safety [in government]'.[30] The decision to form a government, if this became possible, was formally endorsed by the Labour movement within days. MacDonald argued, significantly, that Labour, as the occupant of the opposition front bench, might be supplanted by the Conservatives, if the Liberals took power. After another general election, the Liberals might then end up there. To avoid this hypothetical step backwards for Labour, it was necessary to advance all the way to becoming a minority government. It was a somewhat antipodean reason for Labour deciding to assume administration responsibility but it shows that parliamentary considerations were uppermost in the minds of the party's leaders.

Maurice Hankey, the formidable Cabinet Secretary, had already paid a discreet visit to Howitt Road just after the election, while still in the service of Baldwin, but it was Asquith's speech to his parliamentary party which did most to clarify things by 19 December. The King's private secretary, Lord Stamfordham, had already expressed the view that 'at the present moment I feel that His Majesty should do his utmost not to hamper in any way Mr Ramsay MacDonald'.[31] Thus, the Labour leader adjourned to Lossiemouth for Christmas to continue with the process of cabinet-making. The working class was to come to office, if not power, in a slow and sedate manner.

Parliament met, as arranged, on 8 January 1924. That evening, at a victory rally in the Albert Hall, MacDonald proclaimed that there would be a future of gradual political change. George V formally opened parliament a week later. On 17 January, Clynes moved an amendment to the address which had been drafted by the Conservative government. After a debate, Baldwin lost four days later by seventy-two votes, most of the Liberals combining with Labour to throw out the government. On 22 January, forty-seven days after the election, Baldwin presented his resignation to the King at Buckingham Palace.

MacDonald had already selected the members of his hypothetical government. Labour, out of a desire for constitutional conformity, extended him the traditional prerogatives of a Prime Minister. He had over six weeks to choose twenty cabinet ministers and twice as many non-cabinet and junior ministers. The new Parliamentary Labour Party provided a pool of 190 MPs, half of whom were trade unionists. He concluded that he would 'have to put into some of the offices men [sic] who are not only untried, but whose capacity to face the permanent officials is very doubtful'.[32]

Labour had been totally unrepresented in the Upper House, still a pillar of parliamentary government. MacDonald first thought of Sir John Sankey, a judge, for the Lord Chancellorship. However, Haldane would accept no other post and he also, interestingly, agreed to take charge of the Committee of Imperial Defence. MacDonald offered Lord Parmoor, a former Conservative MP turned Labour supporter, the Lord Presidency of the Council, and Lord Chelmsford, a former Viceroy of India and Conservative supporter, the Admiralty. The ex-Fabian, Sir Sydney Olivier, and Brigadier General Thomson were to be created peers, since they lacked male heirs, in order to take the India Office and the Air Ministry, respectively. One quarter of the senior ministers, then, belonged to the House of Lords, compared with seven in Baldwin's 22-man cabinet.

Charles Trevelyan accepted Education, in which he had been the junior minister until the war. The former Liberal MPs, Noel Buxton and Josiah Wedgwood, were to take Agriculture and the Duchy of Lancaster, respectively. (Arthur Ponsonby, another ex-Liberal parliamentarian, was given the junior post in the Foreign Office.) It was the latter who persuaded MacDonald that he should also take charge of foreign affairs. His closest trade-union friend, J. H. Thomas, was unacceptable to some ILP MPs; they wanted the UDC programme at the forefront of government policy. Thomas, who had been made a privy councillor during the war, received the colonial office.

There remained ten seats at the cabinet table for the leaders of Labour. Clynes, as a former party Chairman, became Lord Privy Seal and Deputy Leader of the House. The Scottish office was given to Adamson, his predecessor in the Chair. Philip Snowden was regarded as a financial expert and was an automatic choice for the Treasury. Henderson, who had yet again lost his seat, became Home Secretary and was returned in a by-election; MacDonald had wanted him to look after the party, in expectation of a short parliament. Sidney Webb was originally marked down for the Ministry of Labour but, at the last moment, he was moved to the Board of Trade. Tom Shaw of the textile workers was given the former position. Vernon Hartshorn, another miners' MP, became Postmaster-General. The third service ministry, the War Office, went to Stephen Walsh, who had been a junior coalition minister during the war. Fred Jowett, the loyal ILPer, was made First Commissioner of Works and, on the day of Baldwin's Commons' defeat, Wheatley was 'finally fixed' as Minister of Health; 'necessary to bring Clyde in. Will he play straight[?]', mused MacDonald.[33]

It was, otherwise, a politically safe and respectable cabinet. MacDonald's proposed government, at senior level, contained eight representatives of the governing class and seven trade unionists. Eleven of its members originated in the working class and nine belonged to the UDC. Socially, the first Labour government must have been perceived by the middle- and upper-classes as a revolutionary breakthrough, given that it contained a bare majority of working men. As the King wrote in his diary on 22 January: 'Today 23 years ago dear Grandmama died. I wonder what she would have thought of a Labour Government!'[34]

The non-cabinet posts absorbed further members of the parliamentary party, including Margaret Bondfield – the first woman in government. Many, however, seem to have been disappointed with their offers. On 19 January, MacDonald had anticipated a sleepless night, having received a 'wild letter' from the spouse of an insulted MP.[35] It was not until two days later that he presented his final list to Henderson, Clynes, Snowden and Ben Spoor, an ILP member who was Chief Whip, this would-be inner directorate generally accepting the explanations offered.

George V had decided from the first to send for MacDonald, as leader of the second largest party, if Baldwin were to lose a vote in the House of Commons. On the eve of the government's censure, the Palace contacted the Labour leader to inform him of procedure. Just after noon on 22 January a privy council was held, at which MacDonald was sworn a member; this was apparently in the presence of Thomas, Henderson, and Clynes – Labour's only privy councillors. The latter 'marvell[ed] at the strange turn of Fortune's wheel, which had brought MacDonald the starveling clerk, Thomas the engine-driver, Henderson the foundry labourer and Clynes the mill-hand, to this pinnacle beside the man whose forebears had been Kings for so many splendid generations.'[36] MacDonald subsequently accepted the King's request to form a government and the two talked for nearly an hour. The former stated 'they [might] fail in their endeavours: but it [would] not be for want of trying to do their best'. The

King, for his part, denied Lansbury's allegation of political intrigues at court, warned MacDonald of the heavy burden of being his own Foreign Secretary and referred to 'the unfortunate incident' when the *Marseillaise* and *Red Flag* had been sung at the Albert Hall rally. The Prime Minister designate explained that he had prevented the Red Flag being sung in the House of Commons. 'It [would] be by degrees that he hope[d] to break down this habit.' MacDonald returned at 4.30 that afternoon, to be sworn First Lord of the Treasury. He then presented a list of his proposed government. The King expressed the hope, in 'another long talk', that he would not have to 'shake hands' with an ambassador from Russia.[37] The following day, the Labour ministers were presented with their seals of office. A select few attended a luncheon party at the Webbs's, where they 'laugh[ed] over Wheatley - the revolutionary - going down on both knees and actually kissing the King's hand'.[38]

George V expected his new ministers to wear court dress. While the cabinet was, apparently, to excuse Wheatley and Jowett from attending at official functions on the grounds of their opposition to flunkeyism, MacDonald believed that 'the spirit of ceremony' enriched them as 'pioneers of a new world'.[39] He was to be punctilious in his observance of the crown in parliament as the form of British democracy. The new Prime Minister, however, wanted to dispense with the nomination of ministers to the royal household. The King favoured the retention of this kind of prime ministerial patronage, and it was agreed that most of the appointments would be a-political but that they terminated with the government. With 'Mrs Philip Snowden' advising that wives of Labour ministers should be invited to afternoon receptions, it is not surprising that the King could write to his mother of the new ministers: 'They have different ideas to ours as they are all socialists, but they ought to be given a chance &. . . treated fairly.'[40]

The King could afford this generosity of spirit. It was clear from the first that parliamentary democracy was to be safe with Labour in office. The arbiters of power were Asquith and the Liberal Party. Baldwin seems to have appreciated that a government such as MacDonald's, regardless of its parliamentary position, would not be too radical.

4   The first Labour government, 1924

On 19 January, MacDonald had written: 'Sometimes feel should like to run away home to Lossie to return to reality & flee from these unreal dreams. I am a Socialist because I prize above all things the simple life & here I am in this, encountering it on the way to Socialism. . . So I swing between my two beings and go on.'[1] Three days later he was Prime Minister at the age of fifty seven.

Labour was to show it could rule responsibly. MacDonald's government would have to deal with a series of strikes and, in the area of domestic social policy, there was to be some reform. Snowden would show himself a highly orthodox Chancellor and parliamentary business was to be dependent upon Liberal and sometimes Conservative co-operation. Foreign affairs would come to absorb much of MacDonald's time and, in the context of Versailles, he was instrumental in securing the withdrawal of the French from the Ruhr. The Labour government was also to recognise soviet Russia but subsequent draft treaties were to alarm the Conservatives and then the Liberals. The collapse of the government was to be precipitated by the failure to prosecute a British Communist and MacDonald would also handle the 'Zinoviev letter' affair badly during the subsequent election. Labour was to lose a sizeable number of parliamentary seats – but not votes – in October 1924 and, within days, the party would be back in opposition.

MacDonald quickly decided to retain the wartime cabinet

secretariat, including Hankey's assistant, Thomas Jones. While he was initially suspicious of the officials at 10 Downing Street, it was Labour's first Prime Minister who ended the practice of political appointments to the private office.

J. H. Thomas ensured that there would be smoking in a Labour cabinet, when the government met for the first time on 23 January at 4.00 p.m. It was left to Lord Haldane to acquaint his new colleagues with ministerial etiquette. The Prime Minister made a request for punctuality and the cabinet then began its business. It was agreed to establish a committee on unemployment and housing under Webb, and another on agriculture. Henderson, as Home Secretary, reported on contingency plans for a strike of engine drivers. It was an inauspicious but highly significant start to Labour in government and, in the months ahead, trade-union ministers would seem to have ignored plans being prepared in Whitehall to deal with a general strike.

MacDonald was refused access to his own security file and thereby deprived, no doubt, of the authorities' view of his wartime activity. Scotland Yard suggested that he might not want to see their weekly Special Branch reports on revolutionary organisations, to which a secretary replied that members of the government were likely to be aware of the pronouncements of, principally, the Communist Party. MacDonald, in an uncharacteristic display of sarcasm, indirectly requested that the police pay as much attention to the political right, which elicited the reply that the Special Branch was not concerned with constitutional organisations. Scotland Yard's reports seem not to have greatly interested the Prime Minister, even when the government was in trouble over Russia. As the target of secret agents during and after the war, it was an area of state activity he may have been rather glad not to control.

As for the chiefs of the three armed services, he had to battle to bring them into line with government foreign policy. In March he succeeded in cancelling plans for a new naval installation at Singapore, despite the efforts of Hankey, whose power base was the secretaryship of the Committee of Imperial Defence, to mobilise support in the Dominion and Colonial Offices for this expansion. MacDonald was interested in encouraging international agreement on disarmament. The Admiralty, however, was allowed to make it clear that its advice on an issue of national defence had not been accepted. Later, the Prime Minister was routed in the Committee of Imperial Defence. He passed on the idea of a tunnel under the Channel to France, only to be met with the chiefs of staff arguing, ironically, that this might require undesirable troop concentrations near the entrance. While MacDonald had been careful to put safe ministers in charge of the Navy and Army, he made his ILP friend, William Leach, Under-Secretary for Air – the Air Force, however, was not then considered a major part of Britain's military capability.

Indeed, MacDonald would later do much to popularise the idea of civilian and, by implication, military aviation. His friend, Lord Thomson, at the Air Ministry asked for twelve hours notice if he wanted a government plane to travel to Lossiemouth and in October, he was even to offer his own 'private machine' for use during the election.[2] However, it was 1925 before the then leader of the opposition was to be taken up in a Royal Air Force plane; from then on, he was a flying enthusiast.

The new government was noticeably unco-ordinated at first. In early February, MacDonald noted that 'officials dominate Ministers. Details are overwhelming & Ministers have no time to work out policy with officials as servants; they are immersed in pressing business with officials as masters.'[3] The Prime Minister, however, seems to have introduced some direction with an inner cabinet. Clynes, Henderson and Spoor would meet regularly with Thomas, Snowden and Webb. By the summer, Labour was being accepted as a credible government, to the extent that local Labour

Parties were concerned about the eclipse of the Conference and Party Executive.

The main component of the Labour Party was the unions but there were only seven trade unionists in the cabinet. These leaders, however, were now even less inclined to countenance industrial action. The Emergency Powers Act of 1920 allowed ministers to maintain essential services in the event of an industrial stoppage and, in 1924, Labour was determined to prove its fitness to govern. Strikers were to be shown that they could not expect sympathetic treatment from a working-class government.

The new government was saved considerable embarrassment when the engine drivers' strike was undermined by Thomas's union. On 4 February, MacDonald had written to the National Union of Railwaymen: 'I do hope we are not going to have a really serious strike. . . If it occurs, it is going to be a very nasty blow to us and is to increase our worries so much as to spoil our prospects. . . Of course, if it must come it will come, but it is beastly hard for us.'[4]

MacDonald and his colleagues were soon faced with a second industrial dispute. In mid-February, the Transport and General Workers' Union, under Ernest Bevin, called a national dock strike. Wedgwood was nominated Chief Civil Commissioner, to prepare for the use of troops. The strike, however, was settled within three days, when a court of inquiry found in favour of the men. Bevin was not amused to be 'put in the position of having to listen to the appeal of [his] own people [in government]'.[5]

The following month, tram workers came out in London for a wage increase and the transport union arranged for sympathetic action on the underground. The government proclaimed a state of emergency on 27 March, after a joint meeting of the TUC General Council and Party Executive had urged it to take over the capital's public transport. MacDonald, however, adopted a conservative reorganisation bill and this allowed the employers to concede a wage increase. In June, workers on the London underground went on strike but a second government proclamation led to a speedy return.

Labour was not actually to use troops to break strikes in 1924. Party activists, however, became alarmed at the government's defence of what was called the national interest, and trade-union leaders came to realise the need to reassert their independence. They should not have been surprised. From the first, Ramsay MacDonald had declared that, in a democracy where community interests were foremost, there was no room for sectionalism and class politics. It may be that the existence of a Labour government encouraged employers to be less hostile to workers' demands, though the small rise in wage rates that year did little more than compensate for price increases.

The number of unemployed had fallen after 1921 but the rate still remained over ten per cent. Labour's 1923 manifesto had contained no pledges of nationalisation. The party, however, promised a 'programme of national work' and 'adequate maintenance' for the unemployed. It repeated the idea of a one-off war debt redemption levy on fortunes over £5,000 and, according to Hugh Dalton, MacDonald believed that it cost the party fifty seats in the election. A capital levy was an anathema to the bourgeois parties and there was no question of a minority Labour government introducing it. MacDonald merely proffered a committee to consider the national debt, which was absorbing over forty per cent of the budget in interest payments.

In April, Snowden cut indirect taxes, the first Labour budget being the work of a radical free trader, but he ate into the financial surplus, since there was also a reduction in direct taxation. The corollary was a cut in expenditure. With Labour accepting the conventional wisdom of balanced budgets, there was no possibility of expensive state-funded social reform. Tom Shaw, however, was to extend the principle of unemployment insurance benefit and the rates were also increased, at a time of rising prices.

Webb's cabinet committee on unemployment studied the problem of the workless ten per cent. It quickly concluded that the hard-hit staple industries were dependent upon a revival of world trade, the economic future being seen simply in terms of a more prosperous past. Webb and his colleagues also learned that the local authorities were satiated with schemes for relief work. The manifesto had targeted development in electricity, transport and land and, after a vote of confidence on 29 May when the Liberals declined to bring down the government, Mac-Donald turned the problem over to a committee under Snowden. Proposals for electricity supply were announced in July and legislation prepared for the autumn. It was also agreed to establish a permanent committee on economic questions, similar to the Committee of Imperial Defence.

Responsibility for housing had been hived off to Wheatley. He declined to work through a cabinet committee and his Health Ministry produced the one domestic success of the Labour government. Wheatley quickly learned the lessons of post-war attempts to subsidise house-building. He provided 44-year financial inducements to local authorities to build homes to be rented, albeit by the respectable working class. He secured dilution in the building trades with fair wages and a fifteen-year programme of work. However, his attempt to control the price of materials was to be overtaken by national political events. In conception, it was an all-encompassing approach and Wheatley managed to steer his policy quickly through the bureaucracy. On both counts, it was Labour's most notable achievement. Snowden was prepared to sanction the reform, since this municipal housing scheme would involve only a gradual drain on the national Exchequer.

Snowden, who played a major role in this government, also allowed Trevelyan's moves towards secondary education for all;

they were to cost little in the immediate future. Old-age pensions were increased, though MacDonald asked that not too much money be spent. A legal minimum wage for agricultural workers was also restored. At the beginning of the summer recess, Mac-Donald expressed himself satisfied with such piecemeal reform. The Executive of the parliamentary party was to claim in October that 'the record of the year [would] be phenomenal'.[6] Such peacetime Socialism, however, paled into insignificance compared with the Liberals' pre-war reforms, while the state remained largely non-interventionist. The government, by its deeds, must have reassured sections of the bourgeoisie that it was far from being an expropriator of wealth.

This hardly pleased the ILP. While 129 Labour MPs were formally members, the left was a minority force within the parliamentary party. It was, however, well represented on the Liaison Committee, where twelve backbenchers, including the two women members, regularly met Clynes, Henderson and Spoor. The major left-wing figure was George Lansbury, who had returned to parliament in 1922 after ten years' absence. He was now the hero of municipal resistance in the London borough of Poplar, having been imprisoned in 1921 for refusing to cut out-door relief, but Lansbury was not a potential leader of the left. He had declined MacDonald's offer of the Transport Ministry on the grounds that it was a non-cabinet post. His pacifism, however, led him to move (unsuccessful) amendments to the army vote, directed at allowing soldiers to abstain from strike-breaking activities. The Liaison Committee served to constrain its more active members and the ILP was reduced to sending missives to MacDonald. The Prime Minister's star may have been falling with some Socialists, but the ILP had supported the formation of a Labour government. When, in February, the Prime Minister declined to stand again for the ILP leadership, Fenner Brockway, as Secretary, forwarded a most effusive letter of thanks for his past work. MacDonald's secretary replied: 'although for the time being he must work in a somewhat large field and perhaps approach old problems with a somewhat more complicated outlook, he hopes to keep in the closest touch with old colleagues and inspirations.'[7] In August, MacDonald agreed to continue as an ILP delegate to the Labour Party Conference, though doubt was expressed about the Labour left 'associating itself with policies and criticisms which the PM [could not] accept'.[8] Clydesiders, such as David Kirkwood, exercised an influence, mainly on Wheatley. He, in turn, certainly at the beginning, seems to have confided in MacDonald. When Wheatley's attempt to deal with the problem of domestic evictions was about to succumb to parliamentary emasculation, James Maxton argued that a general election on the issue should be called.

This was the recognised alternative political strategy for Labour. It was one, however, which MacDonald never seriously considered. Even before the government was formed, he accepted that Asquith would attempt to persuade the King not to grant Labour a dissolution. In his opinion, it was fraught with more danger than minority government.

Domestic policy was believed to be ultimately dependent, given Britain's declining share of world trade, on the state of international relations. This reinforced MacDonald's growing proclivity for foreign affairs in 1924, a subject in which he had taken a great deal of interest since the war. His retention of the Foreign Office, for what he considered would be a short ministry, gravely disappointed Morel, who expected to be in the government. While Ponsonby was to welcome the parliamentary discussion of proposed treaties, foreign policy, in the context of a minority régime, was to be conducted by the Prime Minister with reference only to a few officials. This seems to have been acceptable to the government and Labour Party, though the international department, which was shared with the TUC, would remind MacDonald of earlier positions. It was, in the main, UDC supporters who were to be disappointed with the practical results of his diplomacy.

The main issue was still the Ruhr. France and Germany, however, were wearying of the conflict and mediation by a third party was an increasing possibility. A solution lay in the direction of a French withdrawal.

MacDonald's *Foreign Policy of the Labour Party* (1923) had identified with 'the spirit and purposes of America'.[9] It was the United States' influence which led to an expert examination of Germany's economic plight. In April 1924, General Dawes, soon to be elected American Vice-President, recommended a loan to underwrite reparations. Labour, of course, had opposed such a peace. However, the Foreign Office was to maintain a continuity in policy. MacDonald, as its head, was, therefore, left to determine the manner of modifying Versailles.

As early as 26 January, he had written a personal letter to the French Premier, Poincaré, offering to co-operate. He explained a month later that France's desire for security, which had led to the invasion of the Ruhr, cut across Britain's interest in European trade. The rhetoric of the 'new' diplomacy barely masked the reality of the 'old'. The major powers, including Germany, quickly accepted the Dawes plan. MacDonald soon won over the Belgians, this being a precondition for dealing with the French. Britain then threatened to come out against the occupation. Poincaré was told that he would be allowed to save face if he withdrew from Germany but that there could be no future international sanctions against another default.

In June, the new French Premier, Herriot, reached an understanding at Chequers. MacDonald, however, was forced to travel to Paris in July to resume the talks. A joint memorandum was eventually agreed, for presentation to an inter-allied conference which had been summoned for London on 16 July. By 2 August, the allies had reached agreement, though Snowden, who did not defer to his Prime Minister and Foreign Secretary, was worried about securing the bankers' loan. Three days later, there began an international conference with the Germans. By 16 August the Dawes principle was accepted, with a French pledge to evacuate over the period of a year.

MacDonald hailed it as 'the first really negotiated agreement since the war'.[10] The London conference was an undoubted success and it would secure a French withdrawal, without ignominy, by mid-1925. However, Labour's leader had worked within the terms of Versailles, when he had hitherto been opposed to the whole settlement. In April he had written that 'nothing [gave him] greater pleasure than the relations [he was] establishing with America'.[11] No one, including the UDC, pointed a critical finger at this emerging Atlanticism.

The French wanted an international military guarantee of their security. In 1923 the Assembly of the League of Nations had accepted a draft treaty of mutual assistance. Britain, however, was opposed to this because it feared it would have to come to the defence of all victims of aggressive warfare. The service chiefs were especially suspicious but the Labour government temporised about taking a public stand. MacDonald had long opposed military pacts of the sort which was being suggested in Geneva. However, as Foreign Secretary, he came to accept the inter-governmental League of Nations as better than nothing. By the end of the London conference, he saw little immediate prospect of his desired solution – international disarmament; 'I think if you sat with me for a week at the Foreign Office and looked at the papers I have to examine from day to day', he had replied to a correspondent, 'you would agree that that is so.'[12]

However, he had assented to appear at the 1924 Assembly with Herriot, when replies to the draft treaty were to be considered. The arrival of the British Prime Minister in Geneva on

3 September was accompanied by considerable press excitement. The following day, MacDonald spoke against the draft treaty. He called for the admission of Germany to the League, a proposal which would be sunk by a denial of war guilt from Berlin. On the question of security, he insisted that arbitration was the only way forward. On 5 September, Herriot, however, again insisted on collective security. Nevertheless, a compromise Anglo-French resolution was drawn up and it was accepted by delegates the next day. There followed detailed negotiations in which Lord Parmoor, the British representative, was assisted by Arthur Henderson. On 2 October, the Assembly unanimously recommended a 'protocol for the pacific settlement of international disputes'.

The Geneva protocol, as it was to be called, provided for a disarmament conference the following June. Upon agreement then, the instrument proper would come into force. An international system of arbitration was to be established and the Council of the League of Nations might impose a range of sanctions existing in the covenant. Herriot could see his military guarantee in the protocol, while MacDonald concentrated on the peaceful negotiations scheduled for 1925. The goal of disarmament marked a common way forward.

The British government had insisted upon a recommendation only from the assembly. In the cabinet, opposition built up to Parmoor and Henderson, as they seemed to be committing Britain to military sanctions under the League of Nations. As for MacDonald, he most probably played down this possibility; by 2 October he would have other, domestic, preoccupations. The following month, he declined to sign the report of the British delegation, on the grounds that Parmoor and Henderson had been acting with 'full authority'.[13] The protocol was to be formally rejected by Britain in 1925, the Labour leader thereby being spared association with the possible use of military force.

In the 1923 election, Labour had promised to resume diplomatic and economic relations with soviet Russia. This would end a period of hostility in British foreign policy. MacDonald quickly recognised the soviet government. Rakovsky was appointed chargé d'affaires in London, to resume consideration of a commercial treaty.

Talks did not begin until April. Arthur Ponsonby led for the British side and the Russians soon made clear their demand for a loan. Britain, in contrast, wanted the payment of pre-revolutionary debts. The government, however, also thought that an agreement on trade would reduce the level of unemployment. In July the cabinet agreed to guarantee thirty million pounds, in order to bring the Russians to the point of signature, but the negotiations collapsed on 5 August. Prominent left-wingers, such as A. A. Purcell, of the TUC General Council, and Morel then mediated. The following day, Ponsonby made a surprise announcement to parliament. He reported that a commercial treaty had now been agreed. There was also a second, general, treaty, providing for the settlement of Russian debts. When that had occurred, a third treaty would be concluded, allowing for a British loan.

The principle of the draft treaties was not opposed by the Liberals in early August. However, the Conservatives exploited the last-minute mediation, arguing that the conduct of foreign policy had been influenced by a left-wing conspiracy. This was enough to lead MacDonald to postpone ratification of the two treaties until after the parliamentary recess. However, Lloyd George also campaigned against the Anglo-Russian accord, and, given the long-term rivalry with his party leader, Asquith was to have joined the critics of 'nursery diplomacy' by 22 September.[14]

The Russian draft treaties were to lead to the downfall of the Labour government. It is ironic that Labour, a party which did much to fight Communism at home and abroad, should be tarred

J. Ramsay MacDonald

with the Bolshevik brush, simply for restoring relations with the new Russian régime. Indeed, in early June the King's secretary had sent MacDonald a copy of *Pravda,* obtained from the soviet trade delegation in London, which contained a political attack on MacDonald. However, it was a domestic issue, to be known as the Campbell case, which brought about the defeat of his administration.

On 25 July, the *Workers' Weekly,* published by the Communist Party, called on soldiers to 'use your arms on the side of your own class', in an article to mark anti-war week. The paper was brought to the attention of the authorities. After consultations between the Director of Public Prosecutions and the Attorney General, Sir Patrick Hastings, the editor, J. R. Campbell, was charged on 5 August with incitement to mutiny. According to Scotland Yard, his arrest caused 'considerable excitement in Communist circles'.[15] The following day, Hastings had to answer questions in the House of Commons. Later, Maxton and others told him that Campbell was a war hero and that he had only been acting editor at the time. Like the lawyer he was, Hastings began to doubt the success of a prosecution.

MacDonald had first heard about the arrest from a junior minister. He insisted that he 'must be informed before [any] action [was] taken'.[16] This was an appropriate response, but the Prime Minister showed himself not to be master of events. He did not contact the Attorney General directly and only learned of the prosecution from the newspapers. MacDonald considered the case to be 'ill-advised from the beginning'.[17] However, when Hastings told him on 6 August that 'the whole matter could be dropped, [he] told [him] that, as [he] had begun, [he] had to go through with it'.[18] At a cabinet meeting that evening, MacDonald repeated his view that prosecutions, once entered into, should not be dropped under political pressure. In the course of discussion, however, the Attorney General stated that a letter from

Campbell, which would confirm his temporary editorship, was to lead to the withdrawal of the charge. At this, MacDonald, as he was to put it later, 'agreed that. . . the matter might be dropped'.[19] He took the view that such a letter amounted to an apology for publishing the mutinous exhortation.

On 13 August the case was withdrawn, ostensibly on the grounds that the article merely commented on the use of troops in industrial disputes. This outcome led the Communist Party to boast that 'for the first time[,] the course of justice. . . had been changed by outside political forces'.[20] Maxton appears to have been responsible for Hastings' change of mind. The cabinet had also agreed that it should sanction any future 'public prosecution[s] of a political character'.[21] However, it seems to have been the Communists' claim which alerted the bourgeois press to the fact of political pressure.

It was quickly alleged that MacDonald was fearful of being summoned as a witness for the defence. But, as he told the King's secretary on 22 August when he denied any involvement in the decision, '[he] might have said some things. . . in the witness box. . . that might have added a month or two to the sentence'.[22] The speculation about political interference continued and, on 20 September, it was reported that a Conservative MP would be tabling questions on the Campbell case. The political daggers were being unsheathed.

The Conservatives were to put down a censure motion on the Campbell case on 1 October. However, the Liberals had now come out in opposition to the Russian treaties. It was only a matter of time before the two bourgeois parties coalesced and played one or other red card, in order to bring the government down in such a way that it would appear, in the eyes of the middle classes, to be, at least, sympathetic to Bolshevism.

News of the parliamentary questions had led MacDonald, on 22 September, to look at the minute of the fateful cabinet meeting

of 6 August. He probably then realised that ministers, most likely,
out of ignorance, had not been circumspect about the Attorney
General's discretionary powers. It was the government's principal
law officer, and not the cabinet, who initiated prosecutions. He
would also have observed that there was an inadequate stress on
the letter of apology from Campbell, the thing that had changed
his own mind. Hankey, who would normally have seen it as his
duty to protect ministers from such slips, did not rush to the
rescue. He could have queried Jones's note-taking on 6 August,
though the minute had been formally approved the following
day. MacDonald was under considerable strain from Foreign
Office duties in late September and he directed his political
attention to the Liberals' opposition to the Russian treaties.

Parliament met in special session on 30 September to deal
with the Irish boundary crisis. Hastings acquitted himself well
in the opening questions about the Campbell case. MacDonald,
however, brought about his own political destruction. He gave
a formal reply of political non-interference. The suggestion that
he feared the witness box angered him and he had begun by
stating that '[he] was not consulted regarding either the institution or the subsequent withdrawal of the[se] proceedings'.[23] This
was, as Hankey indelicately put it, a 'bloody lie'.[24] The Prime
Minister had, at some point after 30 July, expressed the view to
Ammon of the Admiralty that he must be informed. Secondly,
he had given the Assistant Director of Public Prosecutions and
Attorney General 'a bit of [his] mind'[25] on 6 August. Thirdly, he
had participated in the cabinet discussion that evening. Mac-
Donald could have told the full truth. However, Hastings, a
barrister who had been elected for Labour in 1922, would have
been revealed as a political reed, the Attorney General would
have been a candidate for resignation and MacDonald revealed
as not up to the job.

Members of Parliament might have gone easy on the government if it had come clean. However, it was on 30 September that the Liberals condemned the guaranteed loan (the envisaged third treaty). MacDonald had been in a defensive mood throughout August and September and he was prepared to fight an election on the treaties. While part of him wanted release from responsibility, another part was prepared to carry the burden of premiership. On 1 October he believed he could secure a dissolution from the King; the Liberals were expected to support the Conservatives' censure motion on the Campbell case. The following day, however, Asquith put down an amendment calling for a select committee. The former Liberal Prime Minister was not yet ready to throw in his lot with the Conservatives and he was, in any case, not too keen on an immediate general election, but he had taken a stand on the Campbell case and there was now a possibility of a united opposition. MacDonald had been determined to face a vote of confidence. However, on 2 October, another law officer told him that his parliamentary answer of 30 September was inaccurate. He concurred with this view in private and instructed Hankey to file a note of his earlier reservations of 22 September with the minutes of the 6 August cabinet meeting.

On 6 October the cabinet decided to oppose Asquith's suggested inquiry. Labour ministers, who must have been clutching at straws, hoped that the amendment would be opposed by the Conservatives, and that the Liberals would refuse to support the censure motion. With the opposition divided, so the thinking went, the party could continue to rule. Before the debate on 8 October, MacDonald personally apologised for misleading the House of Commons. That evening, the cabinet instructed Thomas to wind up with a repeat offer of further information. This tactic was scuppered, however, when Baldwin announced that his party would support the amendment. The die was cast. The Liberals were still hesitant about a general election but, with Labour in a mood to fight for its political life, the responsibility for bringing down the government became the Conservatives'. Asquith's amendment was carried by 359 votes to 198 and the substantive motion by 364 votes to 198. Labour was brought down, on the Campbell case, by the combined ranks of Conservatives and Liberals. The cabinet met at 11.30 p.m., and noted that MacDonald would request a dissolution of the King the following morning.

The Labour government had lasted 259 days. On six occasions the Conservatives had saved MacDonald from defeat in the 1923 parliament, but it was the Liberals who pulled the political rung from under him.

The Prime Minister obtained his dissolution, George V having reluctantly concluded that there was no alternative. 'You have found me an ordinary man, haven't you?'[26] remarked the King during the interview. The following day, in his report to the sovereign on the last parliamentary sitting of 9 October, Mac-Donald claimed the Labour Party '[had] shown the country that patriotism [was] not the monopoly of any class or party'.[27]

He now had to fight the third general election in less than two years. The government was shackled to the Communist menace in the campaign, MacDonald beginning his speaking tour on 13 October by concentrating on the Russian treaties and the Campbell case. Twelve days later, a third aspect of the Bolshevik bogey was to be unleashed on the British electorate. On Saturday, 25 October – four days before polling – the *Daily Mail* published the so-called Zinoviev letter. In this putative document, the Comintern instructed British Communists in subversive preparations.

The letter, dated 15 September, originated with white Russians in Berlin and copies – no original was ever produced – were sent to the *Daily Mail*, Foreign Office and Conservative headquarters at the start of the election. MacDonald was on the lookout for soviet propaganda and, on 16 October in Manchester, he asked the Foreign Office to check its authenticity. Officials were requested to draft a protest which could be published. This reached the Prime Minister seven days later in Aberavon and he hurriedly rewrote the text. It was returned to London uninitialled. On 24 October, Foreign Office officials learned of the *Daily Mail*'s impending publication. They decided to release the letter and protest note quickly, over the name of J. D. Gregory of the Northern Department. Rakovsky was informed of the British government's view later that day. The Russians immediately denied the letter was genuine. However, it was Monday, 27 October before MacDonald commented. At Cardiff, he defended his civil servants' integrity, while suggesting that the Zinoviev letter was 'a political plot'.[28] The press attacked the Prime Minister's confused statement. After the Campbell case, it was another badly mishandled issue. Privately, MacDonald suspected the letter was a forgery.

He was, however, ill served by his officials in Whitehall. While the election was conducted in an atmosphere of press-generated Russophobia, it is unlikely that the anti-Bolshevik plot affected Labour's popular support.

A cabinet committee was to be established, after the election on 31 October, to consider the letter. When the Labour government finally met, four days later, it refused to make a judgement in the absence of an original document. Later, the Conservative government was to vouch for the letter on the basis of secret service reports. Belief in a dirty trick by Tories was to help reconcile Labour to its electoral defeat in the following months.

The government increased its vote to five and a half million, due largely to the fact that it ran ninety more candidates. The Conservatives secured eight million votes, with a larger turn-out, Baldwin attracting a further two and a half million voters. Most of these were former Liberal supporters and the party dropped to less than three million votes. Asquith was never again to sit in the Commons and the 1924 election saw the final routing of the Liberals. This was partly because the Zinoviev letter had frightened the middle classes and the Conservatives were seen as the main anti-Socialist party. However, it was also because there was no obstacle to Liberals switching their loyalty, Baldwin having stated that he was no longer a protectionist. The Conservatives secured a landslide with 419 (of the 615) seats. Labour dropped to 151, a loss of 40 seats. The Liberals became a rump of 40 MPs, reluctantly accepting the leadership of Lloyd George. A Liberal had been MacDonald's sole opponent in Aberavon and the Prime Minister's majority was reduced to 2,100 votes. Labour lost this election but only because the Bolshevik bogey made the Conservatives the first party of the state.

On 4 November the Prime Minister resigned, less than ten months after coming to office. Baldwin then took charge of the 1924 parliament, with a regal brief of 'combating the idea of anything like class war'.[29] MacDonald did show that Labour '[had] the capacity to govern in an equal degree with the others Parties in the House',[30] but his premiership did not pass without being tainted by allegations of corruption.

It was Lloyd George who had created a scandal by selling honours. In 1924 MacDonald was cast in the same light because of the wealthy biscuit manufacturer, Alexander Grant. Grant was a boyhood friend from Morayshire and he was extremely generous with his fortune. When MacDonald became Prime Minister he lent him a Daimler car for the duration, as well as £40,000 to provide a supplementary investment income. MacDonald had a salary of £5,000 but the occupant of 10 Downing Street had invariably been a man of wealth In April, the Labour premier recommended Grant for a baronetcy. This was to be a reward for his many philanthropic contributions and George V duly bestowed the honour. This was not quite political fund-raising courtesy of the monarch but MacDonald showed considerable ineptitude in his use of patronage. On 11 September the *Daily*

Mail revealed that he was the holder of £30,000 worth of shares in McVitie & Price. The following day, he stated that the shares simply covered the running of the car. This was hardly convincing and the story caused Labour considerable embarrassment. Mac-Donald is reputed to have earned the sobriquet 'Biscuits!' but the issue was largely dead by the time of the election. However, it was used 'with force' by his opponent in Aberavon.[31] In December he returned the car and shares (plus £10,000 in securities) to Sir Alexander Grant.

5 *Leader of the opposition,*
1924-9

Three days after Labour's electoral defeat, Harold Laski, a leading Socialist intellectual, wrote to MacDonald: 'At first sight, the vista of the next five years appears unendurable. But I do want you to feel that historically this is a necessary prelude to the greater drama. . . . People who have become accustomed to the epoch of Lloyd George cannot immediately make the transition to the epoch of Ramsay MacDonald. But have faith. Realise that we all care deeply about you, that we have confidence and hope because you stand erectly by us.'[1]

The experience of government was to shorten the political horizon of the Labour Party. Ramsay MacDonald would be re-elected leader in late 1924, he and Lloyd George being the ex-Prime Ministers in the new parliament. With a safe Tory majority, attention would shift to the world of trade unionism. The problems of the mining industry were to lead to Britain's first general strike in 1926. MacDonald was to mediate between the government and the TUC, while privately opposed to industrial action. The Labour Party would have no compunction about the calling off of the general strike and the abandonment of the miners. The ILP, however, was to feel most uneasy about parliamentarism and, when it would attempt a renewal of British Socialism, this was to lead to MacDonald's effective exeunt. He was to concentrate, as Labour leader, on a new party programme for the next election, *Labour and the Nation* (1928) being the quintessence of MacDonaldism. As leader of the opposition, however, he was to

be mainly interested in foreign affairs. MacDonald found Aberavon a demanding constituency and he was to move to Seaham
Harbour in Co. Durham. Stanley Baldwin would go to the country
in May 1929, and, when Labour was returned as the largest
party, MacDonald was to be invited to form a second government.

In November 1924, he reverted to his £400 a year salary as
an MP, though the party was to allow him £800 expenses as
leader. His late wife's trust fund may have yielded a declining
income and he turned again to free-lance journalism. MacDonald
began to charge for articles in the Socialist, as well as the
bourgeois, press, and similarly for speaking engagements. However, he was less inclined than others to exploit his time as Prime
Minister for pecuniary gain.

Early in 1925, MacDonald received a legacy from an admiring
businessman-turned-friend. This would allow him to move into
a house more fitting for a former Prime Minister. Howitt Road
was sold to Alister for £1,200 – less than the market price. For
£6,000, MacDonald bought Upper Frognal Lodge at the top of
Hampstead, though he had to sell some possessions to purchase
it outright. He moved in late May. Upper Frognal Lodge – now
103-5 Frognal – was an impressive twenty-room Georgian house
which MacDonald filled with books. Alister was to draw up the
plans for repair work and construction in the garden. This was
the house of a gentleman, but Hampstead, while a wealthy area,
was attractive to the literati. At 7.30 each morning, MacDonald
would walk on the Heath, his companions including his publisher,
Stanley Unwin. Beatrice Webb noted that 'a few Society dames'
attended his house-warming party and that MacDonald 'looked
very ill and was evidently depressed' in a gathering which comprised the Hankeys, some former ministers and one or two Labour
MPs, plus a 'few Hampstead friends'.[2]

All the family, except Alister, were to live at Upper Frognal

Lodge. Malcolm had unsuccessfully contested Bassetlaw in Nottinghamshire in 1923 and 1924 while still at Oxford. He would become a London County Councillor in 1927. Ishbel was to join him in local politics the following year, having served as her father's hostess in Downing Street. Joan would go to medical school in 1927 and Sheila to Oxford two years later.

No woman entered MacDonald's private world. However, he found female company in 'society', a former Prime Minister attracting his share of social invitations. In 1924, while Prime Minister, he had met Lady Londonderry, a Conservative political hostess, at Buckingham Palace. The Londonderrys – Lord Londonderry had been a junior minister in the post-war coalition and was the Education Minister in the Northern Ireland government – were invited to Chequers. In 1928 MacDonald was to be asked to attend the eve-of-session reception held at Londonderry House in Park Lane. During a Labour Party dinner, he would ask his parliamentary colleagues if anyone wished to accept such an invitation. Arthur Henderson was heard to remark to Adamson: 'Well, Willy, wouldn't you like to go and see the inside of a coal-owner's hovel?'[3] However, MacDonald's relationship with Lady Londonderry, which was to be the subject of much comment, would not take off until 1930.

From 1925, MacDonald found political life increasingly irksome. However, his whole being was rooted in his career as a politician, and politics was all he had. He would turn down an honorary degree from Cambridge in 1926 because of opposition within the university, noting that 'those of us connected with Labour are *sudras* in the eyes of "good society"'.[4] He had already received one from Glasgow and would also be honoured by Edinburgh and Wales (he later received degrees from McGill, Oxford and Manchester). MacDonald had been made a trustee of the British Museum in 1924 and, in 1928, he would be persuaded to accepted Baldwin's offer of a seat on the board of the

National Gallery. However, he could only find peace in long sea voyages and his foreign travel included a trip to the Sahara in late 1926. By 1928 he was thinking that Labour might do better with another leader. However, he did not seriously consider resigning.

Labour had taken a serious knock in 1924. It had become the second party in 1922 and, fourteen months later, the government, but sixty-four Members of Parliament were defeated in Mac-Donald's second general election as leader. In the country, however, Labour received its largest vote in 1924. MacDonald's ten-month government was widely credited with the London conference, but this had been followed by the McVitie & Price mini-scandal, the Campbell case and the Zinoviev letter. As a result of the election which had been forced on Labour, it was clear that the Conservatives would have their own parliamentary way for the first time, excluding 1922-3, in nearly twenty years. It was an ominous prospect.

That MacDonald's leadership should have been called into question is not surprising, nor that he was re-elected unopposed on 3 December 1924, with five against and some abstentions.

The trade-union MPs backed him as the sitting leader, more especially when he was under attack from the left. Henderson, Clynes and Webb apparently discussed the leadership, only to baulk at the idea of another change. The ILPers, especially those from Clydeside, were his strongest critics over the Zinoviev letter, but they still thought MacDonald the best choice. There was quite simply no alternative among the 150 Labour MPs. Snowden disliked MacDonald, and the ex-chancellor was popular with the parliamentary party. However, he considered Henderson the only possible alternative leader. Henderson, for his part, respected MacDonald and seems to have accepted his own role as organiser for the party. Clynes had already been leader and no one seriously considered Webb. That was about it. Wheatley, who had been the first choice of Maxton when the Red Clydesiders travelled to London in 1922, would, quite simply, have antagonised the dominant right. As for the left, it could not have accepted Thomas. Thus, MacDonald stayed.

The economy remained in a post-war depression, the decline of specific industries and districts having a national impact. There was a revival of trade in 1925 and the return of the Conservatives may have been a contributory factor. However, Winston Churchill had returned to the party and, though a financial illiterate, he was made chancellor of the exchequer. Although uneasy about the consequence, he accepted orthodox opinion and in his 1925 budget he returned Britain to the gold standard, in the apparent belief that nothing had changed since 1914. This monetary policy overvalued the pound, thereby making it even more difficult for industrialists to export.

Trade-union membership had picked up in 1924. However, the number of days lost through strikes was still falling from the peak of 1921. The National Unemployed Workers' Committee Movement had organised the first hunger march in 1922. But the decline in unemployment saw the Communist Party concentrate on industrial politics. In 1924 the National Minority Movement became a rallying centre for rank-and-file activity. The left even seemed to be making gains in the TUC. During the Labour government, J. H. Thomas had been temporarily lost to the General Council and, in 1925, Ernest Bevin, then something of a maverick, became a central figure. The TUC had come out against the Dawes plan in 1924 and, at the party conference the following year, Bevin moved, unsuccessfully, that Labour should never again form a minority government. In 1926 the TUC staff was to be separated from that of the Labour Party, under its new General Secretary, Walter Citrine.

In the mining industry, wages had been increased in 1924 but, because of declining profitability, the mine owners proposed to end the existing wage agreement on 31 July 1925. The Miners' Federation refused to negotiate on such terms and their pro-Communist Secretary, A. J. Cook, took the issue to the TUC. The General Council secured the support of the railwaymen and transport workers for an embargo on coal. This threat of industrial solidarity impressed Baldwin. On 31 July, thereafter known as Red Friday, the government intervened with the promise that wages would be subsidised until 1 May 1926. In the meantime, a royal commission was to consider the future of the industry.

It was a clever offer. The miners accepted the commission, chaired by the former Liberal Minister, Sir Herbert Samuel. But when it reported, in March 1926, in favour of wage cuts and reorganisation under private ownership, they rejected the report. This was in full expectation of a lock-out when the subsidies ended.

The government had used the royal commission to buy time. In 1925-6, the Home Office prepared a secret plan for civil commissioners to rule in an emergency. The unofficial Organisation for the Maintenance of Supplies (OMS) received the blessing of the Home Secretary, Joynson-Hicks, for strike-breaking activity. In contradistinction, the TUC made no preparations for a general strike in support of the miners, in the nine months from August 1925. The leaders of the Labour movement believed that the conflict would be resolved through negotiations.

There were many miners in Aberavon but MacDonald responded as a former Prime Minister. He had never believed in the Socialist possibilities of trade-union struggle and, as leader of the opposition, he saw it as his duty to oppose industrial challenges to the state. MacDonald, however, advocated the nationalisation of the mines and harried Baldwin for not intervening earlier. He welcomed the idea of a subsidy to the employers but made no attempt to expose the government's tactics. On the contrary, at an ILP summer school in early August 1925, he privately, as he thought, condemned Baldwin's surrender on Red Friday, arguing that it only encouraged the Communists in their attempts to stir up mass industrial action. MacDonald, however, as a man rooted in Liberalism, was opposed to the suppression of Communism. When, in late 1925, twelve party leaders were given prison sentences for incitement to mutiny, he insisted that even revolutionaries had the right to free speech in Britain. As Labour leader, he continued to speak out in favour of the miners' case, while doing nothing to prepare for the increasingly inevitable confrontation. When, in March 1926, Cook claimed that the Labour Party was committed to following the lead of the federation, MacDonald, in private, expressed vehement opposition. Trade-union action could never be the way forward, especially when Labour was the parliamentary opposition. MacDonald, of all people, was dependent upon there being a negotiated solution.

Mediation was attempted on the basis of the Samuel report. The government, and the TUC, tried to push the miners in the direction of wage cuts, as a precondition for extracting concessions from the owners. The latter, however, had rejected most of the report and they were determined to end national wage agreements. In mid-April, negotiations broke down. Notices were posted, terminating existing contracts at the end of the month. At the eleventh hour there appeared to be a breakthrough. The prospect of a general strike encouraged some ministers and trade-union leaders, including Bevin, to work for a settlement. The employers were forced to concede national wage agreements at a lower level than in 1924 for a quid pro quo of longer hours, which Samuel had opposed. As for the Miners' Federation, it called for negotiations on the implementation of the report, including, it was assumed, Samuel's wage cuts. Both sides moved but the gap did not get appreciably narrower. Over the weekend of 1/2 May, the TUC talked with the government. This was in spite of the fact that a conference of trade-union executives had mandated the General Council to call a national strike from midnight on Monday. In the early hours of 3 May, however, the government broke off the talks. The cabinet had finally united on a policy of confrontation and, when compositors at the *Daily Mail* refused to set a provocative editorial, the government was provided with a somewhat lame excuse.

MacDonald and Henderson participated in the eleventh-hour negotiations, accompanying the TUC to meetings with the government. They had also attended the conference of trade-union executives, which was held in the Memorial Hall from 29 April. On 1 May, MacDonald wound up the proceedings, promising that the parliamentary party would 'be by the miners' side'.[5] It was a hollow undertaking. He privately thought that the 'miners' impossible formula' – 'not a penny off the pay, not a minute on the day' – had forced other unions into a 'general strike psychology'. '[The] strike', he believed, '[could not] settle [the] purely economic problem of [the] bankruptcy of [the] industry'. The government, however, was identified as ultimately the 'chief criminal'.[6] This was a small concession, given the faith most Labour supporters, including miners, had in MacDonald. On the evening of Monday, 3 May, the Labour leader defended the miners in a parliamentary speech. Afterwards, he and Henderson made a fruitless approach to the government. He then returned to Upper Frognal Lodge. MacDonald noted in his diary for 3 May, which he customarily completed before retiring: 'Just home by tube for last time – for how long?'

The first general strike in British Labour history had begun at one minute to midnight.

One million miners had already been locked out. On 4 May, one and a half million transport and railway workers came out on strike, accompanied by printers, some building workers and those in heavy industry and gas and electricity supply. Engineering and shipbuilding workers were not to be called out until a week later.

The TUC closed down all papers, including the *Daily Herald.* MacDonald would subsequently describe this as a mistake. Churchill was ready with the *British Gazette,* which was printed on the *Morning Post*'s presses. On 5 May, the TUC responded with the *British Worker.* The government had initially relied upon radio, and it presumably reached mainly its own supporters through this medium. The private British Broadcasting Company (BBC), under John Reith, was to maintain what it called its 'independence'. Thus, the airwaves were denied to a conciliatory Archbishop of Canterbury and, of course, the leader of the opposition.

Bevin succeeded in creating a Strike Organisation Committee out of the General Council, to run what the trade-union leaders insisted on calling a national strike. Councils of Action emerged in cities and towns, linked to London by a system of despatch riders. The TUC placed no embargo on food supplies, though it largely halted the rail network. On the other side, the OMS used ex-officers and university students to operate road transport. Special constables ensured that essential supplies got through. Troops were deployed from 8 May in the London docks but the police managed to protect buses in provincial centres. Some 4,000 people were to be prosecuted for violent offences, one quarter of them being gaoled. In some areas, strikers did play football with the police.

Churchill used armoured cars to escort food convoys, in keeping with the government's line that the strikers were challenging the constitution. The Chancellor-turned-government-chief-propagandist, who was to earn a literary reputation for reducing all politics to the level of military confrontation, demanded 'unconditional surrender'. Churchill, and his cabinet colleagues, believed in the class struggle, even as MacDonald tried to deny its existence. A former Liberal Attorney General told parliament that the General Council was not protected by the 1906 Trades Disputes Act. Labour's former Solicitor General later denied that there was a seditious conspiracy against the state. On 11 May the government decided to order the banks to freeze trade-union funds. The King, whose sentimental concern for his people embodied a strong degree of realism, successfully counselled against this escalation, on the grounds that it would enrage those strikers in receipt of strike pay. The TUC maintained throughout that it was pursuing only an industrial objective, a sympathetic strike against wage cuts for miners.

The General Strike was, of course, political, in the sense that the state was integrally involved. The owners demanded longer hours, which would have involved the repeal of protective legislation. The government had set up a royal commission and then accepted the Samuel Report. The TUC saw the document as a basis for settlement. In 1926 a sympathetic strike was not illegal, but the trade-union leaders worked with the Labour Party, in order to find a way out. The movement as a whole was committed to the miners and their resistance to wage cuts pointed in the direction of class struggle. This was not revolution, as the government insisted, despite the presence of revolutionaries but it was industrial politics, and the state was arraigned against the working class. The TUC's strategy had been to involve the government in order to put pressure on the recalcitrant coal-owners. Baldwin, however, was now winning a trial of strength with organised Labour, this being something the trade-union leaders had consistently sought to avoid.

A possible solution emerged again in the form of Sir Herbert Samuel. He returned from intellectual musing in Italy to contact an earthy J. H. Thomas on 6 May. The government had earlier declined an offer from Samuel to intervene, Baldwin insisting that the strike had to end before talks could begin. By talking to Samuel, the TUC would be commencing a retreat. On Friday,

7 May, Samuel secretly met a negotiating committee from the General Council. Over the next four days, they searched jointly for a formula allowing wage cuts and reorganisation. A memorandum was eventually agreed on 11 May. On that Tuesday, the general council decided to call off the general strike – after just over a week. The miners' Executive was informed of the Samuel Memorandum that evening. In the early hours of Wednesday, 12 May, it rejected the offer. The miners' leaders were fully cognisant that their members would now be on their own.

At noon that day, TUC representatives informed the Prime Minister that the general strike was over. It had lasted nine days. The General Council received no assurances about victimisation, and, when activists were rejected on 13 May, principally by the railway companies, the strike resumed spontaneously. This forced Baldwin to utter his first conciliatory words. The strikers were to return without ignominy, though many employers still refused to take back some of their workers.

MacDonald had been a witness of history. His involvement was confined to a parliamentary speech, though he was allowed to sit in on General Council meetings. He kept his observations to himself, having no faith in general strikes. The Labour leader favoured it being called off, and anxiously watched the 'end [of] one of the most lamentable adventures in crowd self leadership of our Labour history'. MacDonald feared the worst on 11 May. He saw his 'task. . . to protect the political party from the same crowd rush of emotion which had brought the G[eneral] C[ouncil] to this sorry pass'.[7] It had been his view that the TUC should only have rendered financial assistance to the locked-out miners. By 14 May he was simply relieved that 'the Unions [were] getting out of this all right'.[8] Later, MacDonald described general strikes as 'clumsy and ineffectual'. He hoped the events of May would lead to 'a thorough reconsideration of Trade Union tactics': 'If the wonderful unity of the Strike which impressed the whole world with the solidarity of British Labour would be shown in politics, Labour could solve mining and similar difficulties through the ballot box.'[9]

Such views led Bevin to complain to the Labour Party Executive about 'its leader['s]. . . present policy in relation to the industrial side'.[10] The gap between MacDonald and the transport workers' leader widened, despite the intervention of Arthur Henderson as a conciliator.

The miners remained locked out on 13 May. The TUC, however, had convinced itself that negotiations would resume. A precondition was the lifting of the notices by the owners. The Miners' Federation rejected an offer made by Baldwin on 14 May, whereby a short-term subsidy would be provided to the industry in return for acceptance of the Samuel Report. The employers continued to resist reorganisation and, in June, Baldwin announced a bill to suspend the seven-hour day, which had been enacted in 1919. The government had claimed to be defending the national interest. However, it deployed the resources of the state to defeat the TUC in the general strike and it now intended to legislate to help the employers. MacDonald castigated it for 'abandoning the position of negotiator',[11] not least because it scuppered his attempt to have the South Wales moderates, in the form of Vernon Hartshorn, lean on Cook.

The lock-out dragged on through the summer.

In mid-August, miners' delegates voted to resume negotiations. The owners, however, stood by their demands for reduced wages, longer hours, and district agreements. Proposals from the bishops, which had been endorsed by the miners, had also been rejected by the employers. The federation then acceded to MacDonald's suggestion that he should approach the government. On 1 September he went down to Chartwell for secret talks with Churchill. The two agreed a formula whereby the miners would offer to negotiate about wages and hours in national talks, while recognising the need for district variations. Two days later, Mac-Donald accompanied the miners' leaders to an informal meeting with the Chancellor of the Exchequer. The formula was amended to indicate that the miners would accept a reduction in labour costs in a new national agreement.

On 3 September their officials wrote formally to the government making this offer. MacDonald noted that he had 'changed the whole strategic position of the miners'.[12] The Labour leader had broken the log jam, but the government was to refuse to coerce the owners when they stood out for district settlements only. It was now a case of inflicting a total defeat on the miners. However, generous financial assistance was forthcoming from trade unionists, especially those in Russia. Even so, the miners were starved back to work in November, some coalfields having been drifting back from the late summer. The employers secured all their objectives. With longer hours necessitating fewer men, a logic the federation had been prepared to accept in order to keep wage rates up, unemployment further crippled mining communities already subject to victimisation.

In January 1927, MacDonald told Cook in a private letter that 'in all [his] experience of Trade Union leadership. . . [he had] never known one so incompetent as [him]self'.[13] He also privately expressed a degree of personal sympathy for George Spencer – a Labour MP who had the whip withdrawn, having negotiated a local settlement in Nottinghamshire and then set up a breakaway, non-political local union which was to be ineffective. Yet, at the Labour Party Conference that October, the Miners' President, Herbert Smith, seconding a resolution from the leader on the nationalisation of the pits, said: 'Some of them had lived long enough to know that whenever Mr MacDonald put his hand to a thing it was to uplift the general ideas of the community and make the world a better place to live in.'[14] In the wake of the lock-out, a miners' leader could suggest that, on the question of industrial action, MacDonald had been right all along. It was a poor basis on which to reaffirm the essentially parliamentary character of the Labour Party.

By then, the Conservative government had carried its Trade Disputes and Trade Union Act of 1927, using a guillotine in the House of Commons. It made illegal major sympathetic strikes. The act also encroached on the right of any group of workers to use the strike weapon for itself, since attempts to 'coerce the government either directly or by inflicting hardship on the community' were outlawed. Various forms of industrial action were also prohibited. As for civil servants, they were prevented from joining TUC-affiliated unions. Lastly, and most importantly from the point of view of the Labour Party, trade-union members were required to contract in to political levies. The legislative gains of 1906 and 1913 were substantially reversed.

The Labour movement was bitterly opposed to the passage of the bill but MacDonald and his parliamentary colleagues were impotent. Nor could they do anything about the economy. Following the slight upturn in the mid-1920s, unemployment still remained above ten per cent. It would only drop below this base at one point in the good years, 1927-29. Trade-union membership had begun to fall before the general strike and, in 1928, there would be only 3,673,144 trade unionists affiliated to the TUC. The number of working days lost due to strikes reached an all-time low in 1927, official figures having been compiled from 1906.

In time, the historical significance of the general strike was to be appreciated. It remains debatable whether it ended an era of trade-union militancy, or simply interrupted a longer process of incorporation by the state.

In 1927, Sir Alfred Mond of Imperial Chemical Industries approached the TUC. He offered a vision of Labour participation in industrial management on a basis of economic realism. The so-called Mond-Turner (Chairman of the General Council) talks in 1928-9 on the efficiency of British industry would lead to no definite changes. They were to presage, however, the sort of industrial-relations system the trade unions would seek to construct. Ernest Bevin was an increasingly dominant figure. In May 1928 he invited Ramsay MacDonald officially to open Transport House in Smith Square, Westminster. The new headquarters of the transport workers also provided office accommodation for the TUC and the Labour Party. The Labour movement – symbolically and materially – was back in the environs of parliament. Bevin's union was the Labour Party's landlord, perhaps a symbolic anticipation of 1931.

The ILP had increased its membership from 1922, the decline of the Liberal Party producing some new recruits to Socialism. In 1923, Clifford Allen became Chairman. While he was to advocate that a Labour government should legislate audaciously, he remained a political confidant of MacDonald. The latter had chaired a committee on policy in 1920, only to resign, apparently on the grounds of lack of sympathy with the majority. In 1923-4, he dropped out of the leadership of the ILP. However, he continued to attend the conference as a delegate from Leicester.

The experience of government was to have a profound effect on some leading members of the party. It would give rise to a major debate on Socialist strategy. In this, MacDonald was to be influenced by his experiences as Prime Minister.

In early 1925, the ILP attempted to impose a party whip on its MPs. MacDonald considered this 'open to very grave objection'[15] and Fenner Brockway abandoned the plan. At the party conference later that year, MacDonald asked his critics to remember 'that government was different from getting resolutions through an ILP conference'.[16] Shortly afterwards, he told the now ex-Communist, Walton Newbold: 'I can understand a conscious revolutionist. . . but. . . [not] those who run a policy which can only result in revolution at the same time that they have condemned revolutionary methods.'[17] This was a fair comment, albeit the obverse of a communist criticism of the ILP.

James Maxton became Chairman of the ILP in 1926. With Fenner Brockway as Secretary, the party attempted to reassert its Socialist credentials. The Executive drafted a resolution on 'Socialism in our time' for the party conference. This included the idea of a 'living wage', the nationalisation of the banks, railways, mines, land, electricity and imports and also the redistribution of incomes. MacDonald had already condemned these as 'millstones for mere show round the neck of the Movement'.[18] Even though his friend, J. A. Hobson, was chairing the commission on a 'living wage', the Labour leader refused to speak at a meeting to promote the new policy. He told John Paton: 'I can speak at no Conference promoted to popularise absolutely meaningless phrases to mislead the whole of our Socialist movement'.[19]

Hobson was a theorist of economic underconsumption and, in September 1926, the commission proposed a national minimum wage, to be funded through increased production, with an industrial commission reorganising inefficient sectors. The idea of a 'living wage', however, was seen as an agitational demand for a Socialist party . It was designed to propel a Labour government into an attack on Capitalism. MacDonald was totally opposed to any such conception of a 'living wage'. While he considered Hobson's report to be 'an admirable economic document',[20] the Labour leader failed to appreciate that it was an expansionist critique of fiscal orthodoxy.

MacDonald had already raised with Brockway the question of his attendance at the 1926 Labour Party Conference, arguing that, as an ILP delegate, he might be forced to oppose party policy. The ILP Executive responded that, as its nominee for Labour Party Treasurer, MacDonald was free to speak as he wished. It was yet again a case of the ILP needing MacDonald more than he needed the party. At Margate in October, the ILP's resolution was rendered more acceptable by compositing. Speaking for the Labour Party Executive, MacDonald stated that they would consider the question of a 'living wage' in conjunction with the General Council of the TUC. This was not what the ILP had had in mind. A joint committee was duly appointed, but it decided to concentrate on the crucial question of family allowances. It would not have reported by 1929.

MacDonald had given up his editorship of the *Socialist Review* while Prime Minister and, in January 1926, Clifford Allen took over the position permanently. In February 1927, MacDonald stopped his monthly column, on the grounds that the ILP was not 'working in a disinterested way for the propagation of Socialist opinion'.[21]

Eventually, in March, the ILP leadership decided not to nominate him for the treasurership at the 1927 Labour Party Conference. However, it expressed the wish that MacDonald, as an ILP member, should remain on the Executive. It also declined to invite him to the demonstration before the ILP conference in Leicester. At this, MacDonald decided not to attend, having been at every ILP conference, bar one, since 1896. The year 1927 saw the effective parting of the ILP and MacDonald, though he remained a member. Snowden was to resign in 1928, and most ILPers in parliament and many in the branches still looked upon MacDonald as the last of the 'big four' leaders. For his part, he still agreed with the view of many ILP members that there was a need for an organisation to permeate the Labour Party with Socialism; in August 1928, MacDonald was to tell *Forward* readers: 'I believe that never was there more need for Socialist propaganda than now.'[22] The problem was that MacDonald's conception of Socialism was not that of Maxton and Brockway.

As soon as MacDonald was rejected by the ILP, Henderson told him that the treasurership would remain his. The Party

Secretary suggested that he should become a delegate from Lossiemouth and, at the 1927 conference, MacDonald was to represent the division of Moray and Nairn. It looked like the beginning of the end for the ILP in the Labour Party. The following November, twenty-eight pro-MacDonald ILP MPs secretly agreed that 'the ILP had exhausted its usefulness'.[23] Only one of these MPs, Roden Buxton, attended the 1929 ILP conference. However, they still affirmed the idea of a Socialist Party, and could not publicly take a stand against the ILP.

MacDonald had reacted as a right-wing Socialist. The Maxton/ Brockway leadership of the ILP posed a threat but they could only formally claim less than thirty of the 151 Labour MPs (augmented by twelve owing to by-elections). As Labour leader, MacDonald was concerned, above all, with the exigencies of parliamentary politics.

He had, however, to find an alternative electoral programme. In the summer of 1927, he and Henderson produced a draft for the Labour Party Executive. This was rejected by the parliamentary party. At the Blackpool conference that October, MacDonald suggested that there should be a programme of 'legislation and administrative action' for a future Labour government. He hinted that a general statement of Socialist philosophy would be more desirable, since, after all, theoretical evolutionism served as a justification for practical minimalism in office. Before the Party Executive could appoint a sub-committee, a row broke out about the conference's vote in favour of a surtax on unearned incomes over £500. A Liberal periodical had attacked the details and the consequent opposition of Snowden became known. MacDonald publicly defended the surtax idea and expressed the wish that Labour papers would have revealed the shadow chancellor's original support for the idea.

In October 1927, MacDonald, Henderson and Lansbury began work on a programme with six other Executive members. The most notable was Sir Oswald Mosley who had won Smethwick as an ILPer in December 1926; born in 1896 into a landed family, he had become a Conservative MP in 1918, only to accept the Labour Whip in 1924. Mosley was an advocate of the economic expansionism propounded by the Cambridge economist, John Maynard Keynes. In November he urged a revision of monetary policy on MacDonald. The Labour leader was against specific commitments and, on matters of economics, he deferred to the free-trader Snowden. In MacDonald's eyes, Keynes was iden-tified, above all, with Lloyd George, who had been Liberal leader from late 1926. For reasons of Liberal/Labour Party rivalry, Mac-Donald was unlikely to countenance Keynes. The Labour leader and Mosley produced separate drafts and there was a third from Ellen Wilkinson. The Executive, however, asked MacDonald to complete his document. This he did with the aid of R. H. Tawney, a Christian Socialist educationalist and author of, most notably, *The Acquisitive Society* (1921).

In October 1928, *Labour and the Nation* became the party's new programme. Maxton, without success, warned conference dele-gates that they were 'giving a free hand to the next Labour Government to define any programme it pleases'.[24] It was cer-tainly a moderate document compared with Cook and Maxton's *Case for a Socialist Revival* which had appeared in June.

Labour and the Nation declared the party's final goal to be the 'Socialist commonwealth'. It was, however, even less radical than Webb's 1918 programme, which it replaced. In the foreword, MacDonald wrote of 'transforming Capitalism into Socialism'. In the text, Tawney's moralism was imposed on Webb's gradualism. The party's electoral growth as an all-class movement was theorised in *Labour and the Nation,* and the document was based on the idea of state intervention.

It promised the nationalisation of 'the great foundation indus-tries', land, coal, power, transport and life insurance being listed.

These, however, were to be taken into public ownership 'with careful preparation. . . and with due compensation to the persons affected'.[25] Most industrial capital would, under this plan, escape socialisation. As for finance capital, the proposals were generally vague; the Bank of England was to be controlled by a public corporation. The programme's economic policy was an amalgam of current ideas. However, they had no strategic interrelation, though they challenged fiscal rectitude. Labour would launch an inquiry into credit policy, establish a National Economic Committee to oversee recovery, tackle industrial inefficiency, and create a board to promote work schemes. Purchasing power would also be increased, and the bulk purchase of food imports arranged. More specific promises were also made. The 1927 Trade Union Act was to be repealed, unemployment benefits increased, the eight-hour day for miners repealed, a minimum wage fixed for agricultural workers, and so on.

The party conference debated the document for three days. *Labour and the Nation,* after amendment, was eventually accepted without a vote. In 1928, MacDonald reached a political peak. As well as being party leader, he was confirmed as chief ideologist of British Labourism. Several months later, he replied to a letter from Walton Newbold: 'What we have to do to-day is form a synthesis between sound theory and evolutionary action, and the great handicap is that the private capitalists can move much more swiftly than the public authority. As against their power to move we ought to develop the power to swallow.'[26]

MacDonald was also Labour's leading commentator on foreign affairs. In opposition, he besported himself as a man who might again be Foreign Secretary. The Dawes critic, E. D. Morel, had died in 1924. While the Communist *Labour Monthly* carried an attack in January 1925 on 'the diplomacy of Mr Ramsay Mac-Donald' by UDC (possibly George Young, a dismissed diplomat not reinstated by Labour), most sections of the party were proud of the reputation he had acquired as an international figure. He was even mooted as a recipient of the Nobel Peace Prize, though he would refuse a Swedish nomination because of the recipients of previous awards.

Labour had drawn up a plan in 1925 to reform the Foreign Office. The behaviour of Gregory over the Zinoviev letter was very much in the mind of the party's foreign policy specialists. MacDonald, however, came out against their proposed solution of political appointments: 'the American system of the spoils to the victor with a vengeance [is]. . . a complete reversal of all our ideas regarding the Civil Service.'[27] That his comments on international events were circumscribed by his position as leader of the opposition in Britain is clear from his attitude to the revolutionary civil war in China. In February 1927, MacDonald attacked the British decision to send troops to protect Shanghai. However, he also wrote privately to the British minister in Peking, stating that he had been trying to get Labour to support the government's policy. If either Chinese side 'trust[ed] to the goodwill of the British Government,' he wrote, 'they would have no cause in the end to regret it.'[28]

In 1924 the Labour government had failed to ratify the Geneva protocol. The following year, the Foreign Secretary, Austen Chamberlain, signed the treaty of Locarno, under which Britain and Italy guaranteed a non-aggression pact between France, Germany and Belgium. The Conservative government hoped, of course, that it would not have to intervene in Europe. MacDonald welcomed this security pact. This was in spite of the fact that Chamberlain, in opposing the Geneva protocol, had placed a low emphasis on disarmament.

In a speech to the League of Nations Assembly in Geneva in 1927, the British Foreign Secretary refused to reconsider the protocol. MacDonald, thereupon, described this position, in the *Manchester Guardian,* as a 'disaster. . . to the British Empire itself'.[29]

He intimated that the opposition would support moves to revive the protocol. However, two days later, Snowden attacked the protocol in the same paper. Privately, MacDonald had to remind him that the 1924 document was only a first draft, but such public disagreement prevented Labour using 'its foreign policy as a well-shod battering ram to smash the Government'.[30]

The European powers still tried to rule the world. However, an isolationist United States was growing increasingly powerful, and MacDonald believed it could be a force for good. In 1922, under the Treaty of Washington, the navies of Britain, the United States and Japan had been reduced. The two Atlantic powers agreed to parity in battleships. This was the first effective disarmament agreement and the sort of international relations MacDonald wanted to help bring into being.

In 1927, President Coolidge sought to extend the agreement to lesser categories of ships. However, a conference between the three powers in Geneva collapsed in acrimony. MacDonald put the blame on the two western powers. He attacked the government for using 'war methods rather than peace methods' and told the Commons that Britain should be inculcating the 'habits of arbitration and disarmament'.[31] In December, the American Secretary of State, Kellogg, proposed a multilateral renunciation of war. Fifteen nations, including Britain, signed a pact in August 1928. However, militarist pressure had been building up in the United States. When it was revealed that Britain and France had a mutual understanding on naval disarmament, the American President announced, in early 1929, that his government would commission fifteen more cruisers. MacDonald had attacked the Conservative government at his 1928 party conference. He claimed that the pre-war entente was being reconstructed. By the spring of 1929, he was disturbed at the low point reached in Anglo-American relations.

MacDonald's proposed Russian treaties had been abandoned

J। Ramsay MacDonald

when his government fell. However, Britain continued to have
diplomatic relations with the Soviet Union. The Conservative
government found it convenient to attribute unrest in the empire
to Communist subversion and, in May 1927, police raided the
Soviet Trading Organisation in London in an attempt to find
incriminating evidence on British Communists. None was found
but the government went ahead and broke off relations with
Moscow.

By the late 1920s, then, it looked like Locarno had created
stability in Europe, while the United States and soviet Russia
were isolated to the west and east. MacDonald, as an international
democrat, wanted to bring the world together. He promised to
restore relations with the Soviet Union and looked forward to
strengthening the Anglo-American axis, but his main focus was
on Europe and there he hoped that progress towards mutual
disarmament could be resumed.

MacDonald had been MP for Aberavon since 1922. It was,
however, a constituency which required a great deal of nursing.
When he was Prime Minister, he had been agitated by the
demands made on him. MacDonald, like most MPs, worked for
individual constituents, even helping some to find employment,
and contributed to a wide range of charitable activities. In 1924
Aberavon expected to see more, rather than less, of its parliamentary representative. It is possible that, in the wake of the general
strike, the miners of Aberavon looked with less enthusiasm upon
the Labour Party and certainly the local organisation was weaker.
In April 1928 he told a correspondent: 'The alternative is that I
either give up the leadership of the Opposition and attend to
the constituency, or give up the constituency for one that does
not require such close attention.'[32] It is clear that, of the two
possible options, MacDonald gave no thought to the former.

He was, however, able to consider the latter, when Sidney
Webb decided not to stand again for the 'safe and cheap'[33] seat

of Seaham Harbour in Co. Durham, where Lord Londonderry was a large coal-owner. Arthur Henderson, ever the party organiser, saw it as an an ideal sinecure for the leader, who was required in London. At first, MacDonald rejected the suggestion. Then, in May, the Parliamentary Party Executive endorsed the idea. On 14 July the Aberavon party agreed by four to one to release their sitting candidate. As the new prospective candidate for Seaham Harbour, MacDonald inherited Webb's financial obligations. He would not have to contribute to the local party, to the cost of elections or to voluntary organisations in the division. Local officials merely wanted an annual visit, and three or four speeches at election time. 'We ought to be able to do our work here,' wrote the local party secretary, 'and allow you to do yours in larger issues.'[34]

The 1924 parliament was due to end in late 1929. On 10 May, Stanley Baldwin secured a tactical dissolution, polling day being fixed for 30 May. The government went to the country on the slogan 'Safety First'. It had been an unexciting ministry by the standards of recent British history. Laissez-faire had been reaffirmed by the expansion in production. Neville Chamberlain, as Health Minister, was the principal reforming administrator. The Conservatives had lost fifteen seats in by-elections but, with an overall majority of 185 in May 1929, it seemed as if Stanley Baldwin was set to return to Downing Street.

The major event of his ministry was, of course, the general strike. As leader of the opposition, Ramsay MacDonald had been shown to be apposite in opposing large-scale industrial action. Labour's income declined by a third as a result of the 1927 Trade Union Act. However, the electoral tide continued to run its way. Gradually, the party's leaders came to believe in the possibility of an electoral victory in 1929. MacDonald recognised that the anti-Tory camp contained Liberals, though he was concerned not to lose the banner of progressive politics. In November 1928 he wrote in his diary: 'If the three party system is to remain, it is obvious that the problem of coalitions in some shape or form has to be faced. Our immediate duty is to place every obstacle we can in the way of the survival of the three party system.'[35] Labour may have expected to benefit from the increase in the electorate, but the enfranchisement of women over twenty-one years in 1928 was just as likely to help the government.

Unemployment at over a million had now become a structural problem. *Labour and the Nation,* however, offered little in the way of concrete policy. A slowly emerging Socialism was all that was promised. Capitalism, perhaps with protection, was the Conservatives' solution. Such an ideological polarisation, paradoxically, saw a consensus created in British politics in the 1920s. This was because the class struggle was politically mediated, on the one side, by the Conservative Party under a Stanley Baldwin with the common touch and, on the other, by the Labour Party under a Ramsay MacDonald with respectable aspirations.

David Lloyd George had little in the way of party organisation. He was, however, able to fund inquiries on current problems. On 1 March 1929 he unveiled *We Can Conquer Unemployment.* This Liberal programme provided for public-works schemes in roads, housing, telephones and electricity, employing over half a million workers. Unemployment, according to Lloyd George, would be reduced to normal levels in a year. All this was to be funded by a cost-free loan. Labour, the actual party of the working class, was to reply that their ideas had been stolen, that the programme was financially unsound, that Lloyd George was not to be trusted and that industrial revival was the only solution.

The 1929 general election was a three-cornered contest. For the first time, each party ran more than 500 candidates. It looked as though the Liberals, who were attempting a come-back, might split the anti-Tory vote in many constituencies. The Conservatives stood for continuity, the Liberals for deficit financing, and Labour for more of 1924 – less the disasters. Each party had a distinct programme. However, the Liberals breached the economic commonsense of 1929. Ramsay MacDonald was probably the most impressive choice for prime ministerial office, but the Conservatives were the party of stability.

In Seaham Harbour, MacDonald secured a majority of 28,794 votes. Nationally, the Conservatives polled 8,656,000 (thirty-eight per cent), the Labour Party 8,309,000 votes (thirty-seven per cent), and the Liberals 5,309,000 (twenty-three per cent). The electorate had grown by seven million. For the first time, Labour benefited from the electoral system; it took less votes, in strong working-class areas, to elect a member of parliament. The party obtained 288 seats, twenty short of an overall majority. It was, however, the largest party, as the Conservatives dropped to 260 seats. The Liberals increased their representation, but only to fifty nine. The composition of the Parliamentary Labour Party had also changed significantly. The number of MPs sponsored by local Labour Parties had increased five-fold, to 128. The 115 trade-union-supported members were, for the first time, not a majority. The ILP had won thirty-six seats and the Co-operative Party nine. MacDonald was the undoubted victor but, if he was to form a second Labour government, he would still be dependent on the Liberals.

6   *The second Labour government 1929–31*

Early in 1929, a 62-year-old Ramsay MacDonald had written in his diary: 'My friends get more & more confident that there is to be a Labour Government. . . This time I must develop the work of the PM so as to co-ordinate the State policy of the various departments. . . Unemployment will also require much attention from the PM'.[1]

Labour was to assume office quickly, and MacDonald would appoint mainly former ministers to the cabinet. The government was to be concerned about peace and unemployment, the related solutions being better Anglo-American relations and a revival in trade. MacDonald would be the first British Prime Minister to pay a formal visit to the United States, where a naval conference was to be announced for London. A limited naval disarmament agreement would be achieved in 1930 but, with Japan becoming increasingly militaristic, international relations were to get worse. Other foreign policy matters would be left to Henderson, though MacDonald was to play a leading role at the 'round table' conference on India in late 1930. As for domestic policy, Labour would have to negotiate with the Liberals. However, the government was to suffer mainly from a lack of ideas. Britain had been in a relative structural decline since the war and the system of world trade was under threat. Wall Street was to crash in October 1929 and, in the ensuing global depression, unemployment in Britain would soar.

The problem would be handed to J. H. Thomas but, when

Mosley's radical proposals were to be rejected in 1930 by the government, MacDonald would assume charge. He was to be attracted to the idea of a revenue tariff but would lack the courage to challenge Snowden's free-trade beliefs. No one was to question the fact that a balanced budget should be maintained. This, however, would become increasingly difficult with the rising cost of unemployment benefits and a royal commission was to be established to consider the matter. In early 1931 the Chancellor would predict a current budget deficit. The cabinet was to hesitate about attacking the unemployed and it would be forced to appoint an independent committee to advise on public-expenditure cuts. The government was then to wait, while the forces of Capitalist rationality mobilised. MacDonald would make no effort to remove an ailing Snowden from the Treasury. The Prime Minister was to toy with the idea of a coalition, or national, government but this was mainly a yearning for an end to political conflict. Thus, the Labour government was to drift towards its third year in office.

The Conservative government lost the 1929 election. Baldwin resigned on 4 June, preferring a Labour government to a coalition arrangement with the Liberals.

Clynes, Snowden, Thomas and Henderson had been summoned by MacDonald to Upper Frognal Lodge on Saturday, 1 June. They agreed that Labour should again accept office. The following Tuesday, MacDonald met Baldwin, who was still Prime Minister, at the Athenaeum. The latter promised that he would give Labour a fair chance before again ejecting MacDonald from Downing Street.

The Labour leader had first to disabuse the Palace of the power of the party's executive. On Wednesday, 5 June, MacDonald kissed hands at Windsor, agreeing to the King's request to form an administration. George V queried the name of the party when they discussed some of the proposed appointments; MacDonald replied that he himself had engaged in hard manual labour. His ministerial team was sworn in that Saturday, the new Prime Minister having had only days, unlike 1924, to select his government.

MacDonald had a larger parliamentary party from which to choose this time and he formed a cabinet of nineteen – two less than in 1924.

He had accepted, in early 1929, that he could not again be Foreign Secretary. Henderson, thereupon, put in an early bid for the post. On 4 June, the party secretary threatened not to join the government when MacDonald offered the post to his friend, Thomas. This was to be suggested by the King and it would have guaranteed MacDonald a free hand to look after Anglo-American relations as Premier. He intimated that he might assume full responsibility for foreign affairs for two years. This did not assuage Henderson and MacDonald may even have talked about only taking the Foreign Office. Thomas, however, failed to prevent the offer being withdrawn and, the following day, Henderson was given the post. This was an extremely inauspicious start and the tension between MacDonald and Henderson fuelled the split in the Labour government in 1931.

The Prime Minister was left with nineteen posts from his previous cabinet. Haldane had died and he was able to appoint Sankey as Lord Chancellor. Six former ministers – Parmoor, Snowden, Buxton, Thomson, Trevelyan and Adamson – received their old portfolios. Another four were moved, most noticeably Thomas, who became Lord Privy Seal in charge of unemployment. Six, including John Wheatley, were dropped, and a number of junior ministers, including Margaret Bondfield, were promoted. Lansbury was the only real novice in government. Mosley became Chancellor of the Duchy of Lancaster, outside the cabinet.

Thirteen senior ministers had long-term connections with the Labour movement. In July, the Webbs were to analyse the cabinet. They assigned six to the old governing class, five – including MacDonald – to the lower middle class and six to the working class (with two slightly outside). They concluded that the 'brains', including Sidney, belonged to the lower middle class. The 'predominant element was Proletarian. . . [this being defined as] manual or brain workers'. Labour was seen as the only party able to put 'working-men' into high office.[2] Wheatley and Jowett had been dropped, because of their associations with the ILP, and the second Labour government was 'composed overwhelmingly of the Right section of the movement'.[3] Lansbury, a pacifist, was the only one likely to frighten the bourgeoisie.

The new parliament met on 25 June. A week later the minority government presented its programme for the session.

Foreign affairs were emphasised in the speech from the throne. Labour promised to sign the 'optional clause' providing for compulsory arbitration in the statute of the international court. Diplomatic relations were to be resumed with Russia. The government looked forward to a settlement of the reparations issue and alluded to the evacuation of the Rhineland. It announced talks with the Americans on naval disarmament and expressed the hope that this would lead to a general disarmament agreement.

In domestic affairs the new government had more modest objectives: inquiries into the cotton and steel industries were announced, the reform of the licensing laws was mooted and the law governing parliamentary elections was to be considered. The problems created by the 1927 Trade Union Act were to be solved and the coal industry was to be reorganised. In his speech during the debate, MacDonald promised to consult the leaders of other parties about parliamentary business. He mused about whether members might 'consider [them]selves more as a Council of State and less as arrayed regiments facing each other in battle.'[4]

The government, insofar as it had a vision of the future, saw good international relations as a precondition for domestic prosperity. Unemployment at home and peace abroad were related concerns. Labour believed that a stimulation of trade could best be approached through an improvement in Anglo-American relations. Thus, MacDonald retained this important aspect of the Foreign Office's work.

Herbert Hoover had recently become President of the United States. In mid-June, General Dawes came to Britain as the new ambassador, intent upon another naval agreement. Dawes visited the new Premier in his 'Highland fastness'[5] on the sixteenth when the two men talked at an open window with reporters outside. This open diplomacy, as he would describe it without any sense of irony, led to fresh negotiations between the two great naval powers.

The new administration in Washington had been reconsidering the further fifteen cruisers. Hoover and his Secretary of State, Stimson, also wanted to extend the parity principle of the 1922 treaty to smaller ships. Such talks were seen as a contribution to universal disarmament. This appealed to MacDonald, of course, but the Admiralty was primarily concerned with the naval strength of Japan, France and Italy, and only then the United States. In British eyes, there was an economic need to cut military spending. On the question of parity, Alexander, the First Lord of the Admiralty, was to concede this on the grounds 'that nothing can prevent [the United States] having it – and even exceeding it'.[6]

The 1927 talks had collapsed on how to measure parity. The Americans required larger cruisers, while Britain wished to retain a greater number of smaller vessels. Dawes and MacDonald decided to search for an agreement, then the British head of government could visit Washington as a preliminary to a five-power conference in Britain or the United States. The King warned against rushing into a visit, on the grounds that 'the Americans with their unscrupulous Press [would] try and place all responsibility for the failure on your shoulders'.[7] Both sides slowed down their building programmes. In the following weeks, Britain agreed to come down to fifty cruisers by 1936. The Americans countered in September with twenty-one of their boats but there was still no definite agreement. Hoover, however, relented and agreed that MacDonald could come to the United States.

MacDonald and Ishbel set sail on 28 September. This was to be the first visit of a British Prime Minister to the former colony. They arrived in New York on 4 October and were given a ticker-tape parade along Broadway. The British party then travelled on to Washington, MacDonald entering into talks with Hoover at his mountain retreat.

The President insisted on raising the question of belligerent rights at sea. MacDonald, however, who was under pressure from London, succeeded in keeping the issue out of their joint statement of 9 October. Two days earlier, the British government, with the agreement of the Americans, had called a five-power conference on naval disarmament. This was to be held in London the following January. Hoover had pressed for further British concessions but finally the Americans agreed to continue the search for a compromise. The talks were not particularly productive but the United States was, after all, in the process of wresting the baton of global supremacy from Britain. As for MacDonald, who at heart was probably not displeased to be losing the leading Imperialist role, he chose to haze this historic moment in rhetoric: 'the aim of Anglo-American relations,' he said, '[was] to bring down from the realms of dreams and imagination the aspirations that have been in our hearts for so very long, to establish peace and to found these aspirations on solid agreements with political consequences.'[8]

He left Washington on 10 October, having also addressed the Senate. MacDonald stopped off at Philadelphia, where in 1927 he had been hospitalised with a deadly infection while on a visit.

The following day, he received a group of Socialists in New York. MacDonald appeared at public engagements as the self-styled 'representative of a united nation'[9] and spoke on international democracy. He travelled to Canada on 13 October. For the next two weeks, he toured the dominion formally, as one of the Premiers in an emerging commonwealth. 'In spite of slips about "our dominions" and "our colonies",' he said, 'we never mean anything more than that you and we are a common family.'[10] On 19 October he addressed the annual convention of the American Federation of Labor in Toronto. He told delegates that he was 'still the old workman I was born' and reported that British Labour was 'working out a great public philosophy', using the evolutionary means of the ballot box.[10] MacDonald and Ishbel reached Liverpool on 1 November. Four days later, he reported to the House of Commons on his visit. Baldwin and Lloyd George hailed it as a national triumph. Britain had finally acknowledged the Atlantic axis in international relations and such was the discreet charm of its bourgeoisie that Ramsay MacDonald was the willing agent of this historic rearrangement.

The five-power naval conference was opened in London by George V on 21 January 1930. Britain was represented by MacDonald, Henderson, Alexander and Wedgwood Benn, the Secretary for India. The Prime Minister chaired the plenary sessions at St James's Palace, when they were joined by the American, Japanese, French and Italian delegations. MacDonald had opposed the idea of a 'holiday' in battleship construction until 1936, even though the 1922 treaty was about to run out. However, under pressure from Snowden, he accepted this American idea, clearing the way for an early bilateral understanding in the conference.

In early February, the United States accepted the figure of eighteen (large) cruisers to Britain's fifty (fifteen large and thirty-five smaller) vessels. This interpretation of parity was agreed by the end of the month. In 1922, Japan had agreed with the United

States and Britain to a figure of sixty per cent. In London, how-ever, they demanded seventy per cent in non-capital ships. This proportion had been rolled back by March, when the United States offered not to complete three cruisers until 1935. This left France and Italy. They had agreed to parity with each other in 1922, only to stay away from Geneva in 1927. France believed that it required more cruisers than Italy and wanted a pre-war system of security. Their position had deteriorated from the mid-1920s but MacDonald was opposed to any semblance of an alliance. At most, he was prepared to reaffirm the possibility of action through the League of Nations. The British delegation, however, refused to increase its commitment and the cabinet insisted that parliament should have the final say on participation in military sanctions. It was clear that, because of the French, there could be no five-power agreement.

On 22 April, the United States, Britain and Japan signed a treaty restricting the number of cruisers. France and Italy joined them in agreeing to the battleship 'holiday' until 1936. This renewal, and extension, of the 1922 treaty augured well for international disarmament. It was, however, a false dawn. Less than eighteen months later, in September 1931, Japan invaded Manchuria. The resurgence of militarism in the East was the beginning of a more difficult period of the 1930s. Though the London Naval Treaty was not directly abrogated, the 1930 agree-ment, which owed much to MacDonald, marked the end of post-war demilitarisation.

MacDonald generally left the conduct of other foreign policy to his ministers. Hugh Dalton, the junior minister at the Foreign Office, had to advise Henderson to distribute copies of *Labour and the Nation* to senior officials. The foreign policy of the second Labour government was widely attributed to the Prime Minister, in spite of the fact that the Foreign Secretary enjoyed the custom-ary autonomy of his office.

155

Labour had promised an end to the occupation of the Rhineland. In August 1929 a conference at The Hague accepted the Young plan for German reparations. Snowden secured an increased share of the spoils for Britain and Henderson obtained the withdrawal of French troops five years early. One of his first acts had been to sign the 'optional clause' of the statute for the permanent court of international justice. The Foreign Secretary became an important figure at the League of Nations, forcing the preparatory commission on disarmament to speed up its work. He was elected to preside over the world conference arranged for February 1932. Diplomatic relations were resumed with the Soviet Union in October 1929. The King arranged that the Prince of Wales should receive the ambassador. Subsequently, Henderson negotiated a commercial treaty. He had forced the resignation of the High Commissioner in Egypt, Lord Lloyd, and in the summer of 1929 Henderson negotiated a draft treaty which made some concessions to local nationalists. MacDonald was opposed to the restoration of Egyptian influence in the Sudan but Henderson secured his acquiescence by threatening to resign.

Much foreign policy, of course, concerned the empire. It was formally renamed in 1931, the Statute of Westminster enshrining the notion of a commonwealth in which the dominions had already secured national sovereignty. MacDonald had made Thomas Dominions Secretary in June 1930, extending the practice of hiving off from the colonial office. Here, MacDonald had greater control over Sidney Webb (Lord Passfield). In October 1930 the Colonial Secretary announced in a White Paper that Jewish immigration into Palestine would have to cease. He found himself under attack from international Zionists and MacDonald had to step in to smooth things over. The Prime Minister also became involved in India, the preserve of Wedgwood Benn. In 1924 MacDonald had quickly learned the virtue of caution in Indian affairs and by 1930 he was expressing irritation at protests from friends of India. Dominion status had been promised by the Viceroy in October 1929 and this led the Indian Congress to declare in favour of independence. Six months later, the Conservative-appointed Simon Commission, which included the Labour MPs Clement Attlee and Vernon Hartshorn, recommended a system of provincial government and negotiations on central power. MacDonald, faced with this problem, called a 'round-table' conference, his invariable political solution, to be held in London in November 1930. The nationalists stayed away and for three months the Prime Minister concerned himself mainly with communal relations in the sub-continent. The conference came to an end with the Indian Princes agreeing to join a future all-Indian federation. Even this was too much for Churchill, who resigned from the Conservative front bench, and, as Gandhi entered into talks with the Viceroy, MacDonald looked forward to a second, more representative, 'round table' in the autumn of 1931.

Of the extremely modest foreign policy achievements of the second Labour government, the 1930 London Naval Treaty was the most notable. This was a minor contribution to improving the state of international relations. On the domestic front there was little with which to credit MacDonald. When the government tried to reorganise the coal industry, the Liberals attempted to extract electoral reform as the price of not opposing the bill.

Reorganisation had been promised in the King's speech. The government proposed a reduction from eight to seven and a half hours, when it introduced a bill in late 1929. If the reduction in hours was a concession to the miners, the owners received a strong quid pro quo in the form of export levies and production quotas. On 2 December, MacDonald met Lloyd George, Samuel and Sir John Simon. The government, however, felt unable to adopt their principle of compulsory amalgamation immediately. The Liberal leaders decided to put down an amendment for the second reading. MacDonald contemplated the consequences of defeat but the government survived by 281 votes to 273, two Liberals supporting and six abstaining.

Early in the New Year, Lloyd George hinted that electoral reform might secure his neutrality on the Coal Mines Bill. The King's speech had contained the promise of an inquiry and an all-party committee was established in December 1929, under Lord Ullswater. Labour would undoubtedly have benefited from proportional representation in earlier elections. However, it was bent on supplanting the Liberals and Lloyd George knew that he could not be restored to prominence with the existing electoral system. On 3 February 1930, the Liberal leader privately offered to support the government for two or three years in return for electoral reform. MacDonald favoured the sort of informal understanding which had operated before the war and the government resolved to try and push through its reorganisation bill without a deal.

The cabinet, however, accepted some new clauses on amalgamation. When a Liberal amendment deleting quotas was proposed later in the month, the government won by 280 votes to 271, four Liberals supporting Labour and eight abstaining. Following a defeat on a Conservative amendment, supported by forty-two Liberals, Snowden, Clynes and Thomas agreed, on 18 March, to offer the Liberals an electoral reform bill in order to survive another amendment. MacDonald was the only member of the cabinet committee to oppose such a concession. The government survived the vote and the bill secured its third reading. It was subsequently mutilated in the Lords, and the government had to drop the levy scheme to secure enactment. The Coal Mines Act was an extremely cautious achievement, which co-existed rather uneasily with Labour's commitment to nationalisation.

On the Ullswater Committee, the Liberals were pressing for

proportional representation, while the Labour members advocated a package of reforms to the existing system. While MacDonald continued to oppose the Liberals, some Labour members favoured a rapprochement on the alternative vote. In May, however, the Prime Minister secured the backing of the Party Executive for his position. The committee abandoned its search for a compromise in July. In September, with the threat of Tory protectionism looming, Lloyd George again offered to support the government, but it was the unlikely prospect of a Liberal-Conservative deal which persuaded the cabinet to endorse the alternative vote. In October, the King's speech contained an unspecified commitment to electoral reform. The Party Executive and parliamentary party accepted the concession in December, in order to secure Liberal acquiescence for the repeal of the 1927 Trade Union Act. This received a second reading in late January 1931 and, shortly afterwards, an electoral reform bill was carried. The Liberals, however, refused to accept the repeal of the 1927 Act, and, in July, the government considered using the 1911 Parliament Act because of Lords' resistance to electoral reform. The legislative process was extremely arduous and, when Labour tried to secure gains for the organised working class, it roused Liberal suspicions about sectional politics.

By the second anniversary of Labour's entry into government, however, Britain was engulfed in a global Capitalist crisis.

Unemployment had remained above ten per cent from 1920 and, though there was a brief trade revival in 1929, Britain had failed to participate fully in the world boom of 1925-9. After the war, the British economy experienced a structural problem. Its staple export industries – coal, cotton, iron and steel, shipbuilding and heavy engineering – went into decline.

This had much to do with foreign competition and only more latterly with protectionism. In addition, countries formerly economically dependent on Britain were becoming self-sufficient in industrial production. However, it was the falling price of food and primary products on the world market which was critical. Underdeveloped countries found it increasingly difficult to absorb British exports.

The system of world trade looked as though it might collapse, the nineteenth-century economy having broken in the aftermath of the war. The restoration of the gold standard in 1925 represented an attempt to get back to the position of economic dominance. It was still believed that free trade was a cardinal virtue. Protectionism had been mooted by some Conservatives since the 1900s but its enactment would be more an admission of defeat than a far-sighted policy option.

However, there was also a counter-tendency in the post-war British economy, though few could see it at the time. Science-based industries, such as chemicals, synthetic textiles, cars, aircraft and electrical engineering were becoming more important. They would allow for a partial recovery in the late 1930s. Such new industries were more orientated to the domestic market, which provided an alternative to falling shares in export markets. The decline in international food prices allowed for a consumer boom in Britain. Further, the desire for homes and the more technically orientated industries stimulated construction. Building was additionally encouraged by a population shift to the Midlands and South East. New industries tended to locate in such areas because of greater demand. They were able to move closer to their markets because they were dependent for power on national-grid electricity.

In 1929, however, it was not so obvious that the old was giving way to the new. It was not a gradual process, with workers in the old industries finding work in the new ones. The complex social transition, which was the British attempt to adjust belatedly to a new international context, hinged on an economic rupture of historic dimensions - the Wall Street collapse in October.

At the beginning of 1930, unemployment in Britain stood at one and a half million. It was to rise to two and three quarter million by the end of the year. A figure of three million was pessimistically predicted for 1931. However, it would not be reached until January 1933, when nearly a quarter of the insured population was without work. Many, of course, remained in employment. This was in spite of the fact that the working class was being restructured from north to south. Falling prices helped maintain, if not increase, real wages, where collective bargaining prevailed.

MacDonald had appointed Thomas to take charge of unemployment in June 1929. He assigned him Mosley, to deal especially with the problem. George Lansbury, as First Commissioner of Works, was the second cabinet minister in the team. Tom Johnston, as Under Secretary in the Scottish office, had a regional interest in formulating the government's policy. Thomas's cabinet committee was assigned a small secretariat, and co-ordination was also established between permanent secretaries. The government made it easier to qualify for unemployment benefit and the poor law was renamed 'public assistance'.

Within weeks, MacDonald was privately expressing opposition to the state provision of welfare. In August he noted: 'It is very significant that the poor law and dole elements in Socialism are most strongly supported by its middle and upper class adherents.'[12] In contrast, he believed that the members of the government who were of plebeian origin, such as himself, took a more puritanical attitude. In December 1929, he wrote in his diary: 'I have no heart for these doles. . . To establish people in incomes which represent no effort to get or to do work is the very antithesis of Socialism. The state as Lady Bountiful may be a vital expression of Toryism but it is not the beginning of Socialism.'[13] MacDonald had a Victorian belief in the value of hard work and, despite his Socialism, he had very little sympathy

161

for those out of work, a view that had not been uncommon in the ranks of the Labour movement. Despite his reactionary personal position, the Labour leader did not politically oppose increases in benefit. He did, however, pass on dinner-table comments to Bondfield about workers abusing the system, only to find, in one case which had been documented for him, that the local gentry was at fault. In the 1931 financial crisis, MacDonald's view may have prevented him from sympathising with many of his cabinet colleagues. Then, ironically, it was largely the trade-unionists who stood by the unemployed, while the middle- and upper-class elements tended to support the Prime Minister in his attempt to find a solution.

Socialism meant little in mid-1929 when it came to policy initiatives. Herbert Morrison, at the Ministry of Transport, was encouraged to expand road building. This, however, implied a public-expenditure battle with the Treasury under Snowden. Thomas sought to encourage exports but their volume declined by forty per cent between 1929 and 1931. The volume of imports held up, with the fall in international prices. The Lord Privy Seal's advocacy of rationalisation had little effect on the competitive position of British industry. Thomas had cosy chats with the Bank of England about finance for industry. The government established a committee, under Lord Macmillan, to consider the whole question of credit; its members included Keynes, Bevin and the former Liberal Chancellor of the Exchequer, Reginald McKenna.

The government's main contribution to tackling unemployment was probably the idea of a national economic committee. MacDonald wanted a tripartite economic general staff embracing capital, labour and the state. However, the Economic Advisory Council set up in January 1930, which included businessmen, Bevin and Citrine, and Keynes, Tawney and G. D. H. Cole, was more an economic research committee. It was hardly a counterweight to the Treasury, a necessary institutional condition for a break with fiscal orthodoxy, but Hubert Henderson (assistant, later joint, secretary and Keynes's amanuensis) was to become the Prime Minister's personal economic adviser.

The call for a radical offensive against unemployment came quickly from Mosley, who soon won the adhesion of Lansbury and Johnston. By December 1929, they were in revolt against Thomas. However, Lansbury and Johnston were to refuse to follow Mosley's leadership.

Early in the New Year, the Chancellor of the Duchy sent MacDonald what became known as the Mosley Memorandum. This was a document which asserted that the Prime Minister should take control of economic management through a new department. In the short term, unemployment could be solved by raising a loan of 200 million for a public-works programme. In the long term, the government had to plan the revitalisation of old industries and the creation of new ones.

MacDonald rejected any such commanding role and argued that the machinery of the 'unemployment body'[14] had been affected by a lack of co-operation. He had spoken to Morrison about roads and, while the latter was generally negative about the impact of a programme, MacDonald was prepared to listen to arguments. As for the long term, the government had already agreed that this was a separate area for policy.

The cabinet referred Mosley's Memorandum to a committee under Snowden, comprising Shaw, Minister of Labour in 1924, plus Greenwood and Bondfield, Ministers of Health and Labour, respectively. It reported on 1 May 1930. Snowden argued, basically, that Mosley's ideas were subversive of the constitution, that a government loan would destroy economic confidence and that long-term planning implied a transcendence of Capitalism. MacDonald disliked Snowden's 'hard dogmatism expressed in words & tones as hard as the ideas'[15] but he also dismissed 'all this humbug of curing unemployment by Exchequer grants'.[16]

On 8 May, the cabinet decided to refer Snowden's report to the unemployment ministers. They were instructed to press on with already approved relief schemes. It was agreed that Mac-Donald was to chair this committee.

After two inconclusive meetings, Mosley resigned on 20 May. MacDonald insisted that the cabinet had not backed Snowden but the Chancellor of the Duchy was adamant that his memorandum should be accepted. Mosley was certainly a man in a hurry, with little respect for the niceties of parliamentary government. However, Labour had been in office for nearly a year and unemployment was rising fast. Mosley had been fêted by the Labour Party when he came over in 1924 but, following his resignation, one Labour MP was to remark that 'some people get things too easily & they are ruined'.[17] Two days later, Mosley moved a vote of censure in the leadership at a parliamentary party meeting. Thomas was humiliated by this unprecedented event but MacDonald secured the backing of 210 MPs to 29 for Mosley.

On 28 May the government was threatened by a Conservative censure motion. MacDonald could only offer a conference of local authorities, to speed up public works. Mosley, in a resignation speech, called more forcefully for a measure of protection. However, only five Labour MPs abstained and the government survived with a majority of twenty nine. Mosley continued to press his solution in the party.

On 5 June, a ministerial reshuffle was announced. Hartshorn, having finished with India, was made Lord Privy Seal. Thomas was demoted to the Dominions Office and, refusing to accept responsibility for the division in his team, MacDonald allowed him to continue to look after the policy of rationalisation. Attlee took over from Mosley. There was also a change at Agriculture. Most importantly, MacDonald took overall charge of unemployment, Hartshorn as deputy being responsible for the secretariat.

The number out of work continued to rise. By September, the value of approved public-works projects had doubled to £140 million, following the conference of local authorities at the Guildhall. Only half the sum would be spent by the end of 1930, when perhaps 150 thousand workers had been found employment. Hartshorn's secretariat had quickly concluded that nothing more could be done. In July 1930, its head wrote: 'no human endeavour [would] get the ship afloat until in the course of nature the tide again [began] to flow'.[18]

The argument that unemployment in the depressed regions was due to the world recession could not be blatantly accepted by MacDonald. On 12 July he had asked for an examination of the Mosley Memorandum. The Treasury, however, continued to insist that a government loan would have a deleterious effect on the capital market. The Prime Minister had agreed in June to confer with Lloyd George. The latter immediately pressed for an expanded road programme, such as had already been rejected by Snowden, but the Ministry of Transport's consulting engineer demolished the Liberals' optimistic plans. The Treasury attributed the fall in world prices to the monetary policies of the French and Americans but, when MacDonald expressed an interest in the international expansion of credit, it was argued that action in the League of Nations would be counter-productive. He was clearly searching for a policy but the Prime Minister soon ran up, at each and every point, against the implications of fiscal orthodoxy.

MacDonald had first queried the doctrine of free trade at the beginning of 1930. By the summer, he appeared converted to the idea of a revenue tariff. However, he was only too well aware that such a radical change in fiscal policy would lead to a divisive budgetary debate within the cabinet.

Keynes had been the first to moot the idea of temporary

protection, on the Macmillan committee. He also raised the same proposal on an economists' committee of the Economic Advisory Council. On 30 May Hubert Henderson, in a paper prepared for the cabinet, recommended a ten per cent tariff. In a global recession, domestic expansion implied a taxation of imports. Such a policy was to be offered in an attempt to hold off a fully protectionist régime. Free traders, however, were prepared to admit that there could be no specific policies for dealing with unemployment.

Many British protectionists were motivated simply by sectional concerns. This was particularly the case in agriculture, where cereal growers had to compete with cheap imports. By February 1930, the Ministry of Agriculture was advocating a marketing board and import quotas. In late March a government committee recommended co-operative marketing and, while this would go forward for legislation, there was no decision on quotas. MacDonald had favoured the support of domestic prices but he relented in the face of free-trade orthodoxy. Snowden argued, sarcastically, that it would be 'better [to] adopt wholeheartedly the inflation policy of McKenna or Keynes or the whole-hog protection policy of Baldwin',[19] if it was the government's intention to hit consumers by attacking real wages. Attlee, however, described the Treasury view as antithetical to 'most Socialist proposals',[20] when he reported in favour of state intervention to help arable farming.

In September 1929, as part of the government's economic foreign policy, Graham, President of the Board of Trade, had proposed an anti-tariff agreement in the League of Nations' Assembly. Britain was one of the eleven countries to sign a convention opposing tariff increases until April 1931. In June 1930 the cabinet's free traders sought to reaffirm the government's opposition to protectionism. Graham, however, was instructed in early August to negotiate international tariff reductions before ratifying the convention. At a cabinet meeting in early September, however, he and Snowden secured the support of Henderson for immediate ratification. Thomas and Hartshorn were the only ministers to defend the earlier decision. MacDonald was absent on holiday in Lossiemouth. Thus, the Labour cabinet committed the country to a continuation of free trade through the winter of 1930/31 without the presence of the Prime Minister.

The British government was subsequently to be constrained, by international convention, to the defence of free-trade. By failing to keep control of his government, MacDonald allowed an easy victory to Snowden and his followers. From September 1930, then, Labour had more or less decided to await a revival in world trade as the solution to unemployment in Britain.

This was effectively the policy MacDonald took to the party conference, which opened at Llandudno on 6 October. He still commanded a pre-eminent position in the eyes of most delegates. The day before, the British airship R.101 had crashed at Beauvais in France and among the forty-six killed was the Air Minister, Lord Thomson. The Prime Minister was genuinely upset at the loss of a close friend and he won the sympathy of even his critics when he spoke on 7 October. MacDonald defended the government and the final peroration of his speech began: 'So, my friends, we are not on trial; it is the system under which we live.' As he sat down, he was greeted with 'loud cheers'[21] from the delegates. Though no one, least of all MacDonald, could have known it, it was the last ovation he was to get from a Labour Party Conference.

A pro-government resolution was moved by the municipal workers, calling for the implementation of the unemployment measures in *Labour and the Nation*. Maxton moved an amendment urging a militant Socialist strategy, to include, if necessary, a general election. This ILP position was rejected by 1,803,000 votes to 334,000. MacDonald had intervened in the debate before hurrying back to London. Jousting with Maxton, he said:

'Socialism is not a thing of dogma. . . That has never been the Socialism of the I.L.P. That was an issue which Keir Hardie and the rest of us fought and fought and fought again, and some of my old comrades. . . know that that issue was always a fundamental issue with the ILP.'[22]

Mosley next presented his alternative proposals. A resolution calling for an executive report on his still-unpublished memorandum was narrowly defeated by just over 200,000 votes. The former Chancellor of the Duchy, by a mixture of diplomacy, charm and not a little mystery, secured the support of some big unions. It was the closest the parliamentary leadership came to a defeat during the second Labour government. George Lansbury had been assigned to oppose the resolution on behalf of the Executive. In a speech which took up a theme of MacDonald's, he said: 'let them educate, agitate, and organise – sweep the present Cabinet out and put themselves in, if that would help – until they had got the teeming millions of their people imbued with socialist ideals, and when they had got that, they would not want anybody's Memorandum. . . to bring about Socialism.'[23] Thus, MacDonaldism was rhetorically defended by the minister most popular with the conference.

In October 1930 the Economic Advisory Council's committee of five economists, chaired by Keynes, reported on the depression. It saw business confidence being revived by a reform of unemployment insurance and the balancing of the budget without further direct taxation. This was a conventional bourgeois view and the working class was meant to pay for economic difficulties. The committee, however, also recommended domestic investment, partly through public works but also by controls on the export of capital. This was a much more interventionist approach. Keynes even considered that export bounties might complement a revenue tariff.

MacDonald liked the idea of a revenue tariff. Unemployment

would rise if taxation was increased and he believed, like everybody else, in a balanced budget. The Economic Advisory Council report, however, had little effect on the government. At the time, it was preoccupied with the Imperial conference, which was being held in London.

There was dominion pressure for moves towards empire free trade. Snowden lectured the assembled leaders on the evils of protectionism against the rest of the world, but the cabinet decided that existing preferences on empire products would continue, the Chancellor being forced to admit that some import duties would still be collected. Snowden agreed that the question of dominion wheat imports into Britain should be referred to the next conference, the cabinet having turned down the idea of a quota. It was clear that Lord Beaverbrook's populist crusade was being ignored by the free-traders in government.

Unemployment was still rising inexorably. Even before the government's moderate reforms of the insurance system, the national fund had run into deficit. By mid-1930, most of its borrowing was exhausted. The limit was legislatively increased in two stages. However, by February 1931 this had nearly run out. The deficit on the insurance fund, which had been premissed on much lower unemployment figures, was due in part to the increase in those receiving full insurance benefits but the number in receipt of so-called transitional benefits had risen more sharply. The workhouse was the next, and last, step. An all-party committee had failed to find a solution. A sub-committee of the Economic Advisory Council, chaired by G. D. H. Cole, recommended benefit cuts or increased contributions. It also suggested a means test for those on transitional benefits. This was politically unacceptable, not least for Cole. In the 1930 King's speech, however, the government had promised a royal commission on unemployment insurance. Under Liberal pressure, MacDonald promised interim reports.

Inevitably, events were moving towards a political crisis. Throughout 1930, the government dithered. Every time a possible policy emerged, it was vetoed by the free-traders. With an ideological polarisation between Capitalism and Socialism, many in the Labour Party felt, paradoxically, that, if it was not yet time for Socialism, then unrestrained Capitalism was inevitable. MacDonald had transcended his absolutist commitment to free-trade but he was still suspicious of bourgeois reformers. When he refused to become master of events, they began to take control of the Labour government. With the unemployed the principal sufferers of the world recession, he allowed middle-class opinion to target unemployment benefit as a problem. The Prime Minister, of course, was unsympathetic and when it was to be posed in a different way, namely in terms of the national finances, he would take a firm stand. With Snowden at the Treasury, it was only a matter of time before the economic issue was being defined as an unbalanced budget.

Snowden had inherited an unbalanced budget from Churchill. In 1930, in his first budget, he increased direct taxation. He also announced a tax on land values but this would never be collected. By the end of the year, there was a wide consensus against further tax increases. This implied a cut in expenditure and MacDonald had accepted that this would be necessary in 1931. The idea of a revenue tariff was not seriously promoted, since it was politically divisive. In the new year, the Chancellor predicted a deficit of forty million pounds on the current budget. In 1931/32, this would rise, on current estimates, to seventy million pounds. Snowden was concerned that there might be a run on the pound. Ominously, he singled out unemployment benefit as the area where savings could be made. Unforgivably, especially for a former leading ILPer and a Labour Chancellor who had made concessions on transitional benefits in 1930, he blamed the budgetary crisis on the long-term unemployed.

On 14 January 1931 the cabinet accepted the Chancellor's doom-laden warnings. This was the point at which the Labour government began to commit political suicide. However, while all ministers accepted the necessity of a balanced budget, a majority was to baulk at the means of a cut in unemployment benefit.

Margaret Bondfield, after consulting MacDonald and Snowden, proposed on 5 February that unemployment benefit should be cut by two shillings (ten pence) a week. The first woman cabinet minister also suggested restrictions on the rights of women and other workers. Senior ministers, led by Henderson, reacted strongly. They argued, successfully, that the report of the royal commission should be awaited, that the Minister of Labour should borrow another twenty million pounds, and that transitional benefits should be extended to October.

A majority of the cabinet, then, was for temporising. Henderson and his followers resisted making the unemployed bear the burden of financial retrenchment. However, this feeling was not to be articulated clearly, much less expressed as a coherent political strategy. The defenders of the unemployed simply left it to Snowden, Graham and Alexander to come up with an alternative to Bondfield's proposals. This was to be their position throughout the following six months.

The Conservatives moved quickly to censure the government over public spending. Lloyd George, however, was not willing to have a general election and he proposed an amendment calling for an independent committee to advise on cuts. The government then put its collective head in the noose, instructing Snowden to accept the idea. The three parties, in a grotesque display of parliamentary unity, combined to carry the amendment. There was little opposition from within the Labour ranks. Only twenty-one government supporters voted against, though there were also some abstentions. Later in the month, Mosley, Lady Cynthia Mosley, and four other Labour MPs finally resigned the whip but the New Party was no alternative. In March, Sir George May, formerly of the Prudential Assurance Company, began work with his committee on public expenditure estimates. If he was not a Treasury man, May was just the figure Snowden was looking for to strengthen his hand.

The Chancellor of the Exchequer had had a prostate operation in late February and, during his recuperation, talk of a budgetary crisis subsided. On 7 March, in the new *New Statesman and Nation*, Keynes advocated a revenue tariff for the first time in public, 'in order. . . that [Britain might] resume the vacant financial leader-ship of the world, which no one else [had] the experience or the public spirit to occupy'. He argued that such an import tax would create a budget surplus. While there was as yet no public ad-mission of a budgetary crisis, in ruling circles, where Keynes was really at home, his policy initiative had already been rejected. However, the Treasury again came out against this variant of protectionism. It was 29 March before MacDonald could visit his recovering Chancellor at home in the country. Even though he was head of government, Snowden told him little more than that the 1931 budget would not contain a duty on tea. Even when the cabinet asked subsequently to be consulted, Snowden cited 'the universal practice of withholding information'.[24] Such constitutionalism was accepted by his Labour colleagues.

Things became more bizarre. On 27 April, Snowden presented what he called an interim budget. The deficit, which had been hanging round the government's neck since January, disappeared through an accounting device. Clearly, Snowden was waiting for the May Committee to report.

MacDonald, for his part, also seems to have been waiting – for Snowden to leave the Treasury by the summer. There had been some changes in the government in March but MacDonald was to make no effort to reconstruct his ageing and divided cabinet. Passfield and Parmoor were keen to retire and Henderson and Snowden were desirous of elevation to the Lords before the next general election. There was plenty of opportunity but Mac-Donald was concerned mainly about being left in the Commons to carry the burden of government without senior colleagues. This was a particularly petty and selfish reason, when the times demanded leadership. With MacDonald rarely on the bridge of the ship of state, it was the possibly prostate-less Chancellor who dominated the final months of the session before the summer recess.

In March, the cabinet had divided again on the question of a wheat quota. Addison, who had taken over as Minister of Agriculture, was asked to try and find a solution. He reported that none existed 'within the limits of the Government's policy'.[25] Mac-Donald came out against an opening towards food taxation on 4 June, telling the cabinet that it would not get through parliament. Land taxation had been further provided for in the 1931 budget and, while it was not due to be raised until 1933/34 when all land had been valued, the Liberals suddenly came out against the taxation of developed land on which income tax had already been levied. Snowden wanted to fight on this issue, which was dear to his radical heart, but on 14 June Sir Stafford Cripps, the recently appointed Solicitor General, came up with the compromise of a graduated tax on developed land. After a special appeal from MacDonald to the Chancellor, the cabinet rallied to the idea of a deal with the Liberals. Indeed, the two parties had been co-operating increasingly since March, with Johnston, who took over as Lord Privy Seal, presiding over joint committees on unemployment schemes.

By the second anniversary of its entry into office, Labour had visibly failed to tackle unemployment. The division in the government, however, had yet to work itself through. In parliament there was no economic consensus among the parties, though protectionism was a possibility for the Conservatives. This, however, did not prevent some commentators from calling for a coalition, or national, government for the duration of the crisis.

Such a solution had at times appeared attractive, to Mac-Donald. He began his second administration by expressing the hope that there would be united parliamentary action. This was, of course, a tactical necessity for a minority government, not least when the bourgeois parties might have been expected to play a rough parliamentary game. However, his utterance also showed his commitment to the idea of a superior national interest. MacDonald believed, like all his predecessors, that the office of Prime Minister was being entrusted for a period to a party leader on the grounds that he was able to command the support of parliament.

Lloyd George had been considered a good wartime supremo. He was, however, perceived to be an unacceptable coalition leader in peacetime. By the late summer of 1930, he was to be found talking again of 'national government'. LLoyd George saw this as an extension of his party's support for Labour. It was assumed that he would occupy a major office. MacDonald was not unsympathetic to the concept. He believed that another election, occasioned by the Liberals allying with the Conservatives, would be bad for the country. In private, he expressed a willingness to stand down as Prime Minister.

By November, the *Observer* was campaigning for a three-party government. Snowden, as an absolutist free trader, was widely seen to be standing in the way of government action. When Henderson began to be promoted as a new leader for Labour, MacDonald, in order to frustrate him becoming Prime Minister, began to think about a national government which he would support from the backbenches. He realised that this would further divide the Labour Party. In December, Baldwin suggested Mac-Donald might become Viceroy of India. There was some support for this in ruling circles. When, however, the Prime Minister sounded the Conservative leader about a national government, the latter replied that protectionism was an insuperable obstacle to coalition.

A national government was not a practical possibility in 1930. MacDonald, however, had admitted to himself that his cabinet was getting nowhere. Presumably, this would become even more apparent with time.

He was extremely conscious of his role as leader of the Labour Party. He had already given this position up, in 1914, on an issue of major policy. Then, however, he had simply been the leader of a minor party and he had resigned in order to oppose the government over the war. In the early months of 1931, Mac-Donald did not think his government could last much longer. He wondered about leaving or splitting the Labour Party. It is clear, however, that this was a prospect which had no attraction for him. Indeed, by June he was thinking of the 'luxury'[26] of being, once again, leader of the opposition. He was concerned about senior colleagues who wished to retire or move to the Lords, and, in his heart of hearts, he admitted that the party would improve with a new leader. The main problem with a national government, however, was that it would split the Labour Party, and this would partly defeat the whole object.

While MacDonald was, undoubtedly, becoming attached to the notion of a national government, there is no evidence that he consistently played the role of Labour traitor in 1930/31. As Prime Minister, he, of course, wanted a consensus in parliament for government policy. He was also becoming more dependent on the Liberals but there is no evidence that he was actively constructing a cross-party government, whether of organisations or individuals. MacDonald may have sinned in thought but there was no prime-ministerial conspiracy to destroy the elected government. Nor would there be.

7   The 1931 financial crisis

On the eve of the summer parliamentary recess, MacDonald would note on 31 July: 'House rose with the feeling that it is not for long. As international bankers we are in a precarious position.'[1] A major British financial crisis was looming, which would test the mettle of the second Labour government.

With the question of the budgetary deficit as yet unresolved, it was to be enveloped, in the summer of 1931, in a threatened collapse of the international banking system. Germans banks began to lose their foreign funds in May and, as confidence across the Capitalist world declined, French depositors would withdraw from London. MacDonald and Henderson were to differ on the issue of reparations. Snowden would fear a run on sterling, leading to the pound being forced off the gold standard. The budget deficit was to become a national priority in late July, the Bank of England having secured loans from abroad. Appeasing international bankers would become the government's aim when, in fact, exchange controls were necessary to halt the international movement of capital. In mid-July, Keynes and Bevin, through the report of the Macmillan Committee, would attempt to draw attention to an expected balance of payments deficit. This conception of the problem, however, was to be overshadowed by the May Committee's report, which would go to cabinet on 30 July. It was to predict an even larger budget deficit, to be met by some tax increases but mainly by cuts in expenditure. The unemployed would have to bear much of the burden.

Parliament would adjourn but, with a continuing run on the pound, a cabinet committee on the May Report was to be summoned for 12 August. The Bank of England had given the government fourteen days in which to act. On 20 August the financial crisis would become a political one, when the TUC was to come out against cuts in unemployment benefit. Henderson would consider that loyalty to the Labour movement might involve handing back office to the Conservatives and Liberals. In contrast, the hostility of the TUC was to increase MacDonald's resolve to see the issue through. The opposition parties would be determined that the May Report should be accepted. They were to threaten to bring down the government and requested the recall of parliament. On 21 August the idea of a national government, under MacDonald's leadership, would be mooted by them. The crisis was to reach a climax on 22/23 August. With an American loan promised, the Labour government would split on a ten-per-cent cut in unemployment benefit. It was to be agreed that the government should resign but the cabinet accepted that MacDonald would suggest a conference of the three party leaders. On 24 August the Labour leader was to succumb to the blandishments of the King that he should remain in Downing Street, forming an interim national government of individuals to see Britain through the crisis.

In May 1931 a leading Austrian bank collapsed. This threatened the German banks which had come to its aid and their loss of foreign funds jeopardised reparations payments. The German leaders came to Chequers in early June to enlist the support of the British government. MacDonald suggested a joint rescue to the Americans but Hoover proposed a year's moratorium on all inter-governmental debts on the twentieth. It was 7 July before the United States secured an agreement in Paris because the French wanted reparations to continue. By this time, Germany was on the point of financial collapse.

International bankers, like generals who always fight the last war, recalled the post-war crisis in Europe. Then, inflation had been fuelled by printed money. The depreciation of currencies was halted only by balancing budgets. Fiscal orthodoxy would, once again, be posed as the solution to financial difficulties. The 1931 crisis was shaped largely by the subjectivity of bankers. Prices, certainly in Britain, were falling at a time of monetary restraint.

The financial crisis had an immediate effect on Britain. London banks found that their loans had been frozen in Germany. This encouraged mainly French savers to withdraw their money from the world's leading financial centre. London bankers, however, were able to draw on the gold reserves of the Bank of England. The latter institution, in turn, then had to seek loans from France and the United States.

The Americans suggested a conference in London on the developing European crisis. MacDonald, however, was opposed to the harsh terms of French loans to Germany, while Henderson was convinced that Germany should make political concessions to France. Thus, the international gathering on 20 July was unable to come up with much for Germany in four days of talks. A national liquidity crisis, consequent upon the amended Versailles settlement, was becoming a matter of global financial confidence.

In Britain, the run on sterling forced a rise in bank rate. The Treasury publicly warned that the country could be forced off the gold standard. There was a fear in financial circles that the currency would go into an inexorable slide. On 23 July, Mac-Donald had urged Snowden to look to the budget. At the same time, he instructed Graham to look out for German dumping in Britain.

The government was to seek to restore the confidence of international bankers and to do this by tackling the budget deficit. Ironically, and tragically, this was a minor economic problem in comparison with the international movement of capital in 1931. To do something about the latter would have required extensive exchange controls (such as were introduced in Germany), a policy which would have been antipathetic to British financial interests.

Against the background of the European financial crisis, the policy debate in Britain had continued its desultory course.

On 14 July, the Macmillan Committee on finance and industry reported the results of its deliberations. It did not argue for the abandonment of the gold standard. Keynes believed that confidence in the albeit overvalued pound would be shaken in present circumstances if it was not redeemable at par in gold. The committee, however, did come out in favour of a managed currency. It saw a rise in the price level halting the spiral of deflation but this was very much a recommendation for the future.

The Macmillan Report did, however, draw attention to Britain's balance of payments. The export of manufactured goods had not paid for the import of food and raw materials for over a hundred years but this had been made up by so-called 'invisible' earnings, such as banking, shipping and the interest on foreign income. These had declined with the recession. Crude estimates – a new economic indicator – suggested that Britain was about to enter into a balance of payments deficit. It was this which alarmed Keynes and Bevin in 1931. By way of solution, they proposed a revenue tariff.

This was eclipsed on 30 July, when the report of the May Committee went to cabinet as MPs were preparing to adjourn for the summer. It predicted an immediate deficit on the budget of 120 million pounds. The committee had comprised five rich men and two trade unionists. Their report was a thoroughly ideological document, from which the supposed representatives of Labour gently dissented. It proposed that the budget should be balanced with tax increases of twenty-four million and cuts in expenditure of ninety-six million.

The May Report reaffirmed the idea that an unbalanced budget was a problem. It went on to make a number of unwarranted assumptions. Firstly, the annual payment to the sinking fund of fifty million was considered untouchable. Secondly, reductions in national debt payments - which were to be implemented in 1932 - were not even considered. Thirdly, the increasing number of old-age pensioners was not offset against the declining number of school children. Fourthly, the figure for increased taxation was, of course, arbitrary, as was the proposed level of expenditure. Fifthly, the deficit on the insurance fund had become notorious and May charged this and the cost of 'transitional' benefits to the Exchequer. National insurance was made to bear most of the cuts. The proposed reduction of twenty per cent in benefits was larger than the fall in prices but less than that recommended by the royal commission. In either case, the unemployed were to carry the burden of whatever financial crisis, in spite of the fact that they were already the victims of a Capitalist breakdown.

The Treasury wanted the May proposals for an autumn budget. A cabinet committee, comprising MacDonald, Snowden, Henderson, Thomas and Graham, was established to consider the May report. It was published on 31 July, the last day of parliament's sitting. The government made no statement on May's recommendations and the cabinet committee was not due to meet until 25 August.

MacDonald retreated to his Morayshire home as the Bank of England continued to struggle to defend the pound.

From there, the Prime Minister wrote to Keynes for his views on the May report. He received a reply on 5 August, in which the Cambridge economist privately condemned the document. Keynes argued that May's deflationary attempt would increase unemployment, drive those in receipt of benefits to revolt and allow bondholders to escape sharing the national burden. Though he had hitherto opposed devaluation, he predicted that Britain would have to go off the gold standard. Keynes then, in a moment of economic creativity which revealed his characteristic British nationalism, suggested London hegemony of a new shared currency unit worth, at most, seventy-five per cent of the pound sterling. This was a politico-economic opinion, rather than a technical scientific appreciation. Hubert Henderson, who was more closely involved with the Prime Minister, took a different political view. He considered that May had produced an exaggerated statement of orthodoxy and that this would do harm. The latter, however, had drawn attention to an unbalanced budget in the middle of a crisis of confidence and the government had to act accordingly. The abandonment of the gold standard, he argued, would have unmeasurable consequences. There was, in effect, no well-developed Keynesian view in August 1931, only a number of differing economic assessments.

Among these, the bankers' views were prevailing. They argued that the 26 July loan secured from France and the United States had not restored confidence in Britain. They called upon the government to improve the trade balance but mainly to remove the budget deficit. On 7 August the Bank of England claimed that it had lost most of its original gold and foreign exchange. Snowden thereupon urged MacDonald to return to London so that the cabinet committee could deal immediately with the budget deficit. The Prime Minister had been committed to a reduction in expenditure since late 1930 and, while it is not known what he thought of May's twenty-per-cent cut in unemployment benefit as the solution to the financial crisis, Hubert Henderson had provided a realistic account of the structure of Capitalist power which was operating on the government. MacDonald agreed to cut short his holiday and leave Lossiemouth on Monday, 10 August. He was to journey back to the most momentous event of his political career.

On Tuesday, 11 August, the Bank of England reported that its French francs and United States dollars were being used up. MacDonald and Snowden were told that they had a maximum of fourteen days to take action on the budget deficit. They then decided to summon the cabinet committee for Wednesday and Thursday (12/13 August). The details could be worked on over the weekend and, hopefully, a decision taken on Monday, 17 August. This would be well within the Bank of England's target of 25 August. The deliberations of the government were to be confidential but MacDonald would secretly brief lobby correspondents.

It was presumably on 12 August that Snowden presented the figure of a 170-million-pound budget deficit in a full year to his four colleagues. The Keynesian option of devaluation seems to have been ruled out by all members of the committee, if, indeed, it was even considered. At the second meeting on 13 August, MacDonald proposed some sort of balance between expenditure cuts and increased taxation. He was concerned that the burden should be seen to be shared more equitably; in reality, the judge and the unemployed miner were to make the same percentage contribution to national survival but the coal owner would escape making a major sacrifice.

Snowden presented his budget estimates on Monday, 17 August. He proposed a tax increase of ninety million and an expenditure saving of ninety-nine million. This would render a surplus in the state's finances. Henderson wanted to see the complete picture before participating in a decision. He objected to the consideration of expenditure before taxation. The Foreign Secretary then complained about the proposed cuts in employment benefit. When MacDonald rehearsed the arguments in favour, '[Henderson] could not reply [and] lapsed into sulky silence for a time'.[2] The latter, supported by Graham, then insisted that they were only taking part in a preliminary examination. The report to cabinet, they argued, might not include specific recommendations.

There was clear opposition within the government to the May

Report. Henderson, however, lacked financial acumen and, though he was joined at this early stage by Graham, they had no alternative economic strategy. Without this, they were unable to put up much of a political fight. They sought merely, almost like dogged trade unionists, to defend the economic territory of the working class against, in this case, Treasury encroachment. There was nothing dishonourable, as such, in this position but temporising, by definition, would, at some crush point or other, lead to surrender and possibly ignominious defeat.

The expenditure saving was reduced to eighty-seven million on 17 August. At another meeting the following day, it came down to seventy-eight and a half million. Snowden had wanted to take sixty-seven million out of the insurance fund. He proposed to do this by reducing benefits by twenty per cent, increasing contributions and transferring the cost of the 'transitional' benefits to local authorities. Henderson and Graham secured the removal of the benefit cut on 18 August; there would be a flat-rate deduction of a shilling (five pence) a week, in line with Mac-Donald's argument that all had to contribute. However, they agreed to the increased contributions and the transfer of 'trans-itional' benefits, which would increase the burden on the rates. They also agreed to a reduction in the benefit period. Henderson and Graham, by juggling the Chancellor's figures, came up with an expenditure saving of forty-three and a half million on unemployment benefit. Other cuts were to come in education, the armed services, roads, and so on. There was to be a symbolic reduction in ministerial salaries.

On 18 August, MacDonald, Snowden, Henderson, Thomas and Graham agreed to tax increases of eighty-nine million. Most of it was to come directly from incomes, especially unearned wealth. Four of the committee seem to have voted, at this stage, against a revenue tariff. The minority of one appears to have been Thomas, rather than MacDonald. The Prime Minister, however, was among the four who voted in favour of an import tax as preferable to a cut in benefits but Snowden was able to veto any such protectionism.

The cabinet committee came up with a budget in slight deficit by two and a half million. May's recommended level of taxation had been increased by sixty-five million. His percentage cut in benefits had been replaced by a shilling-a-week contribution from the unemployed. These 'suggestions'[3] were sent to an emergency cabinet meeting, scheduled for Wednesday, 19 August. Ominously, two of the five ministers were reserving their position while the rest of the committee thought that they had a unanimous report. Given this, it was hardly likely that unity could be found in the full cabinet.

On 19 August the cabinet accepted the principle of a balanced budget, as long as the burden was shared. The Labour ministers agreed to the level of taxation. A majority (fifteen) favoured some sort of revenue tariff; ten were for a tax on manufactured imports only and five for taxing all imports. Snowden again threatened to resign, thereby securing his way. The expenditure cuts were endorsed, except for the increase in local rates. Margaret Bondfield was asked to try and find the necessary twenty-million saving by funding the 'transitional' benefits out of the flat-rate deductions and further increasing employees' contributions. There was more – and, indeed, speculative – juggling with Treasury figures on the expenditure side. As for taxation, the Chancellor seems to have had little difficulty in making his officials' view prevail. The cabinet had a sort of provisional budget for the moment but there was no real political unity. Henderson and Graham had yet to state that they were only engaging in a ministerial exercise.

Moreover, the government had not yet thought about the Labour movement, to say nothing of the two opposition parties. The following day, Thursday, 20 August, the financial crisis became a political one.

Opposition leaders had been waiting since Tuesday. On Thursday morning, MacDonald and Snowden informed the Tories and Liberals of the government's thinking. Both opposition parties, as might have been expected, came out against any increase in taxation. The Tories also wanted another thirty million off expenditure and the Liberals would soon join them in calling for cuts in unemployment benefit. This was the parliamentary pressure from the right.

That afternoon, the five-man cabinet committee met the Party executive and the TUC General Council. While the former backed the government in its attempt to find a solution, the trade-union leaders – significantly – were the ones to ask for a deputation to be received later that day. It looked as though the Labour movement was beginning to split, with the unions taking up the left-wing stance.

That evening, the cabinet met to hear reports. It soon learned that the expenditure juggling of the previous day would not work. Bondfield announced that Henderson's flat-rate deduction was not viable. She also suggested that 'transitional' benefits could be means tested. Snowden, ever gracious to his allies, berated her for only finding four million from increased contributions. It looked like the cabinet now had no budget, a position which would be more divisive than that of the previous day.

Later on 20 August, MacDonald and his four colleagues of the cabinet committee met the TUC's representatives. The latter, in a gesture of magnanimity, opposed any further burden being imposed on the unemployed, while also objecting to planned pay cuts for teachers and police. It was the trade-union leaders who came up with, if not an alternative strategy, then a different, balanced, budget. They suggested further capital taxation and the rescheduling of the national debt. A revenue tariff, however, needed the approval of congress. Snowden defended the deflationary strategy of the government to save the international financial system. The meeting quickly came to an end when MacDonald stated that 'their observations did not touch [the] problem arising out of [the] immediate financial necessity'. Later, the Prime Minister noted that the TUC deputation had made 'practically a declaration of war'.[4] The cabinet committee stayed on for a desultory forty-five-minute discussion. Henderson, apparently, advocated some of the TUC's proposals.

Throughout, the Foreign Secretary had been an uneasy participant in the attempt to balance the budget at the diktat of the Bank of England. However, it was only from Thursday, 20 August that he accepted what might have to be done once the TUC had come out against a restoration of confidence at the expense of the working class. Henderson, along with Lansbury, Johnston, Greenwood, Clynes and Graham, accepted that parity should be maintained but, once the cabinet's diluted version of May's benefit cuts had been rejected by the trade-union leaders, he and the other anti-Snowdenites were forced to consider seriously their role as Labour politicians. His loyalty to the iron-founders in particular and the Labour movement in general was remarkable.

While Henderson was no doubt proud to be British Foreign Secretary, especially with the disarmament conference coming up, he owed his parliamentary position to a Labour Party which, historically, was strongly dependent on trade unionism. He was a representative of the Labour movement, and, when it was clear that the working class would be made to pay for a Capitalist breakdown, Henderson began, ever so slowly, to question his constitutional duty as a trustee of the nation's destiny. It began to dawn on him that the government might have to return the offices of state to the opposition parties if this was the only way to maintain the unity of the Labour Party in the financial crisis. The Foreign Secretary had proved his patriotism in the Great War and, when it came to a conflict between country and party in 1931, he was not prepared to overlook the latter, even when he risked losing his position as a cabinet minister.

Ironically, Ramsay MacDonald may have been the first member of the government to consider seriously the choice between country and party, as Britain supposedly drifted towards financial collapse. He wrote in his diary for 20 August that ministers had 'had a rather pointless discussion without concentration on the one point of any importance: "Are we to go on?"'[5] Clearly, the Prime Minister, who must have been wearied by the division in the cabinet, was further demoralised by the opposition of the Conservatives and Liberals, on the one hand, and of the TUC, on the other. After a relatively good night's sleep, however, he was determined, on 21 August, to fight the trade-union movement of Bevin and Citrine. Thus, he noted: 'If we yield now to the TUC we shall never be able to call our bodies or souls or intelligences our own.'[6]

It is significant, and tragic, that it was the trade unions, rather than the opposition parties and, behind them, finance capital, which energised MacDonald to resolve the crisis, especially when an emergent faction of his cabinet was obviously paying political attention to the TUC. MacDonald had long opposed the idea of an exclusively trade-union-based Labour Party. He had resigned the leadership in 1914 rather than trust to its pro-war instincts, believing that a progressive party should draw support from all classes in the nation. Then, he had rejected the party for what he believed was the superior interest of the country. In 1931 he honestly accepted the general interest, as it was defined by British bankers in a crisis made by international speculators, seeing the particular interests of the working class as subordinate. Mac-Donald was prepared to consider again his loyalty to the party, though, formally, the Executive still backed him. However, once the TUC thwarted the government, he was determined to see the crisis through, regardless of the political consequences.

At the cabinet on Friday, 21 August, MacDonald reported that the Bank of England, in a rare display of financial judiciousness, wanted expenditure cuts amounting to half the projected deficit. After a long argument, the TUC's position was rejected by Labour ministers in favour of the Prime Minister's method of restoring confidence.

Two days earlier, the cabinet had reduced the expenditure saving by some twenty million pounds. Bondfield had feared that those receiving 'transitional' benefits would be thrown on public assistance, so unemployment insurance was only planned to contribute twenty-two million to the expenditure cuts. This figure now had to be raised back towards the cabinet committee's envisaged forty-three and a half million. A reduction in benefits of ten per cent was proposed, which would yield twelve and a half million pounds. A percentage cut had been ruled out by the cabinet committee. For the first time, the cabinet was, on 21 August, confronted with the notorious May proposal – albeit ten rather than twenty per cent. Ministers were thereupon divided on the question of a cut in benefits. While MacDonald and Snowden told them it was a pointless exercise to aim for an expenditure saving of only fifty-six million, the cabinet decided to try and achieve this objective. In the opinion of the temporisers, it might still be possible to avoid benefit cuts while balancing the budget in such a way as to meet the absolute minimum requirements of the international bankers.

This figure was presented to the Bank of England on the afternoon of the twenty-first. Its representatives reported that there were only four days' reserves left. It was, therefore, critical to secure further credits in Paris and New York.

MacDonald and Snowden then saw the opposition leaders, Neville Chamberlain and Sir Samuel Hoare for the Conservatives and Sir Herbert Samuel (deputising for an ill Lloyd George) and Sir Donald Maclean for the Liberals. These eminent gentlemen were given the government's final expenditure estimates. After a brief consultation, they reported back that the combined opposition would oppose the government when parliament resumed. It was suggested that the King should be contacted, since there could well be a financial collapse before then. The political crisis was coming to a head, with the Conservatives and Liberals threatening to bring down MacDonald's government.

The four leaders returned to Downing Street later that evening. They requested a recall of parliament and the implication was that Baldwin and/or Lloyd George would take over the government. However, because of their perception of the financial crisis, they had a more immediate political objective. Chamberlain, supported by Samuel offered to serve in a new government formed to handle the national crisis. Whatever the past talk of coalitionism, this was a serious attempt to promote the idea of a national government.

It was an important development and one that might produce a result. The cabinet was deadlocked and MacDonald promised to see the opposition leaders the following day. However, on 21 August the Prime Minister was still not persuaded that he should present an ultimatum to his colleagues whereby he would balance the budget with Conservative and Liberal support, risking a split in the Labour party.

The cabinet met early on Saturday, 22 August. MacDonald asked for a further twenty million in expenditure saving. This was to be made up with a ten-per-cent cut in benefits and seven and a half million from other cuts. Ministers rejected this proposal, Snowden and Thomas alone supporting the Prime Minister. However, they were all extremely conscious of the need to secure further credits and of the threat of the opposition parties to stampede. The cabinet then decided that MacDonald and Snowden should ask the opposition leaders if this twenty million additional saving would satisfy them. The Prime Minister and

Chancellor were to make clear that the Labour government had still not made such a decision. It was a last desperate effort to avoid a split.

And it looked as though it might just work. The opposition leaders hinted that they would accept such a figure if the Bank of England considered it sufficient as a guarantee for credit. MacDonald then sought cabinet permission to put this to the Deputy Governor, and to allow Sir Ernest Harvey discreetly to inform J. P. Morgan and Company in New York, who were acting there for the British government. The cabinet agreed to the extension of this hypothetical chain of relationships. A solution appeared to be in sight when the Bank of England undertook to get in touch with New York. The cabinet then decided that MacDonald should see the opposition leaders if the credit was forthcoming. The government arranged to meet the following day (Sunday) at seven in the evening. It was expected that Mac-Donald would be able to report on the loan. The cabinet would then make a final decision on the budget.

From late Saturday afternoon, financial negotiations took place across the Atlantic. The Conservative and Liberal leaders waited, hoping that they would not have to bring down the government. At the request of his Prime Minister, the King returned precipitately from Balmoral on the overnight train.

This was the moment of truth for the Labour government. The cabinet had acquiesced in a proposed budget, which included the ten-per-cent cut in unemployment benefit. It did so to assuage the opposition parties, who were bent on backing the Bank of England. The solution hung on whether sufficient credits could be obtained from the United States. Since Henderson and his allies were reserving their judgment on the budget, a positive response from New York would place the onus of responsibility for accepting or rejecting on them.

Early on Sunday, 23 August, MacDonald telephoned Malcolm,

then a Labour MP, in Lossiemouth. The Prime Minister gave his son a full report, the latter concluding that the decision of the cabinet that evening was still 'in doubt'. It was possible, according to Malcolm, that his father would secure a slight majority. The government could then handle the financial crisis, though the Prime Minister would subsequently have to deal with the opposition of the Labour Party. It was more likely, noted Malcolm, that he would lose. In this case, the Tories would form a government immediately. Even before a post-crisis general election could be held, the Labour Party would censure all those who refused to back Henderson. Win or lose in the cabinet, MacDonald believed he had already gone too far to be able to remain leader of the Labour Party.

He saw George V later that morning. MacDonald told him that the government was seeking credits, with the promise of a 76-million-pound expenditure saving, but he also warned that Henderson and others would resign over the ten-per-cent cut. If this happened, the government as a whole would resign. The King then asked if he should send for Henderson. MacDonald declined to furnish such advice, upon which George V expressed relief (according to his interlocutor). The Prime Minister suggested that the opposition leaders should be asked to report. The King stated that he would request that they support MacDonald. It is clear that the sovereign intended to back the incumbent Premier, with the assistance of the Conservatives and the Liberals. It is equally likely that MacDonald left the Palace on 23 August believing that he would have to resign by midnight.

George V then sent for Baldwin and Samuel. By one of those accidents of history, the Conservative leader could not be found in the forenoon. Thus Samuel, the acting Liberal leader was able to advise that MacDonald should be maintained in office, with a reconstituted Labour cabinet if necessary. He argued this course 'in view of the fact that the necessary economies would prove most unpalatable to the working class'.[8] If this was not possible, continued Samuel, MacDonald should be prevailed upon to remain as Prime Minister, in charge of a three-party national government 'for the single purpose of overcoming the financial crisis'.[9] The King knew that the first option was probably unlikely. While MacDonald's demeanour earlier that day ruled out any possibility of him staying on, there was a stronger chance that the second option could be realised. It could be represented, through the sovereign's consultations with the opposition party leaders, as the overwhelming wish of parliament. Baldwin turned up in the afternoon. He wanted to assume office with Liberal support, in order to deal with the crisis and then go to the country when, presumably, he would decisively see off both Labour and the Liberals. However, he agreed to serve in a Mac-Donald-led national government if this was to be formed.

Meanwhile, in Downing Street, MacDonald may have discussed his options with Thomas and his youngest daughter, Sheila. According to the latter, he could do one of three things after the cabinet meeting. Firstly, he could go into opposition as Labour leader. However, MacDonald would have dishonestly to oppose government economies and, in any case, he would meet with hostility from within the party for having taken his present line. Secondly, he could become Prime Minister of a coalition government, thereby antagonising the whole Labour movement, and losing the leadership of the party. Thirdly, he could resign the party leadership and, as an 'independent member below [the] gangway',[10] support a new, emergency(?) government. This third option, whereby MacDonald would resign as Premier and Labour leader, was the only one compatible with his support for the cabinet's proposed budget. It was, therefore, assumed that Mac-Donald and his supporters would lose at cabinet that evening. It was certain that he wanted to assume the role of an elder statesman. MacDonald, according to his daughter, was conscious that he would otherwise be accused of 'playing for [government] office'.[11]

He had known since Thursday, 20 August that he was out of step with trade-union opinion. In fact, he was fatalistic about his prospects in the Labour Party. On Sunday, 23 August he was aware that he was committing 'political suicide'[12] by continuing to support the ten-per-cent cut. It was just possible that he could stay as Labour Premier with a reconstructed cabinet. More likely, he would become an ex-Prime Minister, with a seat below the gangway. There is no evidence to suggest that MacDonald intended to throw over the Labour Party and certainly nothing to suggest that he would do so in order to become head of a national government.

However, that is precisely what would happen. Part of the political explanation lies in the pressure that he was to come under from the Palace and the opposition leaders, once the cabinet divided that night on the ten-per-cent cut. The second part of an understanding of MacDonald's handling of the 1931 crisis is his failure to fight for his position within the Labour Party. Even if Henderson and others were to resign, there was no reason, other than the threat MacDonald had already made, for the government as a whole to resign; the TUC had come out against cuts but the Labour Party Executive still backed the cabinet. There was ground to be fought for in the parliamentary party and the fact that MacDonald never considered mounting such a campaign suggests an abdication of political leadership.

The cabinet met that evening, as arranged. After a discussion of the parliamentary position, it adjourned to await news from New York. Upon receipt of a telegram, ministers resumed their deliberations at 9.10 p.m. The Americans offered a short-term credit. However, this could not be guaranteed until the following day and it would have to be matched by an equal French loan. Furthermore, it was dependent upon the Labour government securing support from the Bank of England, the City generally and public opinion. MacDonald and Snowden construed the American offer in a benign light. The Prime Minister then appealed for Labour to join with the opposition parties in supporting the proposals on the table. He argued that the government would be able to explain its actions to the party before the return of parliament.

MacDonald was minuted as concluding his speech: 'The proposals as a whole represented the negation of everything that the Labour Party stood for, and yet he was absolutely satisfied that it was necessary in the national interest to implement them if the country was to be secured. . . If on this question there were any important resignations, the Government as a whole must resign.'[13]

Each minister then stated a position on the ten-per-cent cut in unemployment benefit. Eleven were in favour and nine against. This gave a majority, including MacDonald, of three. The Labour cabinet finally accepted the proposed budget.

On Tuesday, 19 August, six ministers – Parmoor, Snowden, Alexander, Passfield, Lees-Smith and Wedgwood Benn – had voted for the free-trade position. Alexander now broke from this group and they were joined, in what was the MacDonald camp, by Sankey, Amulree, Thomas, Bondfield, Morrison and Shaw. Johnston, Henderson, Clynes, Addison, Greenwood, Adamson, Graham, Lansbury and, of course, Alexander made up the group of nine oppositionists. MacDonald had believed that middle-class Socialists were keen on unemployment benefits, while working-class members of the Labour party saw them as inducing fecklessness. On 23 August the second Labour government showed that his sociological observation, in the context of the 1931 financial crisis, meant little in terms of political outcome. MacDonald was supported by most of the middle- and upper-class members of the cabinet, on the grounds of national responsibility, and opposed by most of those closest to the TUC.

Given the likelihood of some or all of the nine oppositionists resigning, MacDonald stated that he would report to the King immediately. He would tender the advice that a conference of the three party leaders should be held the following morning. This suggestion was to be of critical import but Labour ministers seem to have accepted it with equanimity. The Prime Minister was clearly intending to resign, even though he had won the argument in cabinet by a majority. Yet it would be at the conference of party leaders that MacDonald was to be subjected to the full flattery of the Palace and combined opposition. The cabinet agreed with MacDonald's proposed course of action and authorised him to tell the King that he had received their resignations. It looked as though the Labour Party and its leader were about to hand over responsibility to whomsoever the King might choose – presumably Baldwin, with or without Liberal support.

In the course of the next twelve hours, however, George V would bring into existence a national government led by Ramsay MacDonald which would be opposed by the Labour Party.

The Prime Minister reached the Palace at 10.20 p.m., looking 'scared and unbalanced'.[14] He announced that he would be tendering the resignation of his government. 'The King impressed on the Prime Minister that he was the only man to lead the country through this crisis and hoped he would reconsider the situation.'[15] There is no evidence that such regal blandishment broke his determination to vacate the premiership. MacDonald requested, as head of the government, a meeting of the three party leaders. However, the King had declared his hand and planted an idea in MacDonald's mind.

He reported back to his colleagues in Downing Street at 10.40 p.m. The Labour cabinet agreed to meet again at noon the following day. Ministers were probably hoping for something from the meeting of the three leaders with the King. Even though the cabinet had split, it would seem that both factions were now temporising. No doubt it was difficult, for a number of reasons, to contemplate resignation, and the political autopsy which would take place in the Labour Party. However, to hope that the opposition parties would somehow bale out the Labour government was grasping at straws. It was late when ministers left the cabinet room, all believing that the government was still hanging together.

MacDonald may not have informed them that he had already asked the opposition leaders to meet him as soon as possible. Late on Sunday night, Baldwin, Chamberlain and Samuel came to Downing Street. The Prime Minister told them that the cabinet was hopelessly split. He offered personally to support the proposals of a Conservative government with Liberal support, 'though it meant his death warrant'.[16] He clearly saw himself as an ex-Prime Minister below the gangway. MacDonald specifically refused to lead or serve in a national government. The opposition leaders left believing that they had failed to persuade MacDonald.

In the course of the night of 23/24 August, his determination must have weakened. Perhaps he became frightened by the prospect of being a lone Labour MP supporting a temporary Conservative administration for the duration of the crisis. He had despaired of Labour rallying to the national interest but he had no intention of deserting to another political party. No doubt he must have dwelt on the solid front linking the Palace and parliament, a formidable alliance which would rally the whole establishment and perhaps even the people. By the morning, he was very close to accepting the King's invitation to lead a national government.

MacDonald telephoned Ishbel, who was also in Lossiemouth, at breakfast-time on Monday, 24 August. He outlined his conception of a national government under his leadership to his oldest daughter. According to Malcolm, 'this [National] Government would last about five weeks, to tide over the crisis. It would be the end, in his opinion, of J. R. M.'s political career. . . To break so with the Labour Party would be painful in the extreme.'[17] This was how it would be.

MacDonald's change of mind overnight was largely for personal reasons. He could not face political isolation, during which he would have to defend himself before the party for his conduct as leader of the second Labour government. He had grown away from the party over the years but this had much to do with the way Labour controlled, or rather, failed to control, its parliamentary leaders. The same applies to MacDonald's so-called social corruption, something in which he was not particularly unique. However, it is the case that other politicians, non-Labour and Labour, would not allow themselves to be flattered by the King and leading parliamentarians.

MacDonald was a man who believed he was indispensable as Prime Minister. He saw himself as the saviour of the nation at that critical time, whereas, as Samuel had baldly stated to the King, he was the ruling class's ideal candidate for imposing a balanced budget at the expense of the working class. This was to be MacDonald's political function from 24 August 1931.

At 10.00 a.m., MacDonald, Baldwin and Samuel met the King. George V was determined that the leaders should issue a communiqué to end the political suspense. When MacDonald then said that he had the government's resignation in his pocket, the sovereign expressed the hope that his Prime Minister would remain in office. It was the decisive moment in the 1931 crisis and the point at which MacDonald failed to act on the expectations of all his cabinet colleagues. Baldwin and Samuel, by quickly agreeing to serve in an emergency government, made it difficult for MacDonald, if he was still so inclined, to resist. It was envisaged that, while this temporary administration would continue after a dissolution, the three parties would fight a general election independently. This was agreed in principle within thirty-five minutes.

MacDonald noted later that 'on urgent request of all, I consented to continue as PM under safeguards written on sheet'.[18] This was a reference to a memorandum drawn up by Samuel in the meeting. It provided for 'a co-operation of individuals',[19] as distinct from the coalition of parties of recent political memory. This administration was to implement the measures of the Labour cabinet, agreed by a majority vote on 23 August. When the run on the pound had ceased and the gold standard was once again safe, normal politics would be resumed. The King congratulated the party leaders for ensuring that the country would not be left governless, in the light of the Labour cabinet's collective resignation. The communiqué was issued by the Palace, announcing that a national government was 'under consideration'.[20]

MacDonald hurried back to Downing Street, for what was the last meeting of the second Labour government. It had been assumed at Buckingham Palace that some of his eleven supporters of the previous night would join the new government. He therefore decided not to present the agreed memorandum to his cabinet as a whole. The Prime Minister did, however, announce that the King had asked certain individuals to govern. While he had put the case against his involvement in any such administration, 'he had felt that there was no other course. . . for the purpose of meeting the present emergency.'[21]

He then invited those who wished to make a similar sacrifice to join him. Most ministers, however, indicated their unwillingness. He was left only with Thomas, his old political friend, Sankey, the late middle-class recruit to the party, and Snowden, whose ideological rigidity had brought Labour to this sorry pass. The cabinet, in its last collective decision, then agreed that the government's resignation should be handed to the King that afternoon. On the motion of Sankey as Lord Chancellor, ministers recorded 'their warm appreciation of the great kindness, consideration and courtesy invariably shown by the Prime Minister when presiding over their meetings'.[22]

It was a bizarre end to the second Labour government, the meeting having taken only twenty-five minutes. As ministers trooped out, they had probably still not fully grasped the nature of the political bombshell MacDonald had let off in the cabinet room. Few can have fully realised the historic nature of the occasion for the Labour Party.

The prime minister requested that his three loyal colleagues remain behind. He asked them to become the first members of his new, non-party government, an invitation they quickly accepted. At 2.30 p.m. MacDonald saw his junior ministers, the meeting having originally been arranged to announce the cut in ministerial salaries. While he appealed for some of them to support him, MacDonald had assumed that the stand of the cabinet would be reflected in the lower ranks of the government. As he noted later: 'The Chancellor was getting pessimistic as the desertions went on & I tried to cheer him up, but indeed it was a dreary matter. Still we were right.'[23] He then saw Baldwin and Samuel. At 4.10 p.m. MacDonald handed the King the resignation of the second Labour government. He then kissed hands upon accepting the sovereign's request to form a new government.

8 *The great betrayal, 1931–7*

Eight days later, on 1 September 1931, Ramsay MacDonald replied to a Labour MP's letter: 'If I had agreed to stay[,] [and] defied the bankers. . . you would have been swept out of existence. . . Still I have always said that the rank and file have not. . . the same duty as the leaders. . . I am afraid I am not a machine-made politician. . . and it is far better for me to drop out. . . to make a decent living whilst out of public office.'[1] This was not to be the case.

MacDonald would quickly select the national government, his small National Labour group being outnumbered by the Conservatives and Liberals. He was to make no effort to stay in the Labour Party and in late September the Prime Minister would be expelled. By then, Snowden's emergency budget was to have failed to save the pound and, in the wake of the Invergordon 'mutiny', Britain would go off the gold standard. MacDonald was to believe that he still had to save the pound and he would lead the National government into a general election in late October with the parties divided on the question of protection. He was to receive an overwhelming mandate but the new National government would be supported by a majority of Conservatives. Labour was to to become a minority party and this historic reversal would be blamed entirely on MacDonald. In early 1932 the government was to introduce protection. A free-trade minority would be allowed to oppose a general tariff but, following the Ottowa Economic Imperial Conference, Snowden and the Samuelite Liberals were to resign from the cabinet in September. MacDonald would increasingly become a prisoner of the Tories.

In the area of economic policy, Neville Chamberlain as Chancellor was to be the dominant figure.

MacDonald would again be concerned with international affairs, where the rise of Hitler was to threaten the security of Europe. He would be unsympathetic to France and, though the British Prime Minister was to negotiate an end to reparations in 1932 and would persuade the Germans to return to the disarmament conference, the election of Hitler to the Chancellorship was to lead to Germany's withdrawal from the League of Nations. MacDonald would begin to think more in terms of agreement on arms limitation and, when pressure was to grow for British rearmament, he would back Chamberlain's financial stringency. By late 1934 he was to accept that the rearmers had a case. The following March, MacDonald would find himself committed to increased defence expenditure, at a time when Lansbury was still leader of the opposition. When Hitler was to reintroduce conscription, MacDonald would travel to Stresa, where Britain, Italy and France would agree to prevent further breaches of the Treaty of Versailles. This was to be on the eve of his stepping down as Premier in May 1935.

From the formation of the National government, MacDonald would age physically and mentally. He was to remain emotionally attached to the Labour Party and would hope for a revival of what he considered non-materialist Socialism. MacDonald was to be uneasy in the embrace of the Conservative Party and would attempt to convince himself that he was mitigating the impact of Tory rule. The National Labour group would be nothing more than a personal rump, though he was occasionally to see it as the nucleus of a new Socialism. He would talk of resigning as Prime Minister from 1931 but it was to be a combination of ill health and Conservative hostility which would lead him to hand over to Baldwin. He was to refuse all honours, though the King would persuade him to stay in government as Lord President of

the Council. Fearing retirement, he was to be politically isolated
in the cabinet. He would lose his parliamentary seat in the 1935
general election, though he was to be returned for the Scottish
Universities early the following year. His worries about Abyssinia
and Spain would be ignored by his Conservative colleagues. In
May 1937 he was, with Baldwin, to step down from the National
government. Within months, Ramsay MacDonald would be dead.

The National government had been put together by Mac-
Donald, with the assistance of Baldwin and Samuel, on Tuesday,
25 August 1931. The three former Labour ministers returned to
their posts. The Conservatives were given four positions and two
Liberals made up the cabinet of ten. It was slightly larger than
Lloyd George's wartime régime and, in a broadcast that evening,
MacDonald promised that there would be no coupons in a forthcoming election. 'Those of us who have taken risks', he said,
'will receive either our punishment or our reward.'[2] In private,
he intimated that the four Labour members were going to their
'political deaths',[3] and expressed relief at not having to ask any
of his remaining eight cabinet supporters to join the new
administration.

However, he was having difficulty filling his quota of other
posts in the government. MacDonald had agreed, with Baldwin
and Samuel, a ratio of four-four-two for the cabinet. This became
four-eight-six among other senior ministers, appointed on 25/26
August and 3/4 September. He retained one minister and most
of his law officers but it is unlikely that he would have offered
lesser posts to the likes of Bondfield and Morrison. Junior ministers were also appointed on the latter occasion, the Prime Minister
only keeping one from his previous government. He also
appointed Malcolm as Under-Secretary in the Dominions Office,
the ratio being two-fourteen-seven (several posts being left vacant
pending a general election).

The MacDonald Labourites had a fair share of cabinet seats,

but the Conservatives were the largest party in the government. The Prime Minister's group was even smaller than the Liberals.

MacDonald still considered himself a member of the Labour Party, though he was fatalistic about his future and that of his eleven supporters, seven of whom were MPs. On 24 August, Henderson and Lansbury had met with Bevin and Citrine and party officials in Transport House. The trade unionists expressed their determination to fight the new government. The *Daily Herald* of 25 August accepted that MacDonald was sincere but attacked him for surrendering to the City; the editor, however, would 'do [his] utmost to preserve an absolutely fair attitude. . . throughout the Crisis'.[4] While forming the National government, the Prime Minister wrote to all former junior ministers and Labour MPs about the financial crisis. He indicated that, with the return of normality, the party would be reunited. He had also sent his private secretary to encourage Henderson to take a peerage and, while the latter declined, he stated that '[they] must not take the split too seriously' since he, as Party Secretary, 'was ready to receive Mr MacDonald back again'.[5]

The leaders of the TUC, Labour Party and Parliamentary Party met on 26 August. They resolved to oppose MacDonald's new government in parliament and in the country. A manifesto was issued the following day, endorsing the TUC's stand of a week before. This would rally, not only the cabinet minority of 24 August which accepted fifty-six million in expenditure saving, but also most of the MacDonald majority who voted for the ten-per-cent cut in unemployment benefit. This change of position on the part of former supporters was to be a particular source of irritation to him.

On Tuesday, 25 August the Parliamentary Party had summoned all members to a special meeting on the following Friday. MacDonald's invitation, for some unknown reason, did not reach Downing Street until late on the twenty-sixth and it was Thursday mid-morning before he saw it. Earlier that day, having read of the meeting in a paper to which his letter to Labour MPs had been leaked, MacDonald had written to the Secretary of the Parliamentary Labour Party. He explained that he could not attend because he had arranged to leave that evening for a weekend in Lossiemouth. He did not alter his plans when the invitation arrived belatedly. This was because he believed he would be rejected by the party.

Thus, MacDonald threw over his first, and last, chance to fight for his place in the party by explaining to MPs in person his view of the financial crisis. The government's deliberations had been secret and it is just possible that MacDonald's stature might have swayed a minority of MPs. In such an eventuality, of course, he would have been accused of trying to split the Labour Party.

The Parliamentary Party met in Transport House on 28 August, with members of the TUC General Council present. Labour MPs, with only a few opposing, endorsed the TUC's position. They then went on to elect Henderson as leader of the party, with Clynes and Graham as deputies. Sankey and Malcolm MacDonald, already members of the National government, spoke in favour of its formation. The former, apparently, noted that the meeting was 'very hostile as all the Trade Unionists were there, but [he] defended [his] position in a long speech'.[6] The Labour Party had yet to expel its former leader.

The formation of the National government seemed to have helped towards restoring financial confidence. The loans from New York and Paris were announced on 28 August. However, the run on the pound was not entirely stemmed and, within a week, the Bank of England was calling upon the government to abandon plans for a general election.

When parliament resumed on 8 September, MacDonald survived a vote of confidence. Two days later, Snowden introduced an emergency budget. The deficit was to be met with eighty-two million of increased taxation and a reduction of twenty million on the sinking fund. There was to be an expenditure saving of seventy-million pounds. This comprised the Labour government's fifty-six million, plus another thirteen million from the ten-per-cent cut in unemployment benefit. The sinking fund was a new idea and, ironically, the expenditure cut was eight million less than the Labour cabinet committee had suggested on 19 August. A balanced budget, however, which had been proffered as the only solution, did not end the crisis. Foreign depositors lacked confidence in London banks.

On 15 September, sailors at Invergordon across the Moray Firth from Lossiemouth, 'mutinied' over excessive wage cuts. MacDonald took a strong stand, noting of a cabinet meeting called to deal with the issue: 'Proposals put up [by the naval and military authorities] were namby-pamby. No enforcement of discipline. Thomas let loose upon them. Told them they had to discipline. Labour's three alone stood stiff at first, then all took heart.'[7] However, the Admiralty was forced to promise a revision and the government later produced a universal cut of ten per cent in all public-sector wages and salaries. The gold and foreign reserves continued to drain away. On 18 September further credits were sought in New York and Paris.

These were refused, despite the balanced budget and a National government. The next day, the Bank of England asked to be excused its responsibility for maintaining the gold standard. The necessary legislation was quickly enacted on Monday, 21 September. The pound sterling, allowed to float in the international markets, was to fall by more than a quarter. Thus, devaluation, which Keynes had recommended and the Labour government had gone over the brink to prevent, came four weeks after the formation of the National government. MacDonald's determination had been for nothing. The advice of the Bank of England, which had been taken as absolute gospel, was proved to be worthless. 'Nobody told us we could do this,'[8] remarked Passfield, expressing the general amazement of former Labour ministers. Despite the alarms of the ruling class, there was no apocalypse in Britain as a result of abandoning the gold standard. The onset of currency management, however, signalled the end of British global economic domination. Finance capital, which had successfully imposed its interests on the Labour government as a national priority, was the only loser in September 1931. The price of imports had been falling, and a weaker pound promised to help British exports.

On 30 August, one week after the collapse of his government, the Hampstead Labour Party 'expelled' MacDonald from membership. At the time, he was receiving supportive letters, mainly from older activists; it may be that critics did not write or that the letters were not preserved. His agent in Seaham had already informed him that the local party would be asking for his resignation. MacDonald was not inclined to do this. He thought '[his] friends ought to conduct a campaign of educational propaganda. . . not for the purpose of splitting the Party but of saving it'.[9] He turned down an offer to become the candidate for Moray and Nairn, but he had already concluded that Labour was not fit to govern and, while he told Baldwin on 5 September that '[he had] not left [his] Party and [had] no intention of doing so',[10] MacDonald mooted the possibility of the National government adopting a long-term programme, including protection.

This was after less than two weeks of the emergency administration and the weekend before parliament met. On the Tuesday, the government won the vote of confidence by 309 votes to 249. Though Henderson had begun his speech by alluding to the possibility of MacDonald's return, he articulated the difference between the party and its former leader: 'The Prime Minister appealed to the country. We appeal to that part of the country that we have tried to represent, and I hope that we will appeal on high, strong Socialist grounds.'[11] Only twelve Labour MPs voted for the government, with another five abstaining. The following day, the Prime Minister addressed his rump of supporters in the Parliamentary Party on what he considered to be the reprehensible behaviour of the new Labour leadership.

Snowden's budget widened the gulf. In the parliamentary debate on 11 September, Clynes, who had opposed MacDonald, argued that former cabinet ministers could now object to measures that they had hitherto supported. The following day, the Seaham party came out in support of Henderson. However, it divided, by forty to thirty-nine, on a motion requesting MacDonald's resignation as MP. The Prime Minister replied to the local activists that '[he] would let the matter rest where it [was] for the moment.'[12] By mid-September, he still considered a general election inevitable. Though he had come to believe that a resumption of party conflict was undesirable, he did not see himself as a member of a new National government.

There was a moment of rapprochement with his former colleagues when Britain went off the gold standard. Henderson agreed to support in parliament the floating of the pound. However, 112 Labour MPs voted against on 21 September and he threatened to resign the party leadership. Rumours began to reach MacDonald of possible Labour backing. It was thought that Henderson might cease opposing the National government in return for concessions on unemployment benefit, now that the pound was devaluing. The Prime Minister, however, who was resting away from London, was unable to follow up on this putative political reconciliation. The Conservatives were keen on an election and even on a single-party government to introduce protection. By 26 September, MacDonald had decided that a 'National appeal must be made by those who have formed the National Government'.[13] This was in spite of the fact that the

Liberals were for free trade and against an election. As he wrote to a correspondent two days later: 'although we cannot say it in public, the unsettlement regarding sterling and the uncertainty regarding the position of the Government may, at any moment, bring a new crisis, the results of which may well be starvation for great sections of our people, ruin to everybody except a lot of dastardly profiteers and speculators, and the end of our influence in the world.'[14]

It was now largely a question of formulating an agreed programme for the national government. This, however, was something which MacDonald had promised, in his anti-coupon broadcast a month earlier, that he would not do. On Monday, 28 September, the die was cast. That evening, two Labour MPs asked him to offer an olive branch to Henderson. MacDonald replied that he was hoping to end parliamentary life very soon. Earlier, the Party Executive, with Henderson the sole dissentient, had deemed all supporters of the National government to be non-members of the party. MacDonald would become acquainted with this fact the following day, when he received a letter bearing a signature affixed by a rubber stamp.

The expulsion of MacDonald on 28 September, after a career of thirty-one years in the Labour Party, saw him identified as a traitor. It was, however, to be his decision to go to the country as leader of the National government, which would mainly shape his reputation in British politics.

It took a week for the cabinet to agree a manifesto. On 29 September, Neville Chamberlain, who was Minister of Health, presented MacDonald with a draft election programme. This included provision for protection and the Conservatives knew that it would antagonise the Liberals. The King, however, pronounced that 'party differences should be sunk'.[15] On 1 October, MacDonald made the electoral statement less offensive to the free traders. This was enough for Samuel, as acting leader, but other Liberal ministers asked for time to consider the reformulation. The Prime Minister knew the Conservatives would secure a majority. He asked Baldwin personally to guarantee that he would not impose protection on an elected National government for eighteen months. It is possible that the Conservative leader may have promised this. The cabinet, in MacDonald's absence in Seaham, was unable to agree and, on 3 October, he told the King that 'he was beginning to feel that he had failed and had better clear out'.[16] George V threatened to refuse to accept his resignation. On Monday, 5 October, MacDonald spelt out all the options to his cabinet. In a lengthy discussion, it looked like the government was about to break up. This was until ministers began to accept that they could only secure a mandate by leaving open the divisive question of protection. 'The election will present many difficulties, especially Tariff propaganda & definitions', MacDonald noted later in his diary. 'How sad I feel at the thought of fighting with Tories and Liberals! How I despise the men who ran away. And how hard it is to have to appear to have deserted.'[17] Parliament was prorogued on the seventh and the election set for 27 October.

MacDonald asked for authority to try all possible economic solutions. Baldwin and Samuel endorsed this so-called 'doctor's mandate' and then issued their own, contradictory, party manifestos. If it was not to be a plebiscite on protection, the 1931 election would be a contest biased in favour of the Conservatives.

The National government had a supporter in virtually every seat, the overwhelming majority (523) being Tories. The 160 Liberals had split before nominations closed. Sir John Simon led a breakaway group of forty-one Liberal Nationals, who were prepared to follow MacDonald. The main body of 112 candidates, under Samuel, remained strong free traders. Lloyd George had no love for coalitionism in 1931 and, while he only put a group of seven Independent Liberals into the field, he deprived the rest of his party of considerable financial support. A National Labour committee collected money for MacDonald but there were only twenty candidates from this would-be party. Pitched against the National government, in addition to the Lloyd Georgeites, was the Labour Party, with 515 candidates. It took a strong free-trade position but the electoral programme contained proposals for a planned economy.

Labour concentrated its attack on MacDonald, and the Prime Minister was indeed the issue in the campaign. He represented himself as the leader of the nation, implying that the Labour government had failed to live up to its responsibilities. As the contest proceeded, things became more heated. Snowden, a former ILPer, was even to condemn Labour's far-from-radical programme as 'Bolshevism run made'.[18] The Labour Party was being subjected to the full force of bourgeois propaganda in the aftermath of MacDonald's betrayal.

He had gone to Seaham early, in order to secure his re-election. In this solidly working-class constituency, MacDonald's former agent was now the official Labour candidate. The Prime Minister attempted to reaffirm his Labour pedigree. He also brandished hyper-inflated German banknotes on several occasions, a political stunt which irritated his Labour opponents. He had been expected to lose. However, the national appeal of the government saw its leader returned with a majority of nearly six thousand. MacDonald received 28,978 votes to his opponent's 23,027, most Conservatives voting for a man they had detested when he stood for the Socialist cause.

The turn-out across the country was similar to 1929. Labour, with thirty-one per cent of the poll, lost one and three quarter million votes; it is thought that some women switched to the national candidate, but it seems that the majority of lost Labour voters simply abstained. The combined Liberals, with nearly eleven per cent, dropped three million votes, owing largely to the lack of candidates. The Conservatives, with fifty-five per cent, gained well over three-million votes, most from the Liberals and very few from Labour. The government bloc of parties secured 14,532,519 supporters to the opposition's 6,755,736.

These votes, however, translated badly into seats. The National government had 554 seats to the opposition's 56, a devastating result in favour of the status quo. The Conservatives had 473 seats to the Simonites' thirty five, the Samuelites' thirty three and the MacDonaldites' thirteen. It was the biggest Conservative victory ever. The Lloyd Georgeites were reduced to four, and Labour to fifty two, including one Independent Labour candidate and five ILPers who were not endorsed by the party. Since the ILP was to pull out of the Labour Party within months, the parliamentary group resembled that of pre-war years. Labour was the undoubted loser of the 1931 election. Most of its leaders failed to secure re-election. As Lansbury was the only former senior minister returned, he would be confirmed leader of the Labour Party in late 1932. Thus had Morrison, a MacDonald supporter in August 1931, turned his former leader's portrait to the wall in the headquarters of the London Labour Party.

The 1931 parliament was overwhelmingly Tory, but Mac-Donald sought to retain a National, inter-party government. He was moderately successful at cabinet level, where there were twenty seats to fill. The Prime Minister kept his three National Labour colleagues, though Snowden, who had not fought in the election, had to give up the Treasury. The divided Liberals were given five seats. Baldwin was effectively Deputy Prime Minister and the Prime Minister was forced to make Neville Chamberlain, a protectionist, Chancellor of the Exchequer. There were nine other Conservatives. Thus, the major party had only a bare majority, eleven seats to the Liberals' five and National Labour's four. Among other senior ministers, this ratio became five-one-one, while, among junior ministers, it was fifteen-six-two. The

National Labour group retained its position in the government, but, along with the Liberals, it had declined relative to the Conservatives.

The latter claimed that they had received a mandate for protection, forcing MacDonald to negotiate fiscal policy with the free-trade minority of Snowden the Lord Privy Seal, Samuel the Home Secretary, Maclean the President of the Board of Education and Sinclair the Secretary of State for Scotland. The rumour of tariffs produced a flood of imports. In November 1931 the government imposed duties of up to one hundred per cent on 'abnormal importations'. Samuel and Maclean objected. It was Snowden who protested when Gilmour, the Minister of Agriculture, announced that there was to be a wheat quota and the government moved to protect some horticultural products. With the free-traders uneasy, MacDonald pragmatically suggested selective import controls.

On 11 December a cabinet committee, chaired by Chamberlain, was established to consider the balance of trade. Samuel and Snowden were members but they were outnumbered by Thomas, Simon and Runciman, plus the Conservatives, Cunliffe-Lister, Young and Gilmour. In January 1932 the committee reported in favour of a general tariff of ten per cent. Snowden, Samuel, Sinclair and Maclean opposed the idea in cabinet. However, Simon, Runciman, Thomas and Sankey allied with the Conservatives. MacDonald also threw his weight against the free traders. With the latter threatening to resign, the Conservatives backed off slightly. Hailsham, the Secretary for War, proposed a relaxation of cabinet responsibility. The four ministers would be allowed to oppose tariff reform, while the National government embraced protectionism. This agreement to differ was accepted. MacDonald took the view that the doctrine of collective cabinet responsibility stemmed from the need to preserve party unity; it was necessary in the case of a National government. Chamberlain carried his ten-per-cent tariff bill the following month, Labour and the Samuelite and Lloyd Georgeite Liberals voting against. When Maclean died suddenly in June, MacDonald felt compelled to replace him with a Conservative. There were only three free traders left in the cabinet.

An Economic Imperial Conference opened in Ottawa on 21 July. Seven senior British ministers travelled to Canada but MacDonald remained in London. Over the next four weeks, the goal of empire free trade eluded the member governments. Baldwin was opposed to 'stomach taxes' and there was only limited protection against non-empire foodstuffs. The dominions made some tariff concessions in favour of Britain but this was done by increasing barriers against non-empire producers. This was too much for the free traders at home. Snowden immediately discussed resignation with the Samuelites.

During September, MacDonald agonised about the inevitable damage to the National government: 'The new Government will. . . be, to all intents and purposes, a single-party administration, and. . . a Prime Minister who does not belong to the Party in power will become more and more degrading.'[19] He appealed to the free traders not to resign over Ottawa and to consider their position after the international economic conference planned for mid-1933. The Conservatives opposed any delay in legislating for the Ottawa agreement and, on 28 September, the cabinet split. Snowden, Samuel and Sinclair resigned during the lunch adjournment and they were joined by a junior minister. MacDonald claimed that he had considered resigning. However, in the afternoon he secured endorsement for his continuing premiership from the Simonites and the Conservatives. Afterwards, he noted: 'I have had doubts as to whether I should stay, but only owing to my own personal feelings. It is a lonely job, but of what I ought to do I never doubted.'[20] In reality, MacDonald was afraid to go because he needed the position to fill his personal loneliness.

He had, in the process, revised his own earlier political view that he would become a prisoner of the Tories. MacDonald moved quickly to fill the empty posts; Baldwin also assumed the office of Lord Privy Seal and a Conservative and a Simonite were brought into the cabinet. It now comprised thirteen Conservatives, three Simonites and three MacDonaldites. In parliament, the Samuelites eventually joined the opposition in November 1933. After two years in office, the National government had the support of thirteen disorganised National Labourists, thirty-five increasingly conservative Liberal Nationals and 469 Conservatives. It became, to all intents and purposes, a single-party government, with MacDonald as a figurehead leader.

This was particularly evident in economic policy, where Chamberlain was the dominant figure.

The Chancellor determined the budget each year and, by 1934, he was able to show a surplus. He actually increased the national debt, but his war loan conversion of 1932 reduced the servicing burden on the economy. He secured new revenues from tariffs and was able to reduce the contribution of direct taxation. In the 1931 election, MacDonald had pledged to resign if the National government moved to tax co-operative societies. He was unable to prevent this in 1933. (MacDonald was embarrassed by the undertaking he gave to a constituent, and, when Lord Londonderry informed him that the woman in question had embezzled Labour Party funds in Seaham, the Prime Minister let it be known that he might be driven to use this information.) The following year he had to back down when the Conservatives abolished Snowden's land taxation. As MacDonald expressed it to Simon, 'it mark[ed] the point of departure from a National Government to a Coalition Government'.[21] Progressive electors were losing faith in his government. It was the former Chancellor's 1931 emergency budget which shaped the government's spending plans. That December, MacDonald had argued in cabinet that expenditure savings should be reviewed but Chamberlain was able to continue exercising tight control. In 1932 he cut police pay by ten per cent. Military expenditure was at its lowest since the war. The war loan conversion saw that bank rate reduced to two per cent but the government made no move to stimulate recovery through public spending.

In late 1931, MacDonald had bemoaned 'this extraordinary trade paralysis. It is not the usual depression. It is really the breakdown of a system.'[22] Britain's economic problems, he believed, awaited the solution of a revival in international trade. He had been forced to detach the pound from gold in September 1931 but it was the Treasury which kept the value down until, in 1933, Roosevelt devalued the dollar. Currency management in the sterling area, however, did little to boost international trade. Tariffs were the major contribution of the national government, but they effectively reduced British exports because of increased competition abroad. Trade within the empire became an increasing proportion of Britain's declining overseas business. MacDonald presided at the world economic conference held in South Kensington, London in June 1933. Participants united in deploring the demise of free trade, while operating, to varying degrees, policies of economic nationalism. When Roosevelt refused to stabilise the dollar, this led to the permanent adjournment of the conference. MacDonald was forced to conclude that, whatever the international relations between states, when it came to the world Capitalist system, bourgeois governments were not interested in co-operation. German reparations had been virtually cancelled in July 1932 and, when Britain's other debtors declined to pay off their war loans, the National government was forced to repudiate unilaterally its repayments to the United States in mid-1933. It used, as an excuse, American tariffs. In that year, world trade began to revive. The British government was in no position to claim a share of the credit. The revival at home was due less to the rationalisation of the staple export industries behind tariff barriers and more to the demand for new production in the domestic market. Increased consumption was to reach a peak by 1937, partly because of rearmament but mainly because of house building and new consumer goods.

This boom would not be attributed to MacDonald but, as Prime Minister from 1929 until 1932/33, he could not avoid ultimate responsibility for the way the world recession affected Britain. Unemployment had risen under Labour and, when Mac-Donald allied with the Conservatives, it continued to rise. He was, however, concerned about unemployment benefit and relief works, though virtually a prisoner in his own cabinet. At the depth of the depression in January 1933, he noted of the government's economic policy: 'No vision of general situation & only concern to keep Govt. out of practically everything. Deserted by Labour & Liberal parties, National Govt. inevitably tends to fundamental Toryism.'[23] The means test, which had been intro-duced for transitional benefits in 1931, was unpopular. Mac-Donald, however, was unable to prevent Chamberlain proposing a centrally run system of 'unemployment assistance'. This repre-sented almost a return to the poor law and, when it was enacted in 1934, it gave rise to considerable working-class opposition. The following year, the National government was forced to back down on the level of rates established. Hunger marches were revived in the 1930s by the Communist Party. In 1934, when Maxton had asked MacDonald to receive one such march when it reached London, the latter replied: 'nothing would give me greater pleasure than to gratify you wholeheartedly in the first request you have made, but you. . . know how those of us who are acquainted with the Labour Movement in and out regard the chief promoters of this march'.[24] Though unemployment nation-ally was to fall, because of recovery in parts of Britain, it was, however, still over twelve per cent in 1938.

MacDonald had continued to be interested in international relations. He doubted Simon's ability as Foreign Secretary and the conduct of foreign policy seemed an attractive haven of autonomy with the National government. From 1931, however, the condition of the world would gradually deteriorate. This was reflected in the stands MacDonald took. When Japan invaded Manchuria, he went along with the Foreign Office rather than support the United States. On India, he was forced by the Conservatives effectively to arrest progress towards self-government. However, Europe was again the main arena of British foreign policy in the 1930s, the rise of Fascism in Germany threatening world peace.

When Britain was about to come off the gold standard, Japan committed its aggression in the Far East. China immediately approached the League of Nations, securing support for a withdrawal of troops. The following January, the emperor's forces committed a further aggression in Shanghai. War was likely and the threat to collective security could not be prevented by words alone. The United States wanted Britain to join in a protest against Japan's violation of China's integrity. MacDonald might have been expected to respond favourably but he eventually took the Foreign Office line. Simon did not want to make a British commitment to military action, nor did he want to support a protest he might have to back away from. He was, however, reluctant to say this to the Americans. MacDonald may have suggested another League of Nations' resolution. When Britain proposed that the conflict with China should not be settled by military means, Japan was able to abstain in Geneva in the face of this timid international criticism.

The second 'round table' conference on India had opened in September 1931. This time Gandhi was present as a representative of the nationalists. The Indian Princes had become suspicious of a federation and, with the Moslem minority concerned about its rights, the Hindus began to fear for the future of self-government. The British, with a Conservative, Sir Samuel Hoare, at the India Office, seemed even less committed and Gandhi was ordered home by the Congress – a request he chose to ignore.

MacDonald then took a hand, proposing that a federal constitution should be drafted before legislation granting autonomy to the provinces was passed. On 13 November the cabinet rejected the Prime Minister's scheme. It later decided to legislate for provincial autonomy, but the government was forced to withdraw in the face of Indian hostility and, in a winding-up speech on 1 December, MacDonald reaffirmed support for an all-Indian federation.

No progress was made at a third 'round table' conference in 1932 and, the following year, Hoare handed the issue over to a joint select committee. In parliament, Churchill became an outspoken advocate for the Indian Princes. In February 1935, three months before MacDonald was to resign as Premier, they came out against British plans for a central Executive of sorts. Thus, a Government of India Act was destroyed before it received the royal assent in August – much to the pleasure of the Conservative right wing.

In February 1932, the International Disarmament Conference had opened in Geneva, under the presidency of Arthur Henderson. The British government was unwilling to be dragged into another continental war and it was determined not to support French demands for security through an international police force under the League of Nations. MacDonald had little remaining sympathy for the French, who were widely regarded as having selfishly added to the misery of Germany.

The Germans still wanted to escape from the humiliation of Versailles. To this end, they proposed that the disarmament clauses of that treaty should be applied all round. There was little basis for Franco-German rapprochement and illness kept MacDonald away from the talks until late April. In Geneva he explored the possibility of modest German rearmament, whereby the clauses would be rescinded though France remained militarily superior. His health, however, forced him to return to London. Simon closed the session in July and, when the conference declined to accept the principle of equality of nations, Germany threatened not to return to the conference.

By then, a separate conference at Lausanne on German reparations, chaired by MacDonald, had concluded with an agreement. It had opened in mid-June with MacDonald angling for a 'clean slate', the cancellation of the web of wartime debt. When the French began to move diplomatically, MacDonald injected the idea of a final payment into the negotiations. The Germans, in turn, acknowledged the need for compensation. They had difficulty, however, in selling the proposal at home and the British delegation was rocked by renewed Franco-German rivalry.

Eventually, it was agreed to establish a reconstruction fund. However, the French demanded more than the Germans were prepared to offer. MacDonald tried to coax them to pay more, with the suggested abrogation by the delegates of German war guilt. He offered the French a consultative pact, whereby Britain would talk with them first, before acceding to future German requests for the revision of Versailles. After further negotiations, an agreement was signed on 9 July. It provided for a final German payment in return for a British understanding with the French. Reparations were at an end but the Anglo-French accord only strengthened German nationalism.

In the autumn of 1932, MacDonald laboured to get Germany back to Geneva. He persuaded the British government to tilt in its direction and, in December, Germany agreed to return. It did so in January 1933, the month that Hitler's election to the Chancellorship brought the Nazis to power. This was to alter the whole character of European politics. The era of peaceful reconstruction was at an end. On 2 March, MacDonald noted that 'the intentions of the German Govt. sent secretly from Berlin were so like important events & movements in the summer of 1914'.[25]

Nevertheless, he responded sympathetically when Anthony Eden, the Foreign Office Under-Secretary, returned from Geneva pleading for a British initiative. On 9 March, he and Simon arrived in Paris for talks with the French leaders. Britain, however, refused to sign a communiqué opposing rearmament, on the grounds that this might be seen in terms of an anti-German alliance. In Geneva, MacDonald found the disarmament conference close to breakdown. However, on 16 March he suggested a draft convention, to be considered in the course of a lengthy adjournment. He then left for Rome, where the Italian dictator, Mussolini, had invited him to discuss a four-power pact which would allow for German equality if the international conference failed. MacDonald's initial enthusiasm was further dulled when, on his return through Paris, the French rejected the Italian idea. The consultative agreement signed in early June by Britain, France, Germany and Italy did not address the question of disarmament/rearmament.

At the end of the month, the Geneva conference adjourned for the summer. In October, Germany refused to return. Hitler announced that he was withdrawing from the League of Nations. His foreign policy was overwhelmingly endorsed in a referendum the following month.

This was a turning point for MacDonald. Since 1919 he had opposed the Treaty of Versailles. He tried to negotiate Franco-German relations, seeing the League of Nations as the guarantor of collective security. To this end, he was an early supporter of Germany's entry into the League. It took thirteen years, however, to get rid of reparations. By then, it was too late for the actions of international leaders, in the context of the depression of the early 1930s, to have much effect on the emergence of Fascism in Germany. MacDonald viewed Hitler as a threat to international democracy. When Germany pulled out of the League of Nations, collective security collapsed. MacDonald, of course, continued the search for international disarmament but he was gradually forced reluctantly to consider that, with Germany rearming, he had to abandon the principles of a political lifetime. However, as Prime Minister, he simply accepted that Britain was considerably underarmed and that there was room for improvement. He continued to dissociate himself from the militarists who, in the early-1930s, were a minority force in the Conservative ranks.

Shortly after pulling out of the League of Nations, Hitler insisted that recognition of Germany's right to a conscript army of 300,000 was a precondition for agreeing to a convention on arms limitation. Limitation became the perspective of the British government but the method remained negotiation. MacDonald first thought of inviting Hitler to London for talks. The Germans, not unnaturally, took offence at the idea that they should travel. This only encouraged the Conservatives in the government, who were alarmed at the new German Kaiser. In early November 1933, the Committee of Imperial Defence began to consider the question of rearmament.

As Britain, France and Germany fruitlessly exchanged diplomatic notes in the winter of 1933/34, MacDonald admitted that rearmament might be 'forced upon [Britain] by the refusal of other nations to keep down their arms'.[26] However, he was hesitant about responding to militarism abroad. When, in March 1934, the Committee of Imperial Defence recommended a five-year rearmament programme, MacDonald supported Chamberlain's objection on the grounds of financial stringency. He had, however, become hostile to political talk of disarmament. No doubt he was thinking of Lansbury, when he referred to 'the flabby piety of pacifism'[27] in October 1933.

MacDonald advanced the idea of linking security with a system of arms control in April 1934. The cabinet's disarmament committee, however, was unable to agree a foreign policy initiative. Two months later, the Foreign Office recommended a British guarantee to Belgium. The Prime Minister fought the proposal in committee but the government made a commitment to Belgian defence on 27 June. For MacDonald, it was the early 1910s all over again.

In the late summer of 1934, whilst MacDonald was absent abroad, the Conservative-dominated cabinet reduced the proposed rearmament programme. However, he was coming to share the British fear of German rearmament. He noted after a meeting of the Committee of Imperial Defence in November: 'The militarists are getting too much on top, but up till now defence is so neglected that the time for pulling in has not come.'[28] Chamberlain was in a minority of one, when he opposed a slight increase in expenditure on the Air Force.

Early in 1935, MacDonald agreed that Hankey, long-standing Secretary of the Committee of Imperial Defence, should prepare a White Paper on defence policy. This was published on 4 March and it called for an increase in defence expenditure. This document represented a break with the policy of every post-war government. Inadvertently, it appeared above the Premier's initials. This was enough to stir up the Labour opposition, which was still under the leadership of Lansbury. It is clear that MacDonald accepted that British passivity encouraged German bellicosity; it is not so certain, even in March 1935, that he fully accepted the corollary.

In response, Hitler postponed a visit from Simon. On 16 March he announced the reintroduction of conscription in Germany. The French wanted a League of Nations conference, given that the Treaty of Versailles had been broken but Britain, in a protest noted dated 18 March, only envisaged a new agreement. Six days later, Simon was allowed to visit Berlin. He was greeted by further German demands.

At the behest of Mussolini, Britain and France agreed to send representatives to a conference at Stresa on the growing European crisis. Owing to the illness of Eden, MacDonald was forced to lead the British delegation. The cabinet had decided that negotiations were not to be broken off with Germany. After three days of talks in April, the so-called 'Stresa Front' was established. Britain, France and Italy agreed to act together to prevent any further breaches of the 1919 treaty. The German repudiation was deplored. At the time, Mussolini was preparing his own invasion of Abyssinia. However, neither MacDonald nor Simon mentioned the issue at Stresa, despite advice from Eden that they should do so.

Stresa was MacDonald's last major foreign policy achievement. He had resigned the premiership by the time of the Abyssinian crisis but his lack of criticism of the Italian dictator is politically remarkable. No doubt, this was because of his concern with international relations, where Germany was the major problem in Europe. When he left Downing Street, MacDonald effectively became a detached member of the cabinet. His observations on domestic and foreign policy continued along slowly developing lines but he was also free to indulge the values of the immediate post-war years.

MacDonald had long suffered from depression and in 1927 he had nearly died when on a visit to the United States. However, it was from the formation of the National government that he declined physically and mentally. The real signs of ageing became evident in 1931, the year of his sixty-fifth birthday.

The morning after the vote of confidence on 8 September, the Prime Minister had some sort of breakdown. After the floating of the pound, he had to be spirited away for rest. He had increasing difficulty working but it was all that he had to fill the void of loneliness. At night he suffered from insomnia. Melancholia troubled his days. MacDonald kept his condition from others and no doubt obtained relief from the diary in which he unburdened himself.

In January 1932, glaucoma was diagnosed. This physical disease was greatly to affect his reading. An operation on the left eye required a convalescence of several weeks. His work in Geneva was cut short by the need for an operation on the right eye. MacDonald's disability was sympathetically charted in medical bulletins, but it was in the 1932 session that he waned as a parliamentary performer, in full view of observers of the political scene.

In Lossiemouth after Christmas, he admitted to himself that he had 'crossed the frontiers of age'.[29] However, he refused to consider resignation, believing he was indispensable. In any objective sense, this was less and less the political case, but MacDonald's indispensability was totally subjective. It was how he validated his very existence. There were signs of paranoia during a parliamentary speech in early 1933 and in Geneva he momentarily lost consciousness while speaking. By January 1934, he was comparing himself with an ailing Joseph Chamberlain. Though he wished to avoid public humiliation, he made no serious effort to remove himself from the scene.

Soon his eyes began to trouble him again. His doctors ordered three months' relaxation. In July, he and Sheila left for Canada and Newfoundland. However, travel could no longer restore his health. He again considered retirement but only thought vaguely of political prospects. Back in London for the 1934 session, he deteriorated in his cabinet performance. By the following February, 'the allurement of the end [had become] more enticing'.[30] He was in his sixty-ninth year, and a mere shadow of his former self.

MacDonald had largely been alone as a man in his sixties. There is a persistent story that he had an affair with a Viennese woman in the 1920s and that she later blackmailed him. However, there is only hearsay evidence for this and Oswald Mosley is an unreliable historical witness. MacDonald had women friends but he tended to see them more as daughters.

In 1928, he had met Cecily Gordon-Cumming. They played golf at Spey Bay when he was Prime Minister. He was undoubtedly fond of her and, though she married in 1931, he continued to write regularly for the rest of his life. This was also the case with Marthe Bibesco, a Rumanian Princess and wife of a diplomat. They met during the second Labour government. He came to confide in her and she also remained a friend after he gave up the premiership.

The major woman in his life was Lady Londonderry. In September 1930, Beatrice Webb had noted of MacDonald's visit to the Londonderrys' Highland home: 'Considering that he represents Seaham his friendship with the Londonderrys almost amounts to a public scandal.'[31] Beatrice Webb knew Londonderry as a coal-owner in Co. Durham and considered it gross of a Labour MP to be on such intimate terms. However, MacDonald saw himself above all as the Prime Minister of Britain and his relations with Lord Londonderry were always correct. He shared an interest in Celticism with Lady Londonderry, who was also Scottish. She admitted him as 'Hamish the Hart' to her society in Londonderry House (the Ark) where she played with leading politicians in parties which were much gossiped about. When MacDonald formed the National government, he became closer to this aristocratic partnership. Following the 1931 election, Lord Londonderry became Air Minister in the cabinet. MacDonald had then been returned for Seaham with Conservative help, and the constituency's major coal-owner politically embraced him in the anti-working-class camp. The Prime Minister's relations became more gross. The Londonderrys' Park Lane house became a social centre for the new national coalition. In 1932, the National Labour Party held a major reception there. Lady Londonderry also liked to collect artistic people. At literary gatherings, Mac-Donald associated with Sean O'Casey and James Stephens. She was effusive as a romantic in her private letters to the Prime Minister. After he left the Labour Party, he found solace in her world of pretence. Lord Londonderry, no doubt, considered that this was helpful to his political career. MacDonald's 'love' affair with the wife of one of his Conservative ministers was a symptom, rather than a cause, of his political betrayal of the working class.

MacDonald, of course, still had the support of his family. Alister divorced his wife in May 1936 and his father was delighted when he remarried early the following year. He did not, however, attend the wedding in Caxton Hall. Malcolm had been re-elected for Bassetlaw in 1931 and he was a rising star in the National government as number two to Thomas. In October 1936 he moved to his own house, Hyde Hall, in the country. Ishbel had continued as her father's hostess in Downing Street. She stepped down from the London County Council in 1934 and, in 1936, she became the licensee of a public-house in Speen, Buckingham-shire. She married only after her father's death. Joan had married a doctor in Leeds in 1932 and presented Ramsay with another grandchild the following year. Sheila had been with her father during the 1931 crisis and, four years later, she was active in the National Labour cause.

From 1931, MacDonald became increasingly isolated in the world of politics.

His political concern remained the Labour Party. He believed that, under Henderson and then Lansbury, it was poorly led; in early 1933, he told Ben Tillet, a supporter: 'how little equipped they are, both mentally and humanely to be builders of that Socialist state, which inspired our Movement until men came into it weakened by the vanities which authority and publicity create.'[32] MacDonald considered Labour too economistic and believed that even the unemployed would have responded to a national appeal in 1931. He critically observed the unions regaining a dominant position in the party. The Prime Minister even harked back to 1914, drawing comparisons with his principled stand against the war. Writing in May 1933 to a Yorkshire miners' agent, he referred to 'our Party['s]. . . senseless abandonment of Socialism for a queer mixture of sentimentality and Poplarism'.[33] Earlier, he had written to Tillet: 'If there is any strength and energy left in us when these dreadful times have been got through, we must spend ours in recreating a Socialism inspired by the spirit of the old, so that the Labour Movement will be something much greater than a small-minded squabble conducted in political market places.'[34] He never doubted that it was correct to form the National government but in private moments he occasionally regretted playing the role of national saviour. In May 1934, he noted in his diary: 'Wondering whether by sticking to the Labour majority and protecting the Party from the leadership of the poor specimens who now hold it[,] a greater service to the workers would have been done. . . But at what an awful price of dishonesty. . . Some way of saving the movement & the Socialism it embodied will surely be found.'[35]

MacDonald, of course, was guilty of romanticising the early years of the Labour Party. Further, in 1914 he had resigned the leadership of the party. In contrast, when he formed the National government he was ejected from the position. It was arrogant of MacDonald to dismiss the stand of the Hendersonites as 'sentimentality'. However, his critique of Poplarism antedated 1931. As leader of the party, he had sought simply to prove that Labour was fit to govern. It is surely remarkable that in the 1930s he still thought like an old ILP propagandist. MacDonald remained politically unreconstructed, believing that he was dealing simply with a national emergency and that, at some point in the future, normal politics would resume.

Following the split, there was never any possibility of political reconciliation between MacDonald and the Labour Party. In his handling of relations with former colleagues, he showed that this was the case. In September 1931, he had berated Molly Hamilton for remaining loyal to the party. Following the loss of her seat in the general election, however, MacDonald permitted his former friend to visit him in 1932 after his second eye operation. Harold Laski, who lectured at the London School of Economics, had helped defend MacDonald from Communist criticism in 1929. Three years later, when the former wrote an attack upon the British Prime Minister for an American magazine, MacDonald vindictively arranged that copies should be sent to the University of London authorities. Jim Middleton, who also remained with the party, was probably the only functionary who remained friendly to the former leader. In December 1933, he wrote: 'Life seems to hold more bitterness than one quite thought possible. It hurts badly to see the patience that both you and Henderson are exercising in different camps.'[36] It is certainly the case that the latter believed, at least for a time, that MacDonald might return to the party. However, the Prime Minister was most ungenerous to Henderson. Some thought that the President of the Disarmament Conference should be allowed to return to a Labour-held seat in parliament, in a by-election in summer 1933. It was difficult for MacDonald to endorse the Conservative, who was fighting an anti-Socialist campaign, but he appealed to electors to support the National government. MacDonald was in his bath on 20 October 1935 when he heard of the death of Henderson. He noted in his diary: 'a strange unlovely study of a man with whose vulgar bullying nature I could never make peace. . . I tried hard to think well of him[,] . . . but rushing into my memory came the way he wirepulled himself into the chairmanship of the Disarmament Conference. . . Moreover, it was he who ran way first when the Trade Unionists threatened in 1931.'[37]

MacDonald had been surprised at the Tory landslide in the 1931 election. At the time, he was well aware that the Conservatives were using the National government to make party gains. 'What strange lands I have been pushed into!', he noted on 10 November. 'The first reaction is an increase in my anti-Tory instinct. . . The oppression of my companionship crushes out every other feeling.'[38] He would retain a 'class' hostility to the Conservative party, such as had been displayed in private moments in the past. Thus, he described local Tory bosses, who were keeping him in power, as 'an odd lot of colonels & sycophants repulsively vulgar'.[39] In July 1934, he admitted to himself: 'My heart is elsewhere. . . Colleagues loyal & all that, but I am a Socialist'.[40]

In October 1931 he had realised that a Conservative-dominated parliament made things difficult for him. His only justification for remaining Prime Minister was that he could mitigate the impact of Tory rule. In reality, he was lending credence to the idea of a National government, while becoming increasingly impotent within his régime. In December 1932 he explained his and Thomas's role on the government front bench: 'There are. . . two of us in the very curious position of being amongst the leaders of a Party to which we do not belong and made responsible for a policy which we cannot control.'[41]

In 1931 the Conservatives had refused to give way to some Liberal and National Labour candidates. As Prime Minister, however, it was MacDonald's duty to support pro-government candidates. Invariably, these were Conservatives. When a National Labour candidate was supplanted by a Tory at Wednesbury in July 1932, he refused to send an endorsement. This, however, was an exception. The Labour Party gained ten seats in the 1931 parliament, most of which were at the expense of the Conservatives. With each defeat, Ramsay MacDonald's political authority was further damaged.

He had, at most, twenty-five supporters in both Houses of Parliament in September 1931. After the election, his group was about half that size. The government's appeal to the nation had envisaged the suspension of political activity for the duration of the crisis: 'the immediate tasks are temporary and when finished will be followed by normal political activities.'[42] The National Labour Party, such as it was, existed exclusively to support the National government but, from time to time, MacDonald envisaged it as a new nucleus of British Socialism when the emergency had passed.

There was an attempt to create an organisation. According to a possibly much later constitution, the National Labour Party sought 'social justice' by 'harness[ing] the discoveries of science to the replacing of our economic resources'. It wanted to 'safeguard Imperial unity' and use Britain's strength to promote 'world peace'.[43] The *News Letter,* edited first by Clifford Allen, and then by Godfrey Elton, Malcolm's former tutor at Oxford, appeared monthly. There were few individual members and the parliamentary party had little chance of growing by fighting by-elections. Occasionally, MacDonald asked his party colleagues to define their political role. In July 1932 he even asked Viscount Snowden to 'deliver a good old fashioned address on Socialism with special application to the Opposition policy'.[44] If it is strange that MacDonald should have made such a request, it is bizarre that he should have asked a colleague who was soon to resign on the question of free trade. Half way through the 1931 parliament, MacDonald predicted that, because of poor organisation, National Labour would 'be of little consequence'. 'It might be strengthened very considerably', he went on, 'if some of us were free to do platform work'.[45] In late 1934, he reaffirmed his political commitment in reply to a correspondent: 'I never left my

Socialism; . . . I have never believed in revolution, except in very backward countries like Russia. . . I am only longing for the time when a combination to keep the country from ruin is no longer necessary, so that some plain speaking and principled Socialist propaganda can be launched.'[46] In August 1935, months after he stepped down from the premiership, MacDonald, in a draft article for a book sympathetic to the National Labour Party, reaffirmed that Socialism, as a solution to the problem of distribution, was the force of the future now that Capitalism had solved the problem of production. He condemned the Labour Party for 'substitut[ing]. . . a national-scale of Poplarism for Socialism and a universal Poor Law subscription. . . for industrial planning'.[47] Following the general election in November, male staff in the National Labour Party office were given notice. 'Are we. . . hoping one day to rejoin Labour,' asked a former junior minister of MacDonald's, 'or are we intending to be a left wing of a new centre form of Government[?].'[48] The answer, in both cases, was to be in the negative. There was some attempt to build the National Labour Party after MacDonald stepped down, the second annual conference being held in October 1936. However, it amounted to little.

MacDonald had talked of resigning the premiership from 1931. Baldwin, who was in no hurry to take over, promised to support him until the next election, to be held by 1936. It was not until 1935, when MacDonald had been weakened by ill health and political hostility, that he seriously considered vacating the premiership.

By late January he was worried about the Conservative right: 'How long can I remain at the head of a Government whose appeal to the country is anti-Socialism[?]'[49] The loss of a government seat in early February, due to the intervention of Randolph Churchill in a by-election, led him to fear for the future of the non-Conservative parties. MacDonald discussed this with

Baldwin, who, since 1932, had simply been Lord President, the latter intimating that he was thinking of retiring. MacDonald suggested that they should ease towards a new leadership. However, this was not to come about for more than two years.

MacDonald confided in Thomas, who subsequently revealed the Premier's thinking to Chamberlain. By 21 March, Baldwin had decided not to resign from the cabinet. MacDonald began to think of quitting the premiership after the King's Silver Jubilee celebrations.

Upon returning from Stresa, however, he began to think about cabinet reconstruction but the jubilee orgy in early May constituted the sort of dignified end he sought to his leadership of the government. On 8 May he noted in his diary: 'Here the Empire was a great family, the gathering a family reunion, the King a paternal head. We all went away feeling that we had taken part in something very much like a Holy Communion.'[50] Afterwards, MacDonald discussed the possible shape of the new cabinet with Baldwin. On 16 May, George V suggested that he should remain in the government, in Baldwin's post as Lord President of the Council. It was known that MacDonald would not accept a peerage upon resignation; he even refused a knighthood. The date of Baldwin's succession was fixed on 28 May. On 5 June, MacDonald presided over his last cabinet meeting. He was in his sixty-ninth year and had been in Downing Street for exactly six years. He resigned as Premier two days later.

Baldwin, as Conservative leader, immediately announced his new government. MacDonald was Lord President. His first duty was to officiate at Malcolm's swearing-in as a privy councillor. Father and son were to sit in the new cabinet, the latter as Colonial Secretary. Thomas, to his great relief, was left at the Dominions Office, but Sankey was sacrificed. There were four Liberals but another fourteen Conservatives in cabinet posts. The idea of a National government, however, was still espoused, it being a good political fig-leaf for Conservatism.

Ramsay MacDonald was quickly isolated in the new administration. Conservative ministers treated him simply as part of the machinery of government.

In August, he was worried that the Foreign Office was pushing Mussolini too hard over Abyssinia. However, the Lord President was unable to put his views directly to Sir Samuel Hoare and Anthony Eden, the League of Nations' minister. According to a later note, MacDonald insisted that Mussolini was 'no mad dog'.[51] At Stresa, the then British Prime Minister had been assured that Italy wanted nothing but friendship with Britain. However, Britain was forced to support League of Nations' economic sanctions following the Italian attack but, with the French, it came round to advocating territorial concessions in Abyssinia.

Before this, Baldwin had called an election for 14 November, a decision from which MacDonald found himself excluded. The national parties sought a mandate for moderate rearmament. In his election address, MacDonald admitted that Britain was underarmed; he called for a measure of rearmament, sufficient for national defence and also possible League of Nations' military sanctions. He mocked the position of the Labour Party: 'Our opponents are so devoted to policing the world that they would soon bring us into war, and, at the same time, so devoted to peace that they refuse to provide defence against the enemies they would stir up against us.'[52] He had found it difficult to build a base among Seaham miners and, given the level of unemployment and the means test, to say nothing of a local strike, he lost the seat he had held since 1929. MacDonald secured 17,882 votes but his Labour opponent, his old political friend, Emanuel Shinwell, romped home with 38,380. Malcolm also lost his seat in Bassetlaw.

For Labour nationally, it was a partial settling of accounts. Attlee had become temporary leader and the party secured 154 seats, with over eight million votes. However, nearly twelve million voted for the National government and Baldwin had 432 seats. Only five of these belonged to the National Labour group.

Though no longer an MP, MacDonald remained in the government at the request, again, of the King. In December he told a small meeting of his supporters: 'We stand for Labour within the Baldwin organisation but we shall be OURSELVES.' As one of the six gathered in the privy council office noted: 'We did not look at each other so awkward were our feelings. . . in acute embarrassment we broke up.'[53] The death of a Conservative MP saw MacDonald proposed as the government candidate for a Scottish Universities seat. In his election address, issued from Upper Frognal Lodge, he stated that 'the National front ought still to be maintained for the sake of both home recovery and international peace'.[54] He was elected to parliament in February 1936 'without having to open [his] mouth.'.[55] Malcolm, who had changed places with Thomas because of the latter's unacceptability to some dominions' premiers, was also returned for a Scottish seat, the sitting MP having accepted a peerage.

The death of George V on 20 January had greatly upset MacDonald. He presided at the last privy council, held in the King's bedroom at Sandringham: 'I was the last out & I shall never forget the look illuminated by affection. . . which he gave me & continued it as I went & bowed a second time – my final farewell to a gracious & kingly friend whom I have served with all my heart.'[56] He was less enthusiastic about Edward VIII and, in the abdication crisis which reached its climax in December, he backed the stand taken by Baldwin.

Within the government, MacDonald counted for less and less. He became uneasy about rearmament: 'We are near the border-line between militarism and peace. But it is not a clearly drawn line.'[57] When he made it back to the House of Commons, he was booed by the greatly increased Labour Party on the opposition benches. MacDonald made virtually no contribution to this, his last parliament. He wallowed in his rejection by Conservative colleagues and, in his diary, he began to think himself back into the Labour Party.

Spain was the major international issue of 1936. Earlier, when he was still Prime Minister, MacDonald had considered Spain symptomatic of the general uncertainty in Europe. He wanted to know what Britain could do as a 'pacifying agent', without being 'idealistic' about the state of the world.[58] In 1936 he initially supported Baldwin's policy of non-intervention following the nationalist uprising. However, when it became clear that Hitler and Mussolini were supporting Franco, he began to swing in favour of the Spanish Republicans. By early 1937, he was noting: 'The hard meaning of the European drift with Nazi-ism in the lead is not understood by the Cabinet, but the appalling thing to me [is] that it is democracy which I see to be breaking down.'[59]

In the cabinet, MacDonald only had Thomas and Malcolm as kindred political spirits. In May the Colonial Secretary was found to have leaked budget secrets to business friends. MacDonald, while he refused to believe ill of Thomas, had supported the latter's immediate resignation from the government. He had to accept the latter's withdrawal from the House of Commons in June. MacDonald, as he put it, had lost his 'Fidus Achates, with whom [he] discussed every plan & move & project'.[60] In early May, Snowden had died; MacDonald noted in his diary: 'When last I saw him. . . I told him that nothing he would do. . . would ever make me forget our long friendship and co-operation and even then he seemed as though he would like to bite my hand.'[61] This left only Malcolm. While he was no doubt proud, as a father, to see his son handling delicate relations with the Irish Free State, MacDonald cannot have taken much pleasure in being over-shadowed. In July, during a meeting of the cabinet committee on Ireland, he insisted that the dominions be informed immediately. Malcolm, in contrast, preferred to try and keep de Valera within the Commonwealth through bilateral negotiations. Later in the meeting, MacDonald Senior espoused an evolving view of the Commonwealth, generous enough to be compatible with the Dominions Secretary's political strategy.

His depression had not lifted with the burdens of office. In April he had another eye operation. That November he collapsed at the Lord Mayor's Banquet, though he attributed this to 'bad, thick air and tight lacing at the neck'.[62] In early 1937, MacDonald was ordered yet again to take a long rest.

Meanwhile, Baldwin was planning to leave the government following George VI's coronation in May. MacDonald, thereupon, also decided to step down. He declined a peerage when it was offered by Chamberlain, Baldwin's likely successor. However, he secured Malcolm's retention in the cabinet. MacDonaldism was on its political last legs and the former Prime Minister told Lord Tweedsmuir: 'I hope with all my heart that I shall not be a spectator. . . of any member of my family becoming a Tory of the 20th century.'[63] When Baldwin offered him a seat in the Lords, he declined a second time. Meanwhile, MacDonald busied himself with arrangements for the Coronation on 12 May. He attended his last cabinet meeting on 26 May and refused a peerage yet again when it was offered by the new King. Two days later, MacDonald and Baldwin resigned. The inter-war years, though few realised it at the time, were almost over.

MacDonald, who was still a Member of Parliament, retreated to Lossiemouth for the summer. At some point he attended a party in Glasgow, organised by old ILP friends. He embarrassed his guests when he ended a speech by proclaiming his Socialism. Back in London, on 28 September he lunched with Elton: 'Made it clear that I was not joining the Tory Party and that I did not agree that it was or ought to be the nucleus of a National Govt.'[64] It was as if the previous six years had not unfolded as political tragedy. There were no Socialists at a farewell gathering in Upper Frognal Lodge in early November. MacDonald, however, made a feeble overture to Citrine, with whom he had been able to relate in the 1930s.

On 4 November 1937, MacDonald and Sheila left for what was to be a long holiday in South America. On board the *Reina del Pacifico,* he fell ill during the afternoon of 9 November. He died of heart failure, at 7.45 p.m. the same evening. Six days later in Bermuda, his body was transferred to a naval cruiser for return to Britain. A funeral service for the former Prime Minister was held at Westminster Abbey on 26 November. He was privately cremated at Golders Green and his ashes taken to Lossiemouth for burial in Margaret's grave at Spynie.

James Ramsay MacDonald, who had described himself as a 'dead man',[65] when he was Labour's first Prime Minister in 1924, had found peace at last.

Conclusion

Only his family and a handful of friends really mourned Mac-Donald's sudden passing in 1937. The Tories showed no gratitude for his presumed saving of the country in 1931 and his wartime stance had long been forgotten by Socialists. Some might have been surprised to be told that he had been alive until 9 November, as he had been politically dead for some time.

Yet James Ramsay MacDonald was an important figure in British politics. He had been Prime Minister for just under seven years during the inter-war period, at the head of four governments, having won all but one of the four general elections he fought as alternative or encumbent Premier. Certainly, his first minority government lasted less than a year and his second, which was also a minority administration, split but, in 1931, he was returned with more Members of Parliament behind him than any other peacetime Premier.

Churchill was to maintain the support of all parties from 1940 to 1945, while, in the First World War, Lloyd George had tested the loyalty of the Irish and Labour Parties to breaking point. Ramsay MacDonald should be remembered, if for no other reason, as the political leader who formally suspended the party system in British politics in peacetime, though Baldwin and Chamberlain continued the idea of a national government. Of course, this increasingly became a front for Tory rule and Labour had been in opposition throughout.

MacDonald's authority quickly waned in the 1930s and he became less useful to the Conservatives. Months after stepping down from the premiership, he lost his seat in the 1935 election and was ignominiously forced to rely on the votes of Scottish (mainly Conservative) graduates to remain in parliament. With the exception of the 1918 parliament, he was an MP from 1906 until his death – a period of thirty-one years. He refused all honours and a seat in the Lords, though he was more loyal than, say, Lloyd George, to the monarchy in the person of George V. His two years as a cabinet minister in 1935-7 were a political consolation, MacDonald having headed the four other cabinets of which he was a member. Indeed, he remains the only twentieth-century Prime Minister who reached 10 Downing Street without ministerial experience.

His historical achievement is even greater. MacDonald was, and continues to be, the most lowly born to reach the top of British politics. He followed close on Lloyd George, who, in 1916, was the first 'ranker' raised to the premiership. Ramsay MacDonald started life further from the centres of social power and, though he made it to the top of Hampstead in 1925, he never earned the money of his less scrupulous rival on the progressive wing of British politics. MacDonald was also the only illegitimate Prime Minister. Such a thing mattered in the 1920s, though it had been revealed by an arch-chauvinist who was subsequently convicted of fraud. However, the lack of a father was MacDonald's great driving secret, one that could not be discussed in post-Victorian polite culture. The other outsider among British Prime Ministers is, of course, Disraeli. MacDonald compares favourably with this radical Tory in the amount he wrote and the two men have been matched, possibly, only by Churchill. MacDonald may even have considered Disraeli a sort of romantic hero – after, of course, Gladstone. He is, however, associated most often with Stanley Baldwin, a man he fought in three general elections only to share power with for nearly six years in the 1930s.

It was Churchill who wrote of his two adversaries, after the Second World War, that 'the sympathies of each extended far into the territory of the other.'[1] 'Cato' had condemned the interwar partnership of Baldwin and MacDonald in his anti-appeasement polemic of 1940 and, in the wake of Dunkirk, this interpretation of recent history became well-rooted in popular culture. The inter-war era was to be dubbed by a leading historian in 1955, as 'the rule of the pygmies'.[2]

Whatever may be said of Chamberlain and others, this Churchillian view is unfair on MacDonald. It ignores the importance of his opposition to the First World War and his commitment to international democracy in the 1920s. Secondly, it overlooks the fact that MacDonald saw off the Liberals, making Labour the largest party of the state by 1929. When he chose country rather than party two years later, Labour's most impressive leader lined himself up for historical assassination.

It is understandable that, for over fifty years, the Labour Party has tried to forget MacDonald, while the Labour left is unable to forgive him. MacDonald was a Socialist, according to his own testimony, until the end. He is best tried by his political peers but their politics, in turn, may be compared with his from the 1880s to the 1930s.

MacDonald was born in small-town Scotland in 1866 and education was important, given his precarious petty-bourgeois origins. He became an active Marxist in Bristol in 1885, but British revolutionary authoritarianism quickly repelled him. Morayshire radicalism had been his main influence and he was to remain a member of the political family of Liberalism until 1894.

However, and this point applies especially to MacDonald, he remained a radical in his conception of international relations and British politics generally. He had certainly been a Socialist from the mid-1880s, but, even after 1894, this new British political current continued to have for him a complex relationship with Liberalism. While Socialism was ideologically juxtaposed, the left came to secede from the major bourgeois party in the 1880s and 1890s. However, class relations in Britain were not totally contradictory and the Liberals still occupied the progressive pole of constitutional politics. Failing to find a place in the Liberal sun, the working class was forced to rely upon its own Labourist universe; this was less hegemonic than the Socialist advanced guard might have liked and, at points, had an affinity with Conservatism.

MacDonald became a political secretary in the world of metropolitan Liberalism, though he had joined the Fabian Society about 1886. In the early 1890s, he became a freelance political journalist, and, while he also exhibited an artistic and moral side to his nature, he became a Lib-Lab parliamentary candidate. The hostility of middle-class Liberals saw him join Keir Hardie's ILP. He was one of the new party's candidates in 1895, and, by the time of the next election, a leading advocate of Labour independence. In 1896 MacDonald married into the professional middle class. He was unhappy with the Fabians, and left over the Boer War. This was a great radical cause in 1899-1902, and, indeed, MacDonald had continued to associate with bourgeois intellectuals. On the eve of the war, the trade unions had come round to the idea of Labour representation, and, as a result of Socialist organisation, a Labour Representation Committee was founded in 1900. Ramsay MacDonald was its first Secretary.

The Memorial Hall Conference was hardly considered historic at the time. However, the tariff reform crisis in 1903 allowed MacDonald to negotiate an agreement with the Liberals, which would allow Labour to make a serious electoral bid as an important interest group. He had been involved in the International from 1896, and, in 1905, emerged as an important theorist of British Socialism. This was considered as an advance upon Marxism. MacDonald denied the need for a political rupture, arguing that society was evolving towards Socialism. Such a theoretical dismissal of politics allowed him to slowly build Labour as the alternative to Toryism, when the Liberals were about to be returned to power in 1906.

He was elected to parliament in the Liberal landslide, one of the thirty MPs who constituted the Labour Party; the minority of ILP Socialists had still to woo remaining Lib-Labers from Asquith. MacDonald developed a conception of parliamentary Socialism in the ILP, and, with Hardie, again opposed Socialist unity. In the 1906 parliament he interested himself in the empire, advocating slow progress towards self-government. But Labour made little impact. In the political crisis from 1909, the Liberals were to the fore against the Tories while syndicalists and suf-fragists were outside parliament. When MacDonald was elected leader in 1911, he could only support the government; however, he refused offers of a cabinet seat, but, since he believed in the idea of a progressive party, he did not entirely rule out a future coalition.

With an election expected in 1915, the Liberals might have wooed back some trade unionists, leaving a smaller Labour Party to become more Socialist. Such an ILP-dominated formation under MacDonald, however, would still have been essentially parliamentarist. This was to reckon without the European War. Labour quickly voted for war credits, and MacDonald resigned the leadership. This act owed most to his radicalism.

He was rehabilitated within the ILP, though opposed to simple pacifism. In the middle-class UDC he helped to develop a critique of the old diplomacy. MacDonald tended to mute his criticisms of the war but he opposed Labour's participation in the Asquith and Lloyd George coalitions. It says something for Arthur Hen-derson, who had become Party Secretary, that the former leader was still kept within the fold while Labour was implicated in industrial and military conscription. Revolution in Russia led to Henderson's withdrawal from the government in 1917 and, after October, MacDonald and Webb helped him commit Labour to a democratic peace; it was Webb, however, who drew up the new constitution, which affirmed Socialism in 1918, and also the programme for the post-war election, for which Henderson was preparing the party. Labour only secured fifty-nine seats in the 'khaki' contest but Lloyd George made the Liberals the main casualty. MacDonald and most other prominent Labour figures were defeated.

As Party Treasurer, he concentrated on international Socialist affairs from 1919. He opposed the Treaty of Versailles, though Labour backed Lloyd George in parliament. MacDonald was not a strong critic of the Bolsheviks but, with Moscow determined to build its third International, he came to ally with right-wing Social Democrats; in late 1920 he became joint Secretary of the old second International. The ILP had pulled out of this pro-war rump but when it declined to join the Comintern, it was inevitably forced into the Social-democratic successor in 1923, which Mac-Donald had worked to construct. In a by-election he had lost the only Labour seat of the parliament, but his anti-war reputation saw him prominent in the ILP as the last of the 'big four' leaders.

The Conservatives dumped Lloyd George in 1922 and, in the ensuing election, Labour came back with more seats (142) than the combined Liberals. MacDonald was narrowly elected leader, as the non-trade-union candidate, and Labour became the effective parliamentary opposition. It was the emergent party of the working class in the country, though now with a minority of middle-class MPs. MacDonald was the best leader to unite the trade unionists and the Clydeside Socialists. However, his authority among Labour MPs rested on his reputation, rather than on an organisational base in the party. Baldwin provoked an election on protectionism in December 1923 and Labour was returned with 191 seats. Five years after MacDonald had lost his seat, he was on the eve of becoming Prime Minister.

It was nearly forty years since he had become a Socialist. The Palace overreacted about letting Labour into office, since Mac-

Donald was bent on proving that the party could govern responsibly. He, and the whole ruling class, knew that Asquith could
withdraw parliamentary support at any time. This was reflected
in the cabinet, where John Wheatley was the only minister with
Socialist ambitions. The 1924 Labour government was a turning
point in British political history. However, the party showed
itself respectful of the institutions of ruling-class power. Labour
was careful not to be identified as pro-trade union and there
were few gestures towards social transformation; Wheatley's
house building was the only major reform. The ILP was no doubt
unhappy and Maxton wanted to go to the country on a contro-
versial issue. MacDonald preferred an international stage and
here he made his mark on inter-war history by intervening in
Franco-German relations, almost as an agent of the United States.
It was Russia which undermined the government, the question
of draft treaties was mixed up in the Campbell case and, when
MacDonald was forced to hold an election, the Zinoviev letter
was also badly mishandled. Labour held on to its new working-
class base but the Red scare drove many Liberals into the arms
of Baldwin.

Labour's leader surprised many with his able conduct of the
premiership but the party had shown itself to be an alternative
to the Liberals which could better incorporate the trade unions.
Unfortunately, the ruling class was to overestimate MacDonald's
ability to deliver seven years later.

He was unable to forget that he was a former Prime Minister,
and, when the General Strike occurred in 1926, MacDonald
mediated between the government and the trade unions. He had
never favoured industrial action but, on this occasion, he was
particularly solicitous about what he considered to be the national
interest. MacDonald was already being eased out of the ILP and
in 1927 he effectively left, after more than thirty years. However,
he kept the support of most ILP MPs. He still believed in the

idea of a Socialist organisation, but his Socialism was now obviously empty rhetoric. In 1928 his programme, which amounted to a series of discrete social reforms, was accepted by the Labour Conference. MacDonald went into the 1929 election more powerful than ever and Labour emerged, with 288 seats, as the largest party. However, it lacked a majority and would again be dependent on the Liberals.

For a second time, Baldwin let Labour form a government. MacDonald was even more circumspect in the choice of his ministers. He was the first Premier to visit the United States, the American Navy rivalling in size the British fleet. At the London Naval Conference in 1930, the two powers, plus Japan, agreed levels of disarmament. The following year, when Japan invaded Manchuria, the death-knell was sounded to post-war demilitari-sation. On Egypt, MacDonald clashed with Henderson, though he intervened more effectively on empire affairs. In domestic issues, the government had to reckon with Lloyd George, who had embraced economic expansionism as the solution to unemployment. This did not appeal to Thomas and it led to the resignation of Mosley in 1930. MacDonald then took charge; he had a Victorian distaste for doles and believed that work in Britain depended upon a revival of international trade. Protec-tionism was associated with the Conservatives, but Keynes, who was identified with the Liberals, suggested a revenue tariff. Mac-Donald, however, was not inclined to confront the free-traders in his cabinet.

The government drifted as unemployment increased and in early 1931 a budget deficit was predicted by Snowden. A middle-class prejudice had spread, whereby it was considered that too much was being given to the unemployed. The government, to stay in office, agreed to the May Committee on the state's finances. Lloyd George had begun to talk of national government but Baldwin was unenthusiastic and, while MacDonald obviously wanted parliamentary agreement, he thought more in terms of Liberal support for Labour in office. The government was then confronted with an international financial crisis. European and American bankers, fearful of inflation, argued for the balancing of national budgets. In effect, they wanted to make the working class pay for losses in speculation.

MacDonald was faced with a major challenge in the form of a continuing run on the pound. Exchange controls were ruled out because these were incompatible with London remaining a financial centre of the world. Keynes, in the Macmillan Report, tried to redefine the problem as a balance of payments deficit but it was the May Report's suggested balanced budget which was to prove decisive, published, as it was, on the day parliament rose for the summer recess. The August crisis was soon to split the Labour cabinet and lead MacDonald to form the National government.

Ironically, there was considerable unanimity in MacDonald's government about the international recession. Labour had long been a free-trade party and, in the absence of a Socialist political economy, believed in keeping Britain on the gold standard. Following the defeat of Mosley, the cabinet temporised. It admitted, when it appointed a royal commission in 1930, that unemployment benefits were too high. The government allowed itself to be forced by the Liberals into accepting the May Committee, a device Snowden saw as building a parliamentary consensus for balancing the budget. The Conservatives had threatened a censure motion and, in the absence of a government strategy, it would have been better for the party and for the country if MacDonald had sought a dissolution. Labour might just have lost such an election in early 1931 and remained united.

As it was, the cabinet continued to temporise, and allowed the May Report to be published. All ministers accepted that the budget had to be balanced and most were glad to leave it to a cabinet committee. The new idea of devaluation does not seem to have been considered by the five ministers. The more familiar notion of a revenue tariff appealed to the committee, and later the cabinet, as an alternative to unemployment benefit cuts but, on both occasions, Snowden vetoed the idea. MacDonald could have got rid of his ailing Chancellor earlier in the year. In August, Snowden should have been allowed to resign. He may not have brought down the government, given the Bank of England's pressing advice for action.

The Prime Minister's idea of equity in national sacrifice was widely accepted by his colleagues. Henderson supported the principle but he sought to reserve his position while MacDonald worked out the figures. When the idea of a percentage cut in benefits was taken up, the Foreign Secretary suggested a contribution from the unemployed. May and Snowden had wanted more than MacDonald's final cut of ten per cent and Henderson wanted something less; the differences were only quantitative. Henderson was short on economic ideas and he lacked an alternative political strategy but he had adopted a dogged trade-union stance on behalf of the unemployed. When the TUC came out on 20 August against benefit, wage and salary cuts, he could see the possibility of a defensive action. The Conservative and Liberal Parties had not liked the Labour budget and, at this point, MacDonald was energised to take control of his cabinet. It is unforgivable that he should have been moved only by the TUC's opposition, just as it is commendable that Henderson paid attention to Bevin and Citrine. However, when Bevin and Citrine failed to impose their tentative fiscal ideas on the government, Henderson was left with the option of using his resignation to bring down MacDonald's government. It was a sorry pass for both men to reach.

Over the next four days, when it became necessary to seek further funds abroad, they sought to preserve the unity of the party in government while acting in contrary directions. On 21

August, the opposition parties began to think of a national government. MacDonald considered it counter-productive as it would split Labour, and Henderson seems not to have been alerted to this real danger. He went along with the idea of presenting a draft budget, containing the ten-per-cent cut, to the opposition, the Bank of England and international bankers. The Foreign Secretary may have hoped that it would be unacceptable and he was probably ready to resign if the loan was secured. MacDonald and Snowden construed the news from New York on 23 August in a good light and the cabinet divided on the ten per cent, with Henderson leading a group of nine ministers.

If he had secured a majority – another two supporters – then Labour would probably have resigned as a united party. On the other hand, if MacDonald, who had only two supporters the day before, had gained a more impressive majority, then Labour might just have been able to stay in office. The Prime Minister had underestimated his ability to bring the Labour Party with him if the government accepted the budget. He had threatened to resign if any ministers opposed him and, while this must have concentrated the minds of ministers faced with the loss of office, MacDonald, technically, still had his cabinet behind him. He expected to be leaving office but feared the difficulties of being leader of the opposition, having committed himself to the budget.

The Labour government decided to resign but, crucially, it allowed MacDonald to meet the opposition leaders in the presence of the King the following day. It was expected that there would be a Conservative government with Liberal support but some Labour ministers may still have been clinging to illusions of power. Henderson may not have been aware of the comings and goings of the previous days but he must have known that MacDonald felt insecure as Labour leader. In the absence of any anchor by the party on the latter's actions, he was quickly persuaded on 24 August to remain as Prime Minister. MacDonald had tried to resign but, following the split in the cabinet, he feared political isolation.

A national government with MacDonald as its head was the ideal bourgeois solution; the Tories could implement anti-working-class policies, while appearing to respond to a temporary national emergency. MacDonald was too ready to accept that the pound could be restored in weeks but, since he had believed implicitly in the need for a balanced budget in order to save the country, he acted with a certain political consistency. However, he agreed to the National government on impulse because he needed to believe he was indispensable.

If MacDonald was psychologically prevented from understanding the way he was being used, Henderson should have been more alert to the role envisaged for the Labour Party. However, he effectively ignored the national crisis and, in accepting that there would be a Tory government, showed that his main concern was to preserve the party, albeit as an opposition which had failed the country. Henderson had expressed concern for the unemployed but he must have known that a Baldwin government would have implemented the May Report.

Neither MacDonald nor Henderson was up to the political challenge of 24 August. When the national balloon went up, the latter seems to have thought that, having kept an anti-war MacDonald in the party after 1914, he could do so again. However, this time the Labour leader had chosen to stay in power, in alliance with the opposition parties. Henderson was quickly elected leader and the behaviour of MacDonald made it inevitable that he would become a non-member of the party within weeks.

In two major national crises, seventeen years apart, he had surrendered the leadership of the party. On both occasions, he was opposed by Henderson and the trade unions. In 1914 the latter had become social patriots, making a stand for country in time of war. On the occasion of the 1931 financial crisis, the unions sought to defend the working class in the name of little more than economism. While politically inadequate, this was a more progressive response than during the war. In contrast, while MacDonald had suffered for his opposition to chauvinism, he took a reactionary stand in 1931 largely for personal reasons.

His desertion of the Labour Party was totally unnecessary. The Tories could have taken over and, in MacDonald's eyes, saved the country. Labour would have gone into opposition and he might have retained the leadership. MacDonald simply did not know when to quit and it took the King to keep him in office. At worst, if he had supported the budget and lost the leadership, he could have become a senior parliamentarian. There is no evidence that he mitigated the impact of Tory policies while Prime Minister in the 1930s. However, it is irrefutable that Mac-Donald, under whom Labour had nearly become a majority government in the 1920s, was also responsible, by his decision to seek a mandate in 1931, for pushing it back to its pre-war status as a minor party in parliament, although not in the country.

He must bear ultimate responsibility for this dramatic historical reversal. However, while the Labour Party may attribute its misfortunes to MacDonald, it has to accept that it elected him twice to the leadership for indefinite periods. His radicalism led to the break in 1914 and, while Labour's strategy was to prove it could govern, the split of 1931 occurred because Henderson chose to abdicate.

Labour has not run away from office since. It joined the wartime coalition and, following the defeat of Churchill, Attlee formed two post-war majority governments. Labour lost power in 1951 but on its largest vote ever. The Wilson and Callaghan governments of the 1960s and 1970s were notorious for their anti-working-class policies and, as a result, Labour's vote in 1979 was lower than at any time since 1931. MacDonald, in contrast to later Labour Prime Ministers, failed to implement his ten-per-cent cut. It is surely a measure of the extent to which the Labour Party successfully incorporated the working class, that Wilson and Callaghan chose when to resign the leadership. Against the experience of recent Labour governments, MacDonald may be viewed less unfavourably. After all, he failed to bring the party with him largely because he lacked the will. Subsequent leaders have foisted worse policies on the party.

Neil Kinnock, the current Labour leader, refused office in Callaghan's government and, if he gets to 10 Downing Street in the 1980s or later, he will be the first since MacDonald to do so without ministerial experience. He gained the leadership in 1983 as the candidate of the left but, unlike MacDonald and Harold Wilson, he has taken on socialists in the Labour Party, in the belief that this is a precondition for electoral success. The strange political composite, 'Ramsay MacKinnock', spotted on placards during the miners' strike of 1984-5, may be considered slanderous of Neil Kinnock but, if he continues along his present path, it may come to be considered an historical defamation of Ramsay MacDonald.

Notes

Introduction

1 Tony Benn, *Parliament, People and Power: Agenda for a Free Society*, London, 1982, p. 30.

2 *The Man of To-morrow: J. Ramsay MacDonald*, London; *J. Ramsay MacDonald, 1923-1925*, London; *J. Ramsay MacDonald*, London.

3 *Remembering My Good Friends*, London, 1944, p. 128.

4 *The Rt. Hon. J. Ramsay MacDonald: A Biographical Study*, London.

5 *James Ramsay MacDonald: Labour's Man of Greatness*, London.

6 *Portrait of the Labour Party*, London, pp. 174-7.

7 'What happened in 1931: a record', January-March 1932, p. 1.

8 'Ramsay MacDonald: a portrait', 21 September 1932.

9 Philip Viscount Snowden, *An Autobiography*, London, p. 957.

10 *The Tragedy of Ramsay MacDonald: A Political Biography*, London n.d., but 1938.

11 Colin Stills to James Ramsay MacDonald (JRM), 9 June 1937, Ramsay MacDonald Papers (RMP), Public Record Office (PRO) 30/69/1018.

12 'J. Ramsay MacDonald: an atlantic portrait', April 1938, pp. 452-62; *Remembering My Good Friends*, p. 123.

13 *War Memoirs* (six volumes), London, 1933-6.

14 *Great Contemporaries*, London, 1937; *The Second World War: Volume 1: The Gathering Storm*, London, 1948.

15 *The Life of James Ramsay MacDonald*, London.

16 London, p. 19.

17 *J. Ramsay MacDonald in Thought and Action: An Architect for a Better World*, Albuquerque, New Mexico.

18 *Ramsay MacDonald's Political Writings*, edited and introduced by Bernard Barker, London.

19 *Beatrice Webb's Diaries, 1912-1924*, edited by Margaret Cole, London, 1952; *Beatrice Webb's Diaries, 1924-1932*, edited by Margaret Cole, London, 1956, p. 119.

20 *Diaries and Letters, 1930-1939*, edited Nigel Nicolson, London.

21 Richard W. Lyman, *The First Labour Government, 1924*, London, 1957.

22 Reginald Bassett, *Nineteen Thirty One: Political Crisis*, London, 1958.

23 *A Pattern of Rulers*, London, pp. 61-134.

24 Charles Loch Mowat, 'Ramsay MacDonald and the Labour Party', in Asa Briggs & John Saville, eds., *Essays in Labour History, 1886-1923*, London, 1971, pp. 129-51.

25 Trevor Lloyd, 'James Ramsay MacDonald', in John P. Mackintosh, ed., *British Prime Ministers in the Twentieth Century: Volume One, Balfour to Chamberlain* London, 1977, pp. 156-78.

26 Robert Skidelsky, *Politicians and the Slump: The Labour Government of 1929-31*, London.

27 London.

28 Typescript, 'II The drift of the Labour opposition', RMP, PRO 30/69/1079.

Chapter 1

1   James Ramsay MacDonald to Margaret Ethel Gladstone (later, Mac-Donald) [MEM], 21 June and 14 July 1896, RMP, PRO 30/69/1118.

2   *Highland News,* 15 June 1935.

3   JRM to MEM, 29 June 1896, RMP, PRO 30/69/1118.

4   Ibid.

5   RMP, PRO 30/69/776.

6   February 1886.

7   JRM to Mr Stewart, 18 September 1887, quoted in Marquand, *MacDonald,* p. 21.

8   JRM to MEM, 26 June 1896, RMP, PRO 30/69/1118.

9   Draft chapter on the association, prepared for MacDonald by a researcher in the 1930s, RMP, PRO 30/69/1118.

10 JRM to Keir Hardie, n.d., but ? 1888, quoted in William Stewart, *J. Keir Hardie: A Biography,* 2nd ed., London, 1925, p. 42.

11 *The New Charter,* Dover.

12 Quoted in Stewart, *Hardie,* p. 97.

13 JRM to Crisp, 16 July 1894, in *Southampton Times,* 11 August 1894, quoted in Marquand, *MacDonald,* p. 37.

14 The relevant institution within the ILP was formally known as the National Administrative Council. From an early date it functioned as an Executive and the usage here reflects that characteristic.

15 Beatrice Webb, *The Diary of Beatrice Webb: Volume Two, 1892–1905: 'All the Good Things of Life',* London, 1983, pp. 65-6.

16 *Ibid.,* p. 83.

17 *Ibid.,* p. 94.

18 *Ibid.,* p. 94.

19 RMP, PRO 30/69/1111.

20 JRM to Anne Ramsay, 24 September 1896, in RMP, PRO 30/69/1118.

21 Margaret Ethel Gladstone to JRM, 15 June 1896, RMP, PRO 30/69/778.

22 *Seedtime,* July 1894.

23 J. Ramsay MacDonald, *The History of the ILP: ILP Study Course, No. 1,* London, 1922, p. 8.

22 *Ibid.,* p. 12.

25 *Commonwealth,* September 1896.

26 George Bernard Shaw to JRM, 20 November 1899, RMP, PRO 30/69/1143.

27 Henry Pelling, *The Origins of the Labour Party, 1880–1900,* 2nd ed., Oxford, 1966, p. 205.

28 *Ibid.,* p. 205.

29 *Ibid.,* p. 209.

30 *Ibid.,* p. 207.

31 *Ibid.,* p. 209.

32 RMP, PRO 30/69/1728.

33 J. Bruce Glasier to JRM, 25 October, RMP, PRO 30/69/1145.

34 'The people in power', in Stanton Coit, ed., *Ethical Democracy: Essays in Social Dynamics,* London, 1900, p. 70.

35 Memorandum, n.d., RMP, PRO 30/69/1215.

36 *What I Saw in South Africa,* London, p. 118.

37 Elton, *Life,* p. 115.

38 JRM, *Margaret Ethel MacDonald,* London, 1912, p. 226.

39 JRM, 'A rock ahead', *To-day,* March 1887, quoted in Eric J. Hobsbawm, ed., *Labour's Turning Point, 1880–1900,* 2nd ed., Hassocks, 1974, p. 66.

40 *Socialism and Society,* London, pp. 96 and 100-1.

41 'People', p. 71.

42 *New Charter.*

43 *Ibid.*

44 *Socialism and Society,* p. 101.

Chapter 2

1 Labour Party, *1906 Report,* p. 3.

2 W. C. Anderson to JRM, 3 August 1910, RMP, PRO 30/69/1154.

3 V. I. Lenin, *Selected Works: A One-Volume Selection of Lenin's Most Essential Writings,* London, 1969, pp. 295-7 and 342-3.

4   Labour Party, *1907 Report*, p. 49.
5   *Ibid.*, pp. 20 and 22.
6   *Ibid.*, p. 21.
7   *Labour Leader*, 10 May 1907.
8   Independent Labour Party, *1907 Report*, p. 33.
9   JRM to Bruce Glasier, 31 May 1907, Francis Johnson Papers, quoted in Marquand, *MacDonald*, p. 108.
10 *History ILP*, p. 12.
11 Labour Party, *1906 Report*, p. 15.
12 *Labour and the Empire*, London, pp. 12 and 108.
13 *Ibid.*, pp. 27-8.
14 *Ibid.*, pp. 49 and xi.
15 *Ibid.*, p. 46.
16 *Ibid.*, p. 48.
17 *Ibid.*, pp. 99 and 74-5.
18 *The Awakening of India*, London, p. 266.
19 *Ibid.*, pp 273 and 190.
20 *Ibid.*, p. 297.
21 *Ibid.*, p. 301.
22 *Socialism and Government*, London, p. xxx.
23 *Ibid.*, pp. 109 and 112-3.
24 *Ibid.*, p. 91.
25 *Ibid.*, p. 43.
26 *Ibid.*, pp. 3-4.
27 'Character and Democracy', in various authors, *Social Ideals*, London, 1909, p. 43.
28 JRM's introduction to talk, 'The development of the House of Commons', in J. H. B. Masterman, *The House of Commons, its Place in National History*, London, 1908, p. 29.
29 *Socialism and Government*, pp. 114 & 117.
30 *Ibid.*, p. xxxii.
31 ILP, *1910 Report*, pp. 58-9.
32 W. Anderson to JRM, 3 August 1910. RMP, PRO 30/69/1145.
33 JRM, *Margaret Ethel MacDonald*, London, 1912, p. 137.
34 Diary, 8 July 1910, RMP, PRO 30/69/1753.
35 JRM, *MacDonald*, p. 204.
36 *Ibid.*, p. 226.
37 *Ibid.*, p. 135.

38   Interview, quoted in Marquand, *MacDonald,* p. 134.
39   *Leicester Pioneer,* 8 June 1912.
40   *Syndicalism,* London, p. 55.
41   *Ibid.,* pp. 1 and 5.
42   *Ibid.,* p. 51.
43   *Ibid.,* p. 67.
44   *History ILP,* p. 20.
45   *Socialist Review,* May 1911.
46   RMP, PRO 30/69/779.
47   ILP. *1914 Report,* p. 144.
48   Ross McKibbin, *The Evolution of the Labour Party, 1910–1924,* Oxford, 1974, p. xiv.
49   *Labour Leader,* 10 July 1913.
50   *Hansard,* 1914, Vol. 65, col. 1831.
51   Labour Party, *1916 Report,* p. 3.
52   ILP, *1915 Report,* p. 116.
53   *Socialist Review,* October 1911.
54   JRM to Arthur Henderson, 24 August 1914, RMP, PRO 30/69/1232.
55   Royden Harrison, 'The War Emergency Workers' National Committee', in Asa Briggs & John Saville, eds., *Essays in Labour History, 1886–1923,* London, 1971, p. 222.
56   Memorandum, accompany letter from JRM to J. E. W. Duyes, 30 October 1914, RMP PRO 30/69/1232.
57   H. M. Swanwick, *Builders of Peace: Ten Years' History of the Union of Democratic Control,* London, 1924, p. 36.
58   Diary, 23 September 1914, RMP, PRO 30/69/1753.
59   Ibid., 27 November.
60   Swanwick, *Builders,* p. 90.
61   Diary, 26 September 1915, RMP, PRO 30/69/1753.
62   4 September.
63   *The Times,* 4 June 1915.
64   Diary, 29 January 1916, RMP, PRO 30/69/1753.
65   *Labour Leader,* 25 May 1916.
66   ,*Forward,* 16 December 1916.
67   16 July 1915, quoted in Elton, *MacDonald,* p. 263.
68   *Hansard,* 1916, Vol. 81, col. 99, 20 March.
69   Quoted in Elton, *MacDonald,* p. 252.
70   Diary, 21 December, RMP, PRO 30/69/1753.

71 *National Defence,* London, pp. 16-17.
72 Labour Party, *1917 Report*, p. 44.
73 JRM to Emile Vandervelde, 26 April 1917, RMP, PRO 30/69/1161.
74 Lord Robert Cecil to Lloyd George, CAB 24/14, GT 875, 336.
75 *Socialism After the War,* Manchester & London, p. 41.
76 Labour Party, *January 1918 Report,* p. 96.

Chapter 3

1 26 July, RMP, PRO 30/69/1753.
2 *Ibid.*, 29 December 1918.
3 *Socialist Review*, October 1919.
4 *Theses, Resolutions and Manifestos of the First Four Congresses of the Third International*, ed. Alan Adler, London, 1980, p. 24.
5 24 May, RMP, PRO 30/69/1753.
6 Manchester, p. 92.
7 Diary, 10 November 1920, RMP, PRO 30/69/1753.
8 Sidney to Beatrice Webb, 23 January 1917, in *The Letters of Sidney and Beatrice Webb: Volume III: Pilgrimage, 1912-1947*, Cambridge, 1978, p. 78.
9 Diary, 15 January, RMP, PRO 30/69/1753.
10 Labour Party, *1919 Report*, p. 57.
11 Beatrice Webb, *Beatrice Webb's Diaries, 1912-1924*, ed. Margaret Cole, London, 1952, p. 181.
12 *Ibid.*, p. 182.
13 London & Manchester, p. 71.
14 London.
15 6 September 1919, republished in *Wanderings and Excursions*, London, p. 61.
16 Diary, RMP, PRO 30/69/1753.
17 *Wanderings and Excursions*, p. 116.
18 *Diaries, 1912-1924*, p. 231.
19 Hamilton, *J. Ramsay MacDonald*, 1929, pp. 152-3 & 143.
20 *Ibid.*, pp. 136-7.
21 *Ibid.*, p. 162.
22 *Socialist Review*, January 1923.
23 *Ibid.*, September.
24 *Report*, p. 52.
25 Philip Viscount Snowden, *An Autobiography: Volume 2, 1919-1934*, London, 1934, pp. 581-8; *Hansard*, 1923, Vol. 161, col. 2472.
26 Harold Nicolson, *King George the Fifth: His Life and Reign*, London, 1967, p. 492.

27 *1923 Report*, p. 204.
28 *The Times*, 18 January 1924.
29 19 December.
30 Diary, 10 December 1923, RMP, PRO, 30/69/1753.
31 Nicolson, *George*, p. 496.
32 JRM to A. Henderson, 22 December 1923, RMP, PRO 30/69/1169.
33 Diary, 21 January 1924, RMP, PRO 30/69/1753.
34 Nicolson, *George*, p. 497.
35 Diary, RMP, PRO 30/69/1753.
36 *Memoirs, 1869-1924*, London, 1937, p. 343.
37 Diary, 22 January 1924, RMP, PRO 30/69/1753; Nicolson, *George*, pp. 497-9.
38 *Beatrice Webb's Diaries, 1924-1932*, ed. Margaret Cole, London, 1956, p. 2.
39 Diary, 2 March 1924, RMP, PRO 30/69/1753.
40 Nicolson, *George*, pp. 502-3.

Chapter 4

1 Diary, RMP, PRO 30/69/1753.
2 Egerton P. Wake to JRM, 18 October 1924, RMP, PRO 30/69/1709.
3 Diary, 3 February, RMP, PRO 30/69/1753.
4 JRM to C. T. Cramp, RMP, PRO 30/69/2.
5 Francis Williams, *Ernest Bevin: Portrait of a Great Englishman*, London, 1952, p. 122.
6 Labour Party, *1924 Report*, p. 105.
7 Rose Rosenberg to Clifford Allen, 3 March 1924, RMP, PRO 30/69/1169.
8 Rose Rosenberg to F. Brockway, 23 August 1924, RMP, PRO 30/69/181.
9 London, p. 4.
10 Quoted in Marquand, *MacDonald*, p. 351.
11 Diary, 10 April 1924, RMP, PRO 30/69/1753.
12 JRM to Sir Ellis Hume-Williams, 11 August 1924, RMP, PRO 30/69/183.
13 JRM's secretary to Foreign Office, 24 November 1924, RMP, PRO 30/69/1.
14 *The Times*, 22 September 1924.
15 Special Branch Reports on Revolutionary Organizations, No. 267, 14 August 1924, RMP, PRO 30/69/220.
16 Thomas Jones, *Whitehall Diary: Volume One*, ed. Keith Middlemass, London, 1969, p. 288.
17 *Hansard*, 1924, Vol. 177, col. 605.

18 JRM to Lord Stamfordham, 22 August 1924, quoted in Nicolson, *George,* p. 514.
19 *Ibid.*
20 Quoted in A. J. P. Taylor, *English History, 1914-1945*, Harmondsworth, 1970, p. 289.
21 Jones, *Diary*, p. 287.
22 Nicolson, *George*, p. 514.
23 *Hansard*, 1924, Vol. 177, col. 16.
24 Jones, *Diary*, p. 296.
25 Nicolson, *George*, p. 514.
26 Diary, 9 October 1924, RMP, PRO 30/69/1753.
27 JRM to George V, quoted in Nicolson, *George*, p. 517.
28 *The Times*, 28 October 1924.
29 Nicolson, *George*, p. 520.
30 *Ibid.*, p. 517.
31 Joe Brown to JRM, 5 November 1924, RMP, PRO 30/69/1709.

Chapter 5

1 1 November 1924, RMP, PRO 30/69/2.
2 *Diaries, 1924-1932*, p. 71.
3 Hugh Dalton, *Call Back Yesterday: Memoirs, 1887-1931*, London, 1953, pp. 175-6.
4 Diary, 6 June 1926, RMP, PRO 30/69/1753.
5 Robin Page Arnot, *The General Strike, May 1926: Its Origins and History*, London, 1926, p. 140.
6 Diary, 2 May 1926, RMP, PRO 30/69/1753.
7 *Ibid.*, 11 May.
8 *Ibid.*, 14 May.
9 *Socialist Review*, June 1926.
10 Alan Bullock, *The Life and Times of Ernest Bevin, Volume One: Trade Union Leader, 1881-1940*, London, 1960, pp. 348-9.
11 Diary, 16 June 1926, RMP, PRO 30/69/1753.
12 *Ibid.*, 3 September.
13 JRM to A. J. Cook, 14 January 1927, RMP, PRO 30/69/1172.
14 Labour Party, *1927 Report*, p. 210.
15 JRM to John Scurr and Fenner Brockway, 25 February 1925, RMP, PRO 30/69/1170.
16 ILP, *1925 Report*, p. 124.

17 JRM to J. Walton Newbold, 13 May 1925, RMP, PRO 30/69/1490.
18 *Socialist Review*, March 1926.
19 22 April 1926, RMP, PRO 30/69/1436.
20 JRM to J. A. Hobson, 8 October 1926, RMP, PRO 30/69/1171.
21 JRM to John Strachey, 5 February 1927, RMP, PRO, 30/69/1008.
22 11 August.
23 Robert E. Dowse, *Left in the Centre: The Independent Labour Party, 1893-1940*, London, 1966, p. 140.
24 Labour Party, *1926 Report*, p. 200.
25 London, 1926, p. 27.
26 18 January 1929, RMP, PRO 30/69/1439.
27 JRM to Arthur Henderson, 30 March 1925, RMP, PRO 30/69/1170.
28 JRM to Miles Lampson, 9 February 1927, RMP, PRO 30/69/1172.
29 14 September 1927.
30 JRM to Thomas Johnston, 27 September 1927, RMP, PRO 30/69/1172.
31 *Hansard*, 1927, Vol. 210, cols. 2095 and 2097.
32 JRM to C. Cummings, 18 April 1928, RMP, PRO 30/69/1713.
33 Beatrice Webb, *Diaries, 1924-1932*, p. 169.
34 George Bloomfield to JRM, 26 October 1928, RMP, PRO 30/69/1713.
35 6 November, RMP, PRO 30/69/1753.

Chapter 6

1 30 January, RMP, PRO 30/69/1753.
2 Beatrice Webb, *Diaries, 1924–1932,* pp. 209-10.
3 Philip Viscount Snowden, *An Autobiography: Volume 2, 1919-1934,* London 1934, p. 767.
4 Hansard, 1929, Vol. 229, col. 65.
5 JRM, *The Risks of Peace* (special supplement to *Foreign Affairs,* Vol. 8, no. 1), New York 1929, p. iv.
6 Letter to JRM, 19 September 1929, RMP, PRO 30/69/267.
7 Clive Wigram to JRM, 16 August 1929, RMP, PRO 30/69/4.
8 JRM, *American Speeches*, London 1930, p. 40.
9 *Ibid.,* p. 21.
10 *Ibid.,* p. 118.
11 *Ibid.,* p. 82.
12 Diary, 10 August 1929, RMP, PRO 30/69/1753.
13 17 December.
14 JRM, 'Re Memorandum on Unemployment', n.d., RMP, PRO 30/69/446.

15 Diary, 29 April 1930, RMP, PRO 30/69/1753.
16 JRM to J. Walton Newbold, 2 June 1930, RMP, PRO 30/69/1440.
17 Quoted in JRM's Diary, 20 May 1930, RMP, PRO 30/69/1753.
18 Sir John Anderson to JRM, 30 July 1930, RMP, PRO 30/69/446.
19 P. Snowden to JRM, 28 April 1930, RMP, PRO 30/69/243.
20 Attlee Memorandum, 9 June 1930, RMP, PRO 30/69/243.
21 Labour Party, *1930 Report*, p. 185.
22 *Ibid.*, p. 192.
23 *Ibid.*, p. 204.
24 P. Snowden to JRM, 13 April 1931, RMP, PRO 30/69/1176.
25 JRM, Diary, 17 August 1931, RMP, PRO 30/69/1753.
26 *Ibid.*, 9 June 1931.

Chapter 7

1 Diary, RMP, PRO 30/69/1753.
2 *Ibid.*, 17 August 1931.
3 Cabinet 41 (31), 19 August 1931.
4 Diary, 21 August 1931, RMP, PRO 30/69/1753.
5 *Ibid.*.
6 *Ibid.*, 22 (referring to 21) August.
7 Macolm MacDonald Diary, 23 August 1931, quoted in Marquand, *MacDonald*, p. 632.
8 Herbert Samuel, *Memoirs*, London 1945, p. 204.
9 *Ibid.*.
10 Note of Sheila Lochhead (née MacDonald), quoted in Marquand, *MacDonald*, p. 631.
11 *Ibid.*.
12 Malcolm MacDonald Diary, 23 August 1931, quoted in Marquand, *MacDonald*, pp. 631-2; Ramsay MacDonald Diary, 23 August 1931, RMP, PRO 30/69/1753.
13 Cabinet 46 (31), 23 August 1931.
14 Nicolson, *George*, p. 596.
15 *Ibid.*.
16 Keith Middlemass & John Barnes, *Baldwin: A Biography*, London 1969, p. 628.
17 Diary, 24 August 1931, quoted in Marquand, *MacDonald*, p. 636.
18 Diary, 24 August 1931.
19 Nicolson, *George*, p. 599.

20 *Ibid.*, p. 598.
21 Cabinet 47 (31), 24 August 1931.
22 *Ibid.*.
23 Diary, 24 August 1931.

Chapter 8

1 RM to Mrs Molly Hamilton, RMP, PRO 30/69/1315.
2 Nicolson, *George,* p. 601.
3 JRM to Margaret Bondfield, 25 August 1931, RMP, PRO 30/69/1314.
4 Letter to JRM, 18 September 1931, RMP, PRO 30/69/674.
5 Minute, C. P. Duff, 25 August 1931, RMP, PRO 30/69/1314.
6 Typescript handed to JRM, 24 October 1931, seemingly extracts from Sankey's 1931 diary, RMP, PRO 30/69/1753.
7 Diary, 16 September 1931, RMP, PRO 30/69/1753.
8 Quoted in A. J. P. Taylor, *English History, 1914–1945,* Harmondsworth, 1970, p. 373.
9 JRM to J. H. Sutcliffe, 2 September 1931, RMP, PRO 30/69/1315.
10 Letter, RMP, PRO 30/69/1314.
11 *Hansard,* 1931, Vol. 256, col. 40.
12 JRM to William Coxon, 15 September 1931, RMP, PRO 30/69/1314.
13 Cabinet, 247 (31).
14 JRM to John Hill, 28 September 1931, RMP, PRO 30/69/1176.
15 Nicolson, *George,* p. 629.
16 *Ibid.,* p. 630.
17 5 October 1931, RMP, PRO 30/69/1753.
18 Taylor, *History*, p. 405.
19 JRM to George V, 11 September 1932, Nicolson, *George*, p. 636.
20 Diary, 28 September 1932, RMP, PRO 30/69/1753.
21 Letter, 19 May 1934, RMP, PRO 30/69/680.
22 JRM to Sir George Grahame, 29 December 1931, RMP, PRO 30/69/673.
23 Diary, 29 January, RMP, PRO 30/69/1753.
24 Letter, 27 February 1934, RMP, PRO 30/69/680.
25 Diary, RMP, PRO 30/69/1753.
26 JRM Memorandum, c. early 1934, Robertson Papers, quoted in Marquand, *MacDonald,* p. 757.
27 Diary, 20 October, RMP, PRO 30/69/1753.
28 *Ibid.,* 22 November 1934.
29 *Ibid.,* 19 January 1933.

30 *Ibid.,* 23 February 1935.
31 *Diaries, 1924–1932,* p. 249.
32 Letter, 8 March 1933, RMP, PRO 30/69/1178.
33 JRM to J. Richardson, 30 May 1933, RMP, PRO 30/69/1178.
34 Letter, 8 March 1933, RMP, PRO 30/69/1178.
35 Diary, 20 May 1934, RMP, PRO 30/69/1753.
36 Letter, 31 December 1933, RMP, PRO 30/69/755.
37 20 October 1935, RMP, PRO 30/69/1753.
38 Diary, 20 May 1934, RMP, PRO 30/69/1753.
39 *Ibid.,* 23 October 1933.
40 *Ibid.,* 15 July 1934.
41 JRM to Ralph Glyn, 25 December 1932, RMP, PRO 30/69/1177.
42 Copy in RMP, PRO 30/69/388.
43 Copy in RMP, PRO 30/69/1326.
44 JRM to Philip Snowden, 29 July 1932, RMP, PRO 30/69/1177.
45 Copy in RMP, PRO 30/69/1330.
46 Letter to John Ogilvie, 30 October, RMP, PRO 30/69/680.
47 Typescript, 'II The drift of the Labour opposition', RMP, PRO 30/69/1079.
48 Typescript notes by Earl De La Warr, for meeting 29 November 1935, RMP, PRO 30/69/7.
49 Diary, 27 January, RMP, PRO 30/69/1753.
50 *Ibid.,* 8 May 1935.
51 JRM to Sir Samuel Hoare, 25 November 1935, RMP, PRO 30/69/1753.
52 RMP, PRO 30/69/1748.
53 Harold Nicolson, *Diaries and Letters, 1930–1939,* London 1966, pp. 229-30.
54 RMP, PRO 30/69/626.
55 JRM to H. Dunnico, 4 February 1936, RMP, PRO 30/69/1721.
56 Diary, 20 January 1936, RMP, PRO 30/69/1753.
57 *Ibid.*, 14 January 1936.
58 JRM to Sir George Grahame, 16 October 1934, RMP, PRO 30/69/5.
59 Diary, 3 February 1937, RMP, PRO 30/69/1753.
60 *Ibid.,* 20 May 1936.
61 *Ibid.,* 15 May 1936.
62 JRM to Lord Tweedsmuir, 7 December 1936, RMP, PRO 30/69/1571.
63 *Ibid.,* 13 May 1937.
64 Diary, 28 September 1937, RMP, PRO 30/69/1753.
65 *Ibid.,* 15 July 1924.

Conclusion

1. *Gathering Storm,* p. 18.
2. C. L. Mowat, *Britain Between the Wars,* London, 1955, p. 142.

Appendices

MacDonald's First Labour Cabinet
Formed January 1924

Prime Minister	J. Ramsay MacDonald
Lord President	Lord Parmoor
Lord Chancellor	Viscount Haldane
Lord Privy Seal	J. R. Clynes
Chancellor of the Exchequer	P. Snowden
Foreign Secretary	J. Ramsay MacDonald
Home Secretary	A. Henderson
First Lord of the Admiralty	Viscount Chelmsford
Minister of Agriculture	N. Buxton
Secretary for Air	Lord Thomson
Colonial Secretary	J. H. Thomas
President of the Board of Education	C. P. Trevelyan
Minister of Health	J. Wheatley
Secretary for India	Lord Olivier
Minister of Labour	T. Shaw
Chancellor of the Duchy of Lancaster	J. Wedgwood
Postmaster-General	V. Hartshorn
Secretary for Scotland	W. Adamson
President of the Board of Trade	S. Webb
Secretary for War	S. Walsh
First Commissioner of Works	F. Jowett

MacDonald's Second Labour Cabinet

Formed June 1929

Prime Minister	J. Ramsay MacDonald
Lord President	Lord Parmoor
Lord Chancellor	Lord Sankey
Lord Privy Seal	J. H. Thomas
Chancellor of the Exchequer	P. Snowden
Foreign Secretary	A. Henderson
Home Secretary	J. R. Clynes
First Lord of the Admiralty	A. Alexander
Minister of Agriculture	N. Buxton
Secretary for Air	Lord Thomson
Colonial and Dominions Secretary	Lord Passfield
President of the Board of Education	Sir C. P. Trevelyan
Minister of Health	A. Greenwood
Secretary for India	W. Wedgwood Benn
Minister of Labour	M. Bondfield
Secretary for Scotland	W. Adamson
President of the Board of Trade	W. Graham
Secretary for War	T. Shaw
First Commissioner of Works	G. Lansbury

Changes (June 1930)

V. Hartshorn succeeds Thomas as Lord Privy Seal.

Thomas becomes Dominions Secretary.

Passfield remains Colonial Secretary.

C. Addison succeeds Buxton as Minister of Agriculture.

(October 1930)

Lord Amulree succeeds Thomson (deceased) as Secretary for Air.

(March 1931)

H. B. Lees-Smith succeeds Trevelyan (resigned) as President of the Board of Education.

H. Morrison, Minister of Transport, enters the cabinet.

T. Johnston succeeds Hartshorn as Lord Privy Seal.

MacDonald's First National Cabinet
Formed August 1931

Prime Minister	J. Ramsay MacDonald (N. Lab)
Lord President	S. Baldwin (C)
Lord Chancellor	Lord Sankey (N. Lab)
Chancellor of the Exchequer	P. Snowden (N. Lab)
Foreign Secretary	Lord Reading (Lib)
Home Secretary	Sir H. Samuel (Lib)
Colonial Secretary	J. H. Thomas (N. Lab)
Dominions Secretary	J. H. Thomas (N. Lab)
Minister of Health	N. Chamberlain (C)
Secretary for India	Sir S. Hoare (C)
President of the Board of Trade	Sir P. Cunliffe-Lister (C)

MacDonald's Second National Cabinet
Formed November 1931

Prime Minister	J. Ramsay MacDonald (N. Lab)
Lord President	S. Baldwin (C)
Lord Chancellor	Lord Sankey (N. Lab)
Lord Privy Seal	Viscount Snowden (N. Lab)
Chancellor of the Exchequer	N. Chamberlain (C)
Foreign Secretary	Sir J. Simon (L. Nat)
Home Secretary	Sir H. Samuel (Lib)
First Lord of the Admiralty	Sir B. Eyres-Monsell (C)
Minister of Agriculture	Sir J. Gilmour (C)
Secretary for Air	Marquis of Londonderry (C)
Colonial Secretary	Sir P. Cunliffe-Lister (C)
Dominions Secretary	J. H. Thomas (N. Lab)
President of the Board of Education	Sir D. Maclean (Lib)
Minister of Health	Sir E. Hilton Young (C)
Secretary for India	Sir S. Hoare (C)
Minister of Labour	Sir H. Betterton (C)
Secretary for Scotland	Sir A. Sinclair (Lib)
President of the Board of Trade	W. Runciman (L. Nat)
Secretary for War	Viscount Hailsham (C)
First Commissioner of Works	W. Ormsby-Gore (C)

Changes (July 1932)

Lord Irwin (C) succeeds Maclean (deceased) as President of the Board of Education.

(September 1932)

Baldwin succeeds Snowden as Lord Privy Seal, while remaining Lord President.

Gilmour succeeds Samuel as Home Secretary, and is succeeded as Minister of Agriculture by W. Elliot (C).

Sir G. Collins (L. Nat) succeeds Sinclair as Secretary of State for Scotland.

(December 1933)

Baldwin resigns as Lord Privy Seal, and successor not in cabinet.

Sir K. Wood (C), Postmaster-General, enters cabinet.

(June 1934)

O. Stanley (C) succeeds Betterton as Minister of Labour.

Index

(with thanks to Akis Pittas of Larnaca, Cyprus)